Atheism is the vice of a few intelligent people. ~ **Voltaire**

Why am I an atheist? The short answer is that I cannot accept any of the alternatives. I simply don't find them believable. As for the accusation of intellectual pride, surely the boot is on the other foot. Atheists don't claim to know anything with certainty – it's the believers who know it all. ~ **Barbara Smoker**

It seems to me that the idea of a personal God is an anthropological concept which I cannot take seriously. I also cannot imagine some will or goal outside the human sphere...Science has been charged with undermining morality, but the charge is unjust. A man's ethical behavior should be based effectually on sympathy, education, and social ties; no religious basis is necessary. Man would indeed be in a poor way if he had to be restrained by fear of punishment and hope of reward after death. ~ **Albert Einstein**

The Metaphysics of Aristotle opens with these words: "All men naturally desire to know."

It is a pity that Science must always reject old ideas and cast them away as useless before rediscovering them as something new to be incorporated in its current theories. To discard the alchemist's theories is as intelligent as to dismiss as rubbish Einstein's Theory of Relativity merely because one does not happen to understand his language. Some of our scientific men have realized this, for F. Hoefer in 'Histoire de la Chimie' (Paris 1866) remarks: 'The systems which confront the intelligence remain basically unchanged through the ages, although they assume different forms. Thus, through mistaking form for basis, one conceives an unfavorable opinion of the sequence. We must remember that there is nothing so disastrous in Science as the arrogant dogmatism which despises the past and admires nothing but the present.'

*If Science would but try to understand the conception of the Universe as taught by occultism throughout the ages, taking as its starting-point the teaching of the One Life in Manifestation, its seven planes of consciousness, its infinite forces, and as the basis of its philosophy the Hermetic axiom 'as above, so below,' it would found a system based on eternal Truth instead of on a quicksand of theories. Science will never really understand the truth about life until it reaches this realization, which cannot be attained through its instruments and appliances, but only through the inner powers of the mind. ~ **Unknown***

Obviously, many of the points that we will make in this book fly directly in the face of our mainstream scientific understanding. More and more frontier researchers are discovering that our current scientific Establishment has become akin to a religion in and of itself, where theories that were taught one or more generations in the past have become so institutionalized that any differing opinions are rarely given a hearing of any kind. For anyone who has ever attended a university and built an entire career around one or a series of "pet theories," any definitive evidence that smashes these theories can be utterly shocking and even deeply wounding. Though a non-scientific reader may laugh at the thought of it, when these "paradigm shocks" suddenly explode into view with the arresting finality of Truth, they can literally produce tears, dizziness and nausea in one who has dedicated his or her entire life to studying "the wrong way." Suddenly the security of knowing the "way things work" is gone, and the agonizing new question becomes, "How could I not have seen this before?"

Copywriters notice:

Condition of Sale: All rights reserved. This publication may not be reproduced, stored in a retrieval system, or transmitted, in any form or by any means, electronic, mechanical, printing, photocopying, recording or otherwise, without the prior permission of the publisher.

Permissions: The publisher has made every effort to trace and contact all copyright holders of reproduced copyright materials in this book. The publisher will be glad to rectify any omissions at the earliest opportunity.

Grateful acknowledgement is made to the following for permission to reprint previously published material:

Reclaiming Your Divinity, exposing the ultimate deception by Lightstrorm Published by SHANTI Publishing and Child's Sunvillage, Inc.   USA   208-634-8335   Canada   250-380-3760   lightstrorm@ctcweb.net   www.ctcweb.net/~lightstrorm $5.00 USD Feb. 2005 Chapter 1 reprinted with permission.

Note: Short excerpts that appear in italic are copied from websites and newsletters, be sure to read the footnotes and visit the websites for full text. Many parts of this book make reference to very well known and researched subject of which is nearly impossible to write about better than what others have already done, therefore I choose to provide you with the words of others who enlighten us in the best way possible.

ISBN: 978-0-6151-7127-2

This book is dedicated

to

Tim who for many years I have

tried unsuccessfully to

indoctrinate on the art of magical

and spiritual knowledge

To Emily my daughter who I wish to

to pass all this knowledge to…

And to all the Bill Gates

in the world that can benefit

from all this secret knowledge

that is really not all that secret

if you allow yourself to receive it…

Acknowledgements

Many brave past and present souls and spiritual guides have guided me in writing this book, to bring forth this very special truth, I thank them all, and I give a very special thanks to my partner Carmen, for providing me with a peaceful, tranquil environment to make it so possible for me to research and write this book for you.

To Ralph for being the first person to ever make me notice.

To Leonardo for being the second.

To Jack for providing many insightful tips and great conversation on these subject.

To Jennifer for filling in the information gap when I needed it the most.

To all the authors, thinkers, teachers, healers, and metaphysicians that have added to my thoughts, experiences, and understanding, I am particularly indebted. They often do not receive mention in an author's acknowledgements, but inasmuch as they have shaped so much of my work, they deserve my special thanks.

TABLE OF CONTENTS

COPYWRITERS NOTICE: 6

THIS BOOK IS DEDICATED 7

ACKNOWLEDGEMENTS 8

TABLE OF CONTENTS 9

PREFACE A FEW NOTES WHILE READING THIS BOOK 17

PART ONE QUESTIONING EVERYTHING 23

INTRODUCTION 24

CHAPTER 1 MY EARLY RELIGIOUS/SPIRITUAL YEARS 42

CHAPTER 2 SYNCHRONICITIES - WHAT TRIGGERED ME TO CHANGE FROM ATHEIST TO AGNOSTIC 46

PART TWO FROM ATHIEST TO AGNOSTIC 62

HOW TO GUIDE 62

CHAPTER 3 BENEFITS OF CHANGING FROM ATHEIST TO AGNOSTIC 65

CHAPTER 4 WHAT PRESENT SCIENTISTS ARE SAYING 67

CHAPTER 5 DEATH, WHAT HAPPENS WHEN YOU DIE 73

CHAPTER 6 REINCARNATION & PAST LIVES 76

CHAPTER 7 MENTAL RELAXATION AND MEDITATION 83

CHAPTER 8 ASTROLOGY 101

CHAPTER 9 THE ART AND PRACTICE OF CONSCIOUS CREATION AND OUR BELIEF SYSTEM 108

    AFFIRMATIONS 119

CHAPTER 10 DRUGS 122

CHAPTER 11 ASTRAL TRAVEL, OUT-OF-BODY EXPERIENCE AND NEAR DEATH EXPERIENCES 124

CHAPTER 12 AKASHIC HALL OF RECORDS 130

CHAPTER 13 WHO? WHAT? WHERE? IS GOD 132

CHAPTER 14 HOW TO BECOME IMMORTAL AND /OR IMPROVE YOUR HEALTH 153

CHAPTER 15 THE LAW OF KARMA AND DARMA 156

CHAPTER 16 WHAT IS REALLY GOING ON WITH OUR PLANET? 2012 158

    32 NAMES FOR PLANET X 165

    AKAKOR 167

    ICE AGES -- GRADE SCHOOL SCIENCE 167

My summary: 176

So where are the best places to survive? 180

Y2K vs. 2012 A.D. 181

Things to expect: 186

Can Planet X cause a pole shift on earth as it passes by? 192

Chapter 17 THE MECHANISM OF A PRAYER 194

Part Three Where to find more information 196

Preface.. 197

Chapter 18 DEEPAK CHOPRA THE SEVEN SPIRITUAL LAWS OF SUCCESS 200

The Law of Pure Potentiality 202

The Law of Living 203

The Law of "Karma" or Cause and Effect 204

The Law of Least Effort 206

The Law of Intention and Desire 208

The Law of Detachment 209

The Law of "Dharma" or Purpose in Life 210

Chapter 19 GNOSIS 211

CHAPTER 20 **SATHYA SAI BABA** 216

    How to spend your time.. 217

CHAPTER 21 **BASHAR** 218

CHAPTER 22 **SETH CHANNEL BY JANE ROBERTS** 221

CHAPTER 23 **OSHO** 228

CHAPTER 24 **ROSICRUCIAN ORDER, AMORC** 230

CHAPTER 25 **ECKANKAR** 233

CHAPTER 26 **FALUN DAFA** 234

CHAPTER 27 **FENG SHUI** 238

CHAPTER 28 **PSYCHICS, CHANNELERS, PARAPSYCHOLOGISTS** 244

    Edgar Cayce (1877-1945) 246

    The Sleeping Prophet 246

CHAPTER 29 **DOWSING, PENDULUMS, OUIJA BOARD, TAROT CARDS, DIVINATION, SCRYING, PALMISTRY CHIRIMANCY** 253

CHAPTER 30 **NUMEROLOGY, SACRED GEOMETRY** 258

CHAPTER 31 **BIORHYTHIMS** 261

CHAPTER 32 **MAGICK, WISHCRAFT, PAGAN, WICCA, VOODOO, SHAMANISM** 265

PRINCIPLES OF WICCAN BELIEF 266

THE TEN NATIVE AMERICAN COMMANDMENTS 270

FINDING A GROUP 271

CHAPTER 33 HYPNOSIS 272

CHAPTER 34 GHOST, PARANORMAL 274

CHAPTER 35 ALIENS, UFO'S 275

CHAPTER 36 CROP-CIRCLES 277

CHAPTER 37 PROOFS FOR ATHEIST OF THE EXISTENCE OF SOUL – THE HIGHER LANGUAGE OF SYMBOLS 279

CHAPTER 38 TIPS AND TOOLS FOR IMPROVING YOUR LIFE AND HEALTH 283

EATING TIPS 288

DEEP BREATHING 288

AROMATHERAPY 292

CHAPTER 39 ORMUS/ORMES/M-STATE 303

ORMUS/ORMES DISCUSSION FORUMS 316

THE ORMUS SCIENTIFIC WORKGROUP 317

ORMUS BOOK LIST 318

ORMUS Vendors 320

CHAPTER 40 ORGONE 324

CHAPTER 41 NEW ENERGY TRUTH AND LIES OF OMISSION 329

CHAPTER 42 ALCHEMY 340

    Alchemy Is an Art 342

    What Else Did the Alchemists Know? 342

    What Did Fulcanelli Know? 343

CHAPTER 43 INTENTIONAL COMMUNITIES 346

CHAPTER 44 ADDITIONAL BOOKS, NEWSGROUPS, WEB PAGES 351

    Recommended Web pages 351

    Recommended Books 354

    Advanced psychology manuals 363

    Books that cover many subjects 364

        Spiritual novel - fun to read, teaches a principal in a fun way: 364

    Movies 364

CHAPTER 45 WHERE TO START? 369

DONATIONS 372

Religion is fundamentally opposed to everything I hold in veneration – courage, clear thinking, honesty, fairness, and, above all, love of the truth."

Religion deserves no more respect than a pile of garbage.

~H. L. Mencken, 1880-1956

PREFACE
A few notes while reading this book

Dear reader, first I want to make it very clear that this book does NOT favor any religion at all, and it is not about any religion. If you have not read the quotes on the previous pages, please do so. This book is about spiritual esoteric and scientific knowledge, not religion.

Granted that many religions hold some of the keys to the information of the spiritual (Matrix) realm, but they make no effort in teaching them, for this reason religious books and books such as the bible used by religions should not be completely ignored as valuable sources of information. What most definitely should be ignored is the presentation/interpretation provided by religions.

Keep in mind while reading this book that I was as atheist as you, a none-believer in all that hocus-pocus spiritual, esoteric, religious junk. An engineer by profession, a research scientist and a lawyer, in fact if you are reading this book online on a computer, good chance are that part of the software that allows your computer to run was written by me.

In this book you will find references to LOTS of real quantum physics science, not just what someone says or believes, but real facts that actually explains in plenty of details the how and what is really going on with our existence in this planet, who and what we really are and where are we headed too, you will also find detailed reference of predictions based on scientific evidence of what is happening and will happen in the coming years prior to and after 2012; with plenty of references of where to find the detailed scientific evidence of the how and why of the huge increase in earthquakes, hurricanes, tornadoes, volcanic activity, weather changes, earth changes and much more.

Also keep in mind that you probably got this book as a gift from someone that cares about you, but that has not been able to find the ideal words to talk to you about this subject of maximum importance. If you bought this book on your own, then I probably do not need to convince you much about the value of reading it.

95% of people interviewed in a USA survey said they believe in God, which means 5% are atheists. This books if focuses on enlightening/guiding the 5% that has evaded all information related to the spiritual arena such as all religions, mystics, magic, occultism, alchemy, astrology, numerology, sacred geometry, free energy, stories of Channelers such as Edgar Cayce[1], UFO's, aura[2], yoga, aliens, Breatharian's, Witchcraft, Wicca, dowsing, Ouija board, tarot cards, parapsychology, ghost, hypnosis, apparitions, astral travel, near death experiences, etc. This book is for those who think those

---

[1] **Edgar Cayce** performed in-depth psychic readings for many people, which had an unparalleled accuracy, giving him the oft-quoted status as *"America's Greatest Psychic."* Once in trance, Cayce could medically diagnose people at a distance whom he had never met, and prescribe accurate herbal treatments that neither he nor anyone else had previously heard of. For more information on his work visit www.ascension2000.com and www.michaelmandeville.com

[2] **Aura** The human being does have an egg-shaped "energy body" that is composed of this medium, which many trained seers can both see and heal, and disease conditions will appear in this body first before they become physical.

things are a fraud. And for those people who are rational, open-minded, and believe in the empirical part of scientific method. Try them and decide for yourself, unless you prefer to let others do all your thinking for you. Remember, all great scientific breakthroughs were fought tooth and nail by the "keepers of the status quo" of their time.

One thing I want to make very clear to you is that this book is NOT about religion nor does it support nor sponsor any ancient way of thinking. Many people consider the word spirit or spiritual to be the province of religion, but I insist on making a clear distinction between spirituality and religion. Spirituality has to do with the nonphysical, immaterial aspect of our being, with our energies, essences, and the part of us that existed before and will exist after the disintegration of our body, with the facts of our universe and cosmos, also know as quantum physics[3]. Religion has institutionalized spirituality and done so in a most perverse way possible, and much of what goes on in its name concerns perpetuation of the institutions more than the welfare of the individual.

There are two ways of knowing reality. The first way of knowing is the rational, deductive, argumentative, intellectual thinking that is the hallmark of science and our patriarchal Western culture. Some called this the One Mind. The second way is the non-rational,

---

[3] Quantum physics is the new science that is providing scientific proof of the fourth density (also referred as dimension) and known as the spiritual realm.

image-driven, intuitive way of thinking which is commonly accepted as part of mysticism and religion. Try to use both ways of knowing when trying to understand the topics presented in this book. Do NOT be afraid to accept the truth about yourself when a minor fault or shortcoming of yours is exposed. We are all here on a learning journey to explore and learn new things; among these is the way of knowing reality. And most important to recall/remember the gods we really are, more on this subject on chapter 13, Who, What, Where? is God.

In this book we[4] provide you with additional sources of ways to sense in addition to your five senses. A new window/door into another reality which in time you will realize it is the true reality and that this one that you are living now is just an illusion a dream created by your mind which responds to the Matrix[5] programming.

Though you do NOT know it now, there IS magic[6] in all we do, if only you knew that there is magic in all your actions, you would

---

[4] I say we, since the source of the information presented comes from many masters.

[5] Matrix will be described throughout this book. Also see David Icke, Children of the Matrix for an excellent detailed explanation.

[6] **Magic**.- The physical world however is very dense and of a much lower vibration than the inner Mind worlds of the Astral and Mental spheres, and therefore more Energy, concentration and focus is required in order to bring about a manifestation observable in the physical world. Many people will have heard of "Magic". We should note straightaway however that by true Magic as practiced from time immemorial we do not mean the stage illusionists, prestidigitators, conjurors and other such people from the areas of stage entertainment, but rather Magic in its very truest, very highest

change your actions to work in your favor. Magic is simply Conscious Creation; you do Magical things by consciously willing it so. More on this on Chapter 9 "The Art and Practice of Conscious Creation and our Believe System."

One last note: Most of the knowledge in this book is not mine, I am not the master mind who created it, nor do I think any of the masters ever created any of it, they and myself only provide what we learn from the ALL, we simply share with you the secrets of the universe as WE have found them to work for us.

To my surprise the first few times I was brave enough to try some of what I thought at the time crazy and perhaps stupid experiments in to the spiritual arena, I was quite surprised to find that they did work, that miracles[7] do happen, in fact the word miracle is to me synonymous with ignorance, since there really is not such a thing as a miracle. A miracle is something that happens that does not have a scientific explanation yet; it is something that is not labeled yet by modern science, since modern science barely knows or accepts such evidence as scientific at the present time. But it will, and is doing so faster than you think. Magic is your ability to manifest your own creation.

---

and most sacred form. Magic is in reality a sacred science, the word "Magic" originating from the "Magi" who fully understood and applied natural Universal laws in order to bring about effect that many might consider to be miraculous.

[7] A word commonly used for lack of a scientific word to describe it property

*If only humans knew what lies ahead on the Divine path; time would not be squandered on Earth pursuing trivial, material, egocentric things, while never learning. ~ **Adrian Cooper***

When indifference builds a fortified wall around us; we become spiritually nearsighted and sociologically hard-of-hearing. Then when help and answers do come, we neglect to listen and fail to see the obvious solutions that were right in front of us all along. Despair can be rectified through exposure to Natural Elements, the company of loving friends and family, augmented by a complete retreat from cities and electronic equipment. A Smug-Indifference however, born of Pride and Egoistic thought process, it a hard nut to crack. The know-it-all type of person is difficult to reach and as we can plainly see, their "inner-rooms" are filled to capacity, bursting with all-they-know, consequently there is no room left for new ideas. They cannot escape, trapped inside all that clutter of knowledge, thus there is no way out of that crowded-house. **The Myth, Magic & Murder of ORMUS, By Elder H. Alfred Goolsbee**

PART ONE

QUESTIONING EVERYTHING

INTRODUCTION

I have written this book for the individual that does NOT believe in any of all that spiritual nonsense hocus-pocus junk we all hear all the time; for the ones that hates all religions, the one that pukes when he/she hears god-bless-you or Jesus is my savior, the one that would burn the newspaper just because it has a horoscope section in it, for those that make sure their TV and radio does not stop on any religious channels, and for all of those who have spent many years in universities, the ones that really know that there is nothing magical about life other than the truth of scientific research and hard work to go along with it.

In this book you will find very valuable information from an ex-atheist (me), a scientist and lawyer that spent many years studying to be the best in his field, but one day something happened and I had to research all that was not really real (at least I thought so at the time.) due to the fact of one too many odd unexplainable experiences throughout my life that beg for an explanation that made sense in a clear and concise scientific way.

You will also find an auto-biography; since many have encouraged me to write one; therefore I will take this opportunity to write about myself a little bit, since by doing so, you will get a good understanding of what made me change my believe system. I do this not from the standpoint of my ego, but more so from the point that I like you to know what you are capable of accomplishing, if only you set your mind to it.

From a very early age I have done what most consider impossible: I simply was too busy doing, to learn that it was impossible or a miracle as some would put it. By the time I learned from society that it could not be done, I had already done it! Like reading at age 4 or finding a high paying job as an engineer for a mid-size company at age 15.

I will tell you first about a few so called impossible things that I have accomplished that many would think is not true. I want you to know about my experiences first. I like you to understand that what follows in this book does NOT come from someone that is mentally disturbed, crazy or fanatic in any way. I was an average atheist with very good reasons (I thought) to be an atheist. Only logic made me change my believe system, and a few experiences that had only one logical explanation; and that was that there must be more to life than what I was allowing myself to perceive. My message to you is: Do yourself a favor and open-up your mind a little bit and read all this book and the books and webpage links recommended. My promise to you is that you will not regret it. It is a compilation of approximately 20 years of research and study into subjects we commonly do not talk much about, in a simple way that an atheist can easily understand, benefit from and relate to.

Here is a brief description about my work and educational engineering life. The purpose of it is for you to get an understanding of how I think, and how I used logic. I spent 24 years prior to writing this book as a hardware and software engineer, if you know anything about software and hardware you will know that it is ALL logic, it all operates on ON or OFF signals. No matter what a computer does, it all boils down to a signal being on or off, usually referred to as a 1 or a 0. To build a software one must constantly think of the logical flow of information (1 or 0). What I am trying to say to you is that I the author of this book, analyses things with logic not just with feelings and emotions.

I will start my auto-biography at age 4.-

At age 4, I desperately wanted to learn how to read, I wanted information and was not getting it from my parents, I wanted to go to school, I wanted a teacher; therefore one day at church, I sought intuitively (more on intuition later in this book) the most intelligent person I could find, went up to him and informed him that I wanted him to teach me how to read. Needless to say he was quite surprised and not to keen on helping me, therefore I had to insist quite a bit. My insistence was enough to motivate him to talk to my mother. So in the presence of my mother he agreed on a once a week class for one hour in his home. Upon my arrival at his home after his work day ended at 5 pm he was quite harsh, perhaps even rude to explain the rules to me. He started by telling me that he worked hard all day, that this was his free time to spend with his wife, that the class will be for one hour only, that he expected me to leave immediately after the class, that if I even dream of playing, that would be the last class and that I would have to learn all he told me by the following week or to not come back again. The first class was about the alphabet; needless to say I would better know it all well by next week or else... Second week was on how to combine the letters with vowels. Note: This was Spanish, my first language. Third week was reading a basic book, which again had the same rule; be sure you know how to read it by next week or do not come back. Fourth week was on some non-logical things about Spanish. Fifth and last week was on using the dictionary. I remember well a good piece of advice he gave me: "Well now you know how to read, I have done my part as I had agreed, now all you need to remember is that: "Anything you want to know you can find it in a book." That was it; I was on my way to reading, now the problem was finding literature to read. So I started reading everything I could find in Spanish, but quickly also learned English in school.

My next big goal was convincing my parents to let me enroll in first grade. This was not easy, since the local school only accepted children after age 5. Needless to say I drove my parents crazy until they enrolled me in school. Little did I knew then how much I would grow to hate the school system.

At age 9 when I started 4th grade at a private school after endless complaints about public school and one previous private school, I walked in to class and the teacher put me down for being a Jehovah's Witness. Turns out she hated them. This was war! By now I had a double personality, one was the fake religious one and the other was I will do what I want and when I want (still do), so I proceeded to insult her. It was quite obvious she was not very intelligent at all. In fact she was quite stupid, which I had no qualms about telling her. In fact I called her stupid day in and day out, and challenged her to do something about it. Well, all she could really do was send me to the principal's office and complain about my behavior. One day after two weeks of my verbal abuse to the poor ignorant stupid teacher, the principal asked me why I called her stupid. I promptly responded, because she is stupid. Can you not see how stupid she is? Just look at her stupid person standing there and not saying a word. Only a very stupid person would not defend themselves. I challenged her even further. I said, "Can you prove to the principal that you are not stupid or can you prove that she is not stupid;" this went on for a while. I asked the principal to fire her, but he responded that he could not afford anything better. He was also a politician and did not want to make any waves. So he asked me what I suggested he should do. I said, "well since you are not willing to replace her and you sure do not want this to get out!, how about you put me in your wife's class. I like her and she likes me." He picked up the phone and called his wife, who was the teacher for the 11th and 12th grade, explained the very serious situation, and after a few minutes she quickly agreed to have me in her class. So I went directly from the 4th grade to the 11th.and 12th grade. Even this was quite boring, since it only took me a few months to read all the class books for both years. After all, the stuff they taught was quite simple back then, I sure hope school systems have improved... I even went as far as creating many excuses to not attend school nor write, since I hated writing.

At age 7-10 I managed to do a few more so called impossible tasks. I grew up in a very poor family. My parents had immigrated from Cuba in 1960 to run away from Fidel Castro's regimen, they lived in the province of south Florida in the united states of America. I felt the pain of my parents financial crunch each and every day. I knew that we were poor and that my parents did all they could do, therefore I set my own plan on how to earn money, since I had not been trained yet that this could not be done, I set myself to do it. I noticed a lady one day who came to our door selling AVON[8]. I asked her if I could sell for her and she agree to give me a few catalogs. So I went to work with the catalogs, I passed them around to all the women I could find, they said: "I want this and that;" and took it as a joke, but it was NO joke. I showed up with the product and demanded payment. Soon enough I was known as the kid that

---

[8] AVON a company that sells a large variety of cosmetics, jewelry and perfumes. www.avon.com

sold AVON products, and the sales were good, I got to the point that I earned more in a week than my father. Same lady came later on with another product line from a company that sold cleaning products for homes and business. Recession, bad times or not, I sold thousands of dollars which I used to support my family and buy books and magazines.

At age 11 I was done with school, therefore I decided to never go back to school again and in fact I have never done so again, except for a few very advanced courses in computer science and for teaching very advanced courses in computer science. The last day of school, after dinner with my parents, I firmly informed my parents, especially my father that I was not going back to school the following year; that if he did not like my decision, that I would leave home right that minute and that the subject was not open for discussion, that my decision was final. All he said was: "so what are you going to do?" I replied, "I will get a job, something will come up, and it did!!!"

A few weeks later something quite magical happened, (now I know it by the title "Conscious Creation," in fact I am dedicating a whole chapter in this book to this subject.) I was at a friends house in our neighborhood, he had just started on a two-year course at a technical college, the college provide a two-year course titled: "Engineering Technologist," the course was the first two years in electrical engineering but with a emphasis on an associate degree as a technician, which provided all the knowledge required to be a electronic technician, which at the time was good enough to repair radio and television transmitters and receivers. It encouraged the student to get their radio amateur license and commercial operator's license, which I did by age 13. My friend after describing how much money he was going to earn after completing this two college years, said I am going to fix myself a peanut butter and jelly sandwich with milk, would you like some? To which I replied yes. Before he left to the kitchen, I asked what you are going to do with these booklets. He said, I guess I will throw them away, why you want them? And he left to the kitchen. The course was provided in magazine size 15-30 page booklets, they stacked up to about 3 feet high for the two years course. Till date, I do not know how I read the first one so fast; by the time he got back I had read it cover-to-cover. In it I found a very nice description of what one could do with the knowledge after taking the two-year course. From this point on I went twice a week to his home to pickup the booklet's and homework, when I had question I would ask him and he would ask the teacher, I even did the exams for him.

At age 12 I got an 8-5 job at a woman's clothing manufacturing plant. The Jewish owner knew me well and wanted to pass on his business savvy. He made me a deal, he said that my job would be to do the work of whomever did not show up to work that day. Since I did not know this was not supposed to happen. I did exactly as he suggested, I was the secretary, the receptionist, the accountant, the plant manager, the shipping clerk, the clothe ironer, the label printer, the clothe designer, and much more. He called me too many of his meetings for me to listen in, he even went as far as offering me to manage the whole plant in a few more years. After all none of them had any clue of my real age. One day the insurance guy came in and asked me if I had already insured for the companies family insurance plan, he asked me if I had any children and if I was married, he said what are you 19-20 years old, to which I quickly replied aaaaa... yeaaa 19, from that day on I added 7 years to my real age, in fact I went as far as forgetting my real age. At break time and lunch time I would study my booklets. Later on I would spend most of the night studying them. I studies all weekend long. I learned many aspect of running a company, from marketing, to sales, to managing 200+ women at the same time that I studies my first two years of electrical engineering. I worked in this company for 2 years.

Shortly after I started working there I noticed a lady that came each day for Cuban coffee from the company's automated express coffee machine. So did my co-worker that laid the fabric to be cut together with me; he said you sure like her, don't you? All I could say, I sure do. He suggested that I go over there and introduce myself and asker her out for lunch, so I did. Since I did not know that older ladies (she was 38) were not supposed to date young boys. She replied sure lets do lunch, well after a few lunches she had some plans of her own, she said one day I have some food left over from last night, why don't you come with me to my apartment, so I did, I do not remember exactly how, but she ended up with some red wine on her dress, to which she asked for help to unzipped it down. The rest you can imagine, we had a sexual relationship that went on for years...

At age 14 I informed the owner that I was going to quit the job and that he had 30 days to find a replacement, to which he immediately replied I will triple your pay as of this minute. I was not interested in the money since I already had a television and radio repair shop setup in my home and knew some how that I was going to do well. In fact I already had passes around to all the workers my new business cards.

At first my mother would drive me around to pickup the TV's, but after a while I started driving without a license, I knew I could get away with it, since I had done it since I was 12. This also led me to the knowledge that there were things I could get away with. I got so good at repairing TV's that after a short while I had TV repair mans that could not fix the new modern transistor sets bringing them to me for repair. Word got around and I had 30-40 TVs a week brought to me. This quickly became boring, though those stories you here about the repair man and your wife are true, I had in those two years quite a few house call to fix the TV in the bedroom, in fact you could say I was on my way of becoming a gigolo; more so than the TV repair men; which till day I regret I did not, sure would had been more fun and profitable, but my mind was elsewhere creating another future for myself.

At age 15 one month before my 16th birthday, I managed to get a job as an engineer for a newspaper automation equipment manufacturer. I simply did not know that it could not be done; that at age 15 one could not get an engineer's job. I worked at this company till I became way too stressed to continue and my greedy mind wanted more money. I was traveling all over the world, installing and fixing complex automated equipment for the largest newspaper companies in the world. I even got to attend board meetings to pitch for the equipment. The company sent me with their top sales person to help on the sale of their equipment.

A few years latter after several other quite interesting and challenging jobs and businesses I had another most amazing and incredible miraculous job. One day I was job hunting and got one that paid me for almost 5 years for working a grand total of approximately 4 weeks out of a total of 5 years pay, I got a pay check week after week and did not work at all; in fact they told me to not call them if they did not call me first. I took this time to create my next miraculous job at IBM. NASA was my first choice, but by then I was learning what I was not supposed to be able do, therefore IBM seem still within range; back then I did not know they were the largest computer company in the world. I used these 5 years to work and study more, I spent quite a bit of time continuing to study hardware and software engineering, to the point that I managed to get a consulting job at IBM. My office at IBM was less than 100 meters away from Bill Gates office. We worked on what is now the XP operating system. Later on I did a few more impossible tasks, like getting other companies to triple, quadruple, quintuple and even more my consulting fees. All done with the art of conscious creation[9] that back then I did not know by label and name.

At age 25 I was a very good and loyal U.S. government tax payer, but the U.S. government since I was 12 years old had nothing better do to than sue me time after time and take my hard earned money away. In fact when my mother retired at age 67 they finally coursed her to pay for the lawsuit they lost against me at age 14, for earning a living and being paid wealth fare at the same time. All this led me by force to study none the less than 12,000 hours of law to learn how to defend myself from an extremely corrupt government system that was and continues to only be interested in oppressing and controlling the people at all cost, including those that are not even in USA/US soil. No attorney in the U.S.A. will defend you against the

---

[9] Conscious creation is the magical art of getting what you want, when you want it, the way you want it, even if it is considered by society an impossible task. You can do it by unlearning what society, school, religions, parents and peers have thought you.

U.S. Government properly because he/she knows quite well this is the last time he/she will work as an attorney, therefore there was only one choice for me and that was to go Pro-se[10].

The education on law led me to many other unexpected avenues, such as a thorough understanding on how the government and political system works, and how secret societies thru the ages have fully controlled all governments in a meticulous way, that these secret societies possessed knowledge not commonly known to the masses. This triggered me the desire to also posses this secret knowledge, and let me to the many years of research to truly understand who these people were, what they knew, and what their goals were. In time I found out that that the biggest and best secret of them all was that there is NO secret information whatsoever for those who seek the knowledge and wisdom. What had happen is that the information was once keep close guarded, due to the fact that the ignorant masses would destroy it out of fear, and this seem like it was being keep secret from others, when in fact, all this societies have always made a tremendous effort of recruiting new members to teach them their so called secrets, and yes in deed with the requirement of swearing that under the penalty of death one will never divulge the information to others. This has all changed with the advent of the Internet, since now one can find quite an amount of detailed information on the Internet.

---

[10] Pro-se in Latin represent yourself.

Throughout my life I have done many other so-called impossible things. Most outside the scope of this book to discuss; such as having a successful loving relationship with more than one partner at a time; something believed by most people to be impossible.[11] I have also managed to change career more than once and make a good living at it; again something that most people believe cannot be done. And I have managed to live semi-retired by choice since by my late thirties in a rural mountain retreat in Ecuador, South America.[12]

Same as I done you can too. You will find in this book detailed information to set you into the life of your dreams as of NOW!!! It will provide you with the tools necessary to have a clear understanding of the hard to find rules and laws of the universe, the stuff they do NOT teach in schools, churches nor universities, what your parents should have known and should have taught you, but did not. In a simple and informative way to understand, with plenty of reference and Internet webpage links for you to find further detailed information. You WILL find on this book details about the secrets of life and death. Information on what happens when you die and how you can now prepare for death, even on how to not die if this is your choice, yes if your choice is to keep on living; there are ways to do it.

---

[11] See www.LovingMore.org for details on how you can do it too

[12] See Los Visionarios intentional community www.LosVisionarios.org for more details on where I live now.

Here is a brief explanation of what you will find in this book.

Chapter 1.- **The story of my religious/spiritual life.** In this chapter I will tell you how I ended up labeling myself as an atheist and how why I hated all that had to do with religion or anything that remotely resemble it.

Chapter 2.- **Synchronicities.** What triggered me to change from atheist to agnostic. In this chapter I will tell you what triggered me into researching spiritual matters. Here you will find a list of experiences that I had that slowly triggered me to research further...

Chapter 3.- **Benefits of changing from atheist to agnostic.** In this chapter I will describe to you some of my personal experiences and how I have benefited from them.

Chapter 4.- **What present scientists are saying.** An important thing to notice is that conventional scientists throughout history have been switching from an atheist position to a spiritual one, but we the atheist have not been listening.

Chapter 5.- **Death, what happens when you die.** Many have always know this quite well, but unfortunately many do not. It is really not difficult at all to grasp what happens, and what happens is quite good...

Chapter 6.- **Reincarnation & Past Lives.** Once you understand what life is, how your soul integrates with yours bodies, you will also understand how and why we reincarnate in this world, what our previous lives where and how to do they interact with our present one.

Chapter 7.- **Mental relaxation and meditation.** Learning how to control ones emotions, how to stop anger, hatred, envy, jealousy and all other negative emotions is a must for a healthy peaceful joyful existence. One of the many tools to get to this stage is meditation. Meditation has been taught for thousands of years, but unfortunately many still have no idea on how to do it. It really is quite simple and the results quite astonishing.

Chapter 8.- **Astrology.** Astrology is simply a scientific tool just like any other one. Simply put it works, how or why no one really knows. But what matters is that it is a very useful tool. If you used properly it will help you live a much more joyful harmonious life. It is a tool to point you in the right direction; the rest is up to you.

Chapter 9.- **The Art and Practice of Conscious Creation and our Belief System.** Haven't you always wanted things to go your way? Haven't you always wondered why some individual get all they want. It even fells unfair. Well now you can to!!! And it really is not all that difficult. All it takes is a bit of additional knowledge of the laws of physics, which one could also call them spiritual laws.

Chapter 10.- **Drugs.** Ever wonder why millions of individuals have taken them? Why the war on drugs? Could it be there is some secret hiding in the farce that they are bad for you? Did you ever believe the frying pan brain commercial? Or all the anti-drug commercials? Perhaps there is a bit more than meets the eye. You should find out and make your own decisions if they are for you or not.

Chapter 11.- Astral Travel, Out-of-Body experience and Near Death Experiences. Many have done it, <u>many do everyday</u>. Why should you not know for yourself what else is there outside this reality.

With a bit of practice and patience you can be on your way to exploring other worlds and realities.

Chapter 12.- Akashic Records. The Akashic Records is one of the billions of places where you can stop by on your astral travels. There you can find answers to anything you want to know about our past existence in this planet, and about future possibilities that await us. Sound to fantastic does it not? Well others do it, so can you.

Chapter 13.- **Who? What? Where? Is God.** This is an easy one to answer. Simply put, you are god, yes you are a god. No more any less, you to are god. The rest is all folklore and stories maliciously put in your mind by religions and governments to control you from finding out this truth.

Chapter 14.- **How to become immortal and/or improve your health.** First of all you are already immortal. Your body may die but not you, you are a god, and a god cannot die. Since you are a god, with the proper information you can make your body as healthy as you want it to be. May take you some time, since your have been playing this game of life and death for quite a while.

Chapter 15.- **The Law of KARMA and DARMA.** These are two very basic laws that everyone should be taught from a very early age. You could simplify them by the saying "What goes around, comes around."

Chapter 16.- **What is really going on with our planet? 2012.** Many are starting to wonder if the planet changes that we are all staring to notice are man made or not. Are those prophesies going to come true? Is it a punishment from god? The true answer is found in the fact that our solar system has its cycles in the universe too. At the peak of these cycles earth may experience violent changes, such as massive earthquakes, volcanoes, hurricanes, etc. The ancient prophesies simply say what happen in the previous cycles and give an idea of what may happen in the next cycle. What they do not say is that we can change the course of events. Being aware and prepared will save many lives.

Chapter 17.- **The mechanism of a prayer.** The big question is does a prayer ever work? The simply answer is yes sometimes they do, but more often not. Praying is a tool, and as any other tool, one must know the intricacies of how it works in order to benefit most from it.

From chapter 18 on you will start getting an introduction to the vast array of spiritual information available. Unfortunately not all spiritual information is plain and simple to understand. There are many very ancient languages, which have made for very poorly translated advance reference books, such as the bible, which has been maliciously altered by the Catholic Church. Beginners should skip all these ancient books; go for fresh new clearly explained information. Old ancient books are the worse possible place to get started. Religions have exploited for centuries books such as the bible for their own malicious benefits; needless to say one should skip any thing that relates to religion. It is like going directly to a trade journal on the very first day of class, one could not expect to understand much and never mind actually doing something useful with the information, in fact it could even be quite dangerous. From Chapter 18 through 33 you will find an extensive list of possibilities of where to get started. The last chapter of this book, Chapter 44 will guide you to pick where to get started.

Chapters 34 through 37 provide an introduction to some subjects of interests that merit to be mentioned. Ghost, Aliens, UFO's, Crop Circles and many other Paranormal existences are quite real, but they should not be the focus of your education in the arena of spiritual personal advancement. Nice to know, but try not to get to caught up on it.

Chapters 38.- through 42 provide several tools you should know about, investigate them and put them to use if you see them fit for you. Ask and listen to your heart, that internal part of you known as the sub-conscious, some called it our internal mother or father. Let it guide you, it always knows best.

Chapter 43.- **Additional books, newsgroups, web pages, etc.** This chapter provides yet a few more choices of where to get started. Have fun; start with a good movie or a light novel. Spiritual education should always be fun to learn; otherwise it may be your heart telling you that you are in the wrong path.

Donations. If you feel this book guided you in the right path and you feel you want to help others, please by all means consider a donation. Donations are the only means of getting this valuable and timely information to those who need it most. Buy a few copies of this book or other and pass it out to those you feel need to know.

*We would be 1,500 years ahead if it hadn't been for the church dragging science back by its coattails and burning our best minds at the stake. ~ **Catherine Fahringer***

*For my own part I would as soon be descended from that heroic little monkey, who braved his dreaded enemy in order to save the life of his keeper; or from that old baboon, who, descending from the mountains, carried away in triumph his young comrade from a crowd of astonished dogs – as from a savage who delights to torture his enemies, offers up bloody sacrifices, practices infanticide without remorse, treats his wives like slaves, knows no decency, and is haunted by the grossest superstitions. ~ **Charles Darwin, 1809-1882, The Descent of Man, 1871***

*I call Christianity the one great curse, the one great intrinsic depravity, the one great instinct for revenge for which no expedient is sufficiently poisonous, secret, subterranean, petty – I call it the one mortal blemish of mankind. ~ **Friedrich Nietzsche***

Chapter 1

My early religious/spiritual years

I grew up hating everything that had to do with religion; my parents forced me to attend their Jehovah Witness religious gatherings several times a week. Even on our very few vacations away from home, they were to boring fanatic religious gatherings. The only people they would have as friend were from their church and even worse the only friends I was allowed to have had to be from the same fanatic religion.

Jehovah Witness have it all quite figure out on how to not lose members from their flock of sheep's. I was taught that all is bad and a sin, things like movies, reading the newspaper, dancing, playing any sports with none members, going to the beach alone, going on a date without a chaperon, smoking anything, be it a pipe or a cigar, drinking alcoholic beverages, talking to the neighbors, using drugs regardless of which one, sex other than married and in the missionary position, masturbating, even reading magazines, all this and much more was evil and in many instances reason for temporary or permanent dismissal from the congregation (church), and what is worse, forbidden to ever talk to any of their members ever again, except for very close relatives such as parents, which even though not required is very common to include them. That a supreme being called Jehovah had his eyes on us all the time and would punish us, that ALL none members where going to be destroyed in the Armageddon and not allowed on his kingdom, and worse of all that this Armageddon was around the corner in the following short few years, and that any education other than theirs was a waste of time, that studying medicine or law for example was not going to be of any use in this new kingdom in heaven, therefore going to college was heavily discouraged. They never gave real world fact such as how many other competing religions there are, not ever compared facts other than the ones they could easily control. They had and have two magazines for those of the more curious inquisitive minds, both magazines are led to believe they have all the scientific world information one should ever need to read, and they are often enough to keep the flocks busy and with little time left for thinking or researching any other information. What little time they have left they spend it spying on one another. This was my hell on earth since the day I was born to the date I gathered enough courage to leave once and for all this fanatic religion. Believe me it was quite difficult, since for starters I was falling in love with one girl I really liked, she and her family cared for me quite a bit, and I only had one friend outside the church.

Studying to be a scientist was heavily discouraged; I was thought that the end of the world was soon to come, that god would provide all to every one that abide by his rules, that there was not going to be any diseases, therefore no doctors and no need to study medicine, which was my first choice in education. Since god was to provide everything there was no real need for me to study any further than the basics through school.

All this made me hate everything to do with religion more as each day passed that I was forced to be there. There way of teaching was extremely seductive and based only on fear.

My mother would use any means she could to course me into participating, even by faking all sorts of illnesses, such as heart problems. Even from the very early age of 5, I was deceived to believe she had a heart problem. She is now close to 80 years old, and no heart problem whatsoever, it was all a lie to control me.

I was thought that all other religions were useless and quite wrong in all their teaching, which led me to dismiss all of them, and in fact I found this to be quite true, most religions if not all are based on fear and of taking money from their members in more than one way.

As you can imagine all this led me to concentrate is science and ignore anything that had to do with spiritual believes, religion, etc. I even changed the radio station when it had the daily horoscope, quickly passed to the next page on the daily the newspaper if I saw the horoscope. If any one approached me with their religious propaganda I will quickly throw it away and got quite mad and frustrated on how naive and stupid people were.

We should be agnostic about those things for which there is no evidence. We should not hold beliefs merely because they gratify our desires for afterlife, immortality, heaven, hell, etc. ~ **Julian Huxley, Religion Without Revelation**

Doubt everything. Find your own light. ~ *Last words of Gautama Buddha, in Theravada tradition*

I am against religion because it teaches us to be satisfied with not understanding the world. ~ **Richard Dawkins**

I do not find in orthodox Christianity one redeeming feature. ~ **Thomas Jefferson, 1743-1826**

I condemn false prophets; I condemn the effort to take away the power of rational decision, to drain people of their free will - and a hell of a lot of money in the bargain. Religions vary in their degree of idiocy, but I reject them all. For most people, religion is nothing more than a substitute for a malfunctioning brain. ~ **Gene Roddenberry**

Chapter 2

Synchronicities - what triggered me to change from atheist to agnostic

Below I will describe some of the experiences that I have had thru my early years that have led me to read many books, search many libraries, visit many places, and try many experiments. Slowly I went from an atheist to who I am today. Perhaps you also have had similar experiences but have used logic and have discarded them, even without thinking much about them. I suggest that after you read this chapter you go back to your archived memory of passed experiences and evaluate them with a new point of view; perhaps you too will see the magic in them.

At age 4-5 I had a screwdriver on my hand, the screwdriver tried to penetrate me, it was quite a struggle to make it go away from me. It was like a force was pushing it towards me. I could not make any sense of the experience and I discarded it to my long-term memory.

At age 7-8 I had my first very detailed remote viewing experience, which led to the capture of a thief. It was so real that for many years I analyze the whole experience and often said to myself, o you must have missed something, you much have seen it in person or made it up, it cannot be real, that cannot happen, it is imposable. Then I would rehearse in my mind the facts of where was I at the time which blocked all the view to what I saw and later describe, and the fact that I was laying down on a sofa all that time, that I had not moved from the sofa, and that I had very close up detailed clear view of all the events that transpired on that theft. I just was not ready to neither understand nor admit to myself that I had actually had a remove viewing experience. For many years I chose to block this memory, since I was not able to deal with it. Only years later my mother admitted to having such experiences herself on her younger years, that helped me accept that my experience were also real.

Right after puberty at age 9 and up to about age 13 I started from time to time to have visions of the future. I was able to tell what was going to happen a few seconds before it did, like if I had dreamed of it a while earlier. I tried several times to prove to myself via writing in advance what was going to happen, but I could not narrow something to write, not to mention that writing was the least of my skills and interest at the time. Therefore as time went on I discarded this as some sort of brain failure.

At age 16 I meet a neophyte Rosicrucian[13], he was on his initial steps at the time. From time to time, he would tell me some of his experiences, but they were so far out, that I could hardly relate to them. He was also quite an atheist; he would talk down on all religions and was a very poor teacher, though I thank him quite a bit, because he planted many seeds in my mind and for that I will always be grateful to him.

---

[13] Rosicrucian Order of AMORC.- www.amorc.org

At age 17 I always had a strong interest in psychology and sexology, which led me to often search the library and store books for books on these two subjects, one day after reading all the books that were available on my local book store, I asked myself, if I was to ever be a true expert on the subject of sexuality, how could I justify always ignoring this one book titled: "Sexual Astrology[14]" that I had notice many times and moved to the side, and since there were no more books available and I had plenty of time, I decide to take a quick peek to prove to myself that this books was utterly stupid nonsense garbage, so I went to the index and quickly found that it was divided in 24 sections, one for male and one for female for each of the 12 astrological signs, I quickly found my sign and proceeded to start reading the chapter on my astrological sign, which started on a very thorough description of how a person from this sign sexually feels and behaves, to my huge surprise and amazement it was describing me much better that I could do myself even till this date. So I deducted that it had to be trickery of words, that this was completely impossible, how could a books describe me so well, all I could think was that most people must be the same and that all the chapters were similar, therefore any chapter would apply to anyone, so I proceeded to read a bit of another chapter, but it was different, and another and it also was different, an hour or two had gone by and the store was about to close, so I decided to buy the book just for the purpose of figuring out this trickery of words. To my surprise I read the whole book cover to cover and every single chapter was quite different, and when I reread my sign it was

---

[14] Sexual Astrology: A Sign-by-Sign Guide to Your Sensual Stars by Joanna Woolfolk

just way to accurate to disprove it, in fact it was at least 98% accurate and the other 2% was areas of my sexuality that I was yet to explore, but that I would not mind exploring. So I went on reading the chapter for my friends, especially those I had had sex with, and was also as surprised to find out how accurate they were. I started learning people's astrological signs and putting the information to the test, this is what lead me to having a relationship with two ladies at a time. One day I met one and asked her sign, I immediately recalled that this sign was open to bisexual relationships, therefore I asked her if she would be interested in having a female partner in addition to myself, to which she quickly answered yes, so we both proceed to find one, the rest you can figure out... That opened up the door to some fantastic sexual encounters, since now I knew the dark secret of people's sexuality. I went as far as doing the believed by most impossible affair of having sex with a group of six ladies at the time, and I must add all of their free will. My point is that astrology can teach you lots of things even about yourself that will surprise you.

At age 20 my girlfriend starter reading a few old Wishcraft reference books she found at a antique store, and she started doing some experiments while I was not at home, which led her to all sorts of problems, which really scared her a lot, she described her experiences to me, but I had no ears to believe her, in fact I forbade her to continue any of this nonsense or I would leave her, to which she agreed since it had scared her quite a bit and she had no intentions of pursuing this for the time being. But she did get far enough to convince me one day on an experiment of seeing auras, so successful I was at seeing auras that I had a very hard time not seeing them, I did not like the experience the least bit and had to make a very strong effort to stop seeing them, since days later I was still seeing them on people, animals, plants, you name it, it got to the point that it was really distorting my sight.

At approximately age 22 I made close friends with a fellow that also described to me some of his weird experiences, like having his body floating above his bed after reading one too many books on how to make extraterrestrial contact. In his research into how to make extraterrestrial contact he found some experiments he thought of value and convince me to try them out with him, so one day we tried a few of them; now I know them by the more common name "meditation.[15]" Therefore I will use the word meditation from now on. So I lay down in bed in a very quite room and followed what he told me to do with my mind. I do not remember what he said, but I do vividly remember the experience. Here it goes: I closed my eyes, relaxed all my body, then all of the sudden I started to view a movie, like in a theater, but this was NO ordinary movie nor a theater, this was the absolute best animated cartoon movie ever, it was the most real thing you could possibly imagine, and get this it was all in 360 degrees, I do not mean around in 360 degrees, it was like having a million eyes, I was able to see in all directions at the same time, and I was almost part of it, since I was so close to it. Keep in mind that I had never used drugs at the time; more on drugs later on. From this experience many questions quickly pop into my mind, one of course was the fact of 360 degree vision, how can this possibly happen? But this was not the question that really bothered me the most, what

---

[15] Meditation.- Lots can be said about this word. Basically for me is a way to make the mind work on only one subject at a time or NONE at all.

really bothered me was: where did the movie come from? Who created the characters? The script? Did my brain created it? Or was it a telepathic transmission? I chose to believe that my brain must have the ability to do such incredible tasks; after all we all have heard that we only use a very small fraction of our brains. This led me to research how I possible can use my brain more. What if I could tap into this amazing brain power and use it in real life? This led me to other experiments with this particular meditation technique; the movies did not play again, but other amazing things happen, like attending some quite excellent classical music concerts, with time I realized that I could change the music, that in some situation I could play a whole orchestra in my mind. A few years later I went on vacation to Europe and visited the house of Mozart. I was very surprised to learn that he composed symphonies at a very young age; history says that he composed his first symphony at the early age of 5, this of course could not be true or could it? If it was true, did I stumble into the same abilities as Mozart? And even if so, where did the music come from for those concerts?

This same friend introduced me to another friend who was a professional Reiki massage therapist, among the best; he even owned the largest massage school in the area where I lived at the time. It was quite obvious that he had the power to manipulate some type of energy and was able to project it into my body, it was so strong that I often though he was using some sort of equipment to project this energy into me. I asked him and he explained this was an ancient practice and that the energy was known by the name of chi in China and other Asian cultures... My friend had also mentioned that they had a mutual friend who was a professional astrologer, he had describe him well enough that one day as I was getting a massage behind closed door, I was able to identified him by his voice, so I had time to plan a trick for him to prove to myself that astrology was not that good even though deep inside and from previous experience from the Sexual Astrology book I knew better. As I walked out to meet him I decide to act quite different from who I really am, we quickly got into the conversation of astrology and I managed to challenge him to prove to me that astrology was real, and he was quick to accept my challenge, he said, I will prove to you it is real, in fact I happened to have the right reference book here with me to prove you so. I will tell you the exact date, place and time where you were born; to do so, I will ask you a few question, to what I quickly answer, they better be question that do not give you obvious leads, he smiled and said they will not, so he proceeded to asked me question such as what are my favorite type of foods, how did I relate to my parents, about my siblings, work, study habits and a few other question, as I answered he kept on searching through his book, to my surprise he very accurately told me, the day, month, year and time I was born, in fact at the time I did not know the time I was born and had to ask my mother for confirmation. Needless to say I was one-hundred-percent convinced. Keep in mind that no one that I knew at the time knew my real age, other than my mother, not even close family members knew my real age, since I grew up far away from them, my date of birth was a secret that was not even on my ID, but the astrologer was able in just a few minutes to ping point it down to the time of birth.

About the same time one evening around 9 PM my friend and I were quite bored driving around trying to find something entertaining to do, he remembered that there was a parapsychologist name Iris Saltzman[16], who he had read about in a book and had tried to get an appointment with her, but she was fully booked for private meetings for the following 3 years, though she did give open sessions once a week at this time and we just happened to be in the area. For starters we had a hard time finding her, since she was in this large office building where all the lights were off and we did not know exactly where her office was at, in fact I kept on complaining to my friend that we should leave the building at once before security guards would find us. After walking for what seem an eternity in the building we found an office with the lights on, so we knocked and went in, there were approximately 30 people sitting and a old lady behind a desk talking, another lady was at the door and asked us for $15 dollars and our date of birth and to please sit down since it had already started, so we did not talk to anyone else and just sat down. She started by going into a lengthy introduction of what was it that she did and how was it that she did it, she explained in quite a bit of detail that she used astrology and her psychic abilities, better know as parapsychology, she said that this evening was only a demonstration and that she would give each person a brief reading, that she was in a trance and that this work

---

[16] Iris Saltzman 2225 North University Drive Pembroke Pines, Florida 33024 (954) 986-1303 www.psysearch.com/Iris.html

was quite dangerous to her health and that she asked that no one leave until she was done. She started one by one, but we were all the way on the back, since we came in last. So we listen to an observed peoples reactions, to say the least everyone was in a state of shock, since her abilities were overwhelming, I for one was saying to myself, no way can she tell me a thing, this people must all come here often and she must know them, that all started to change when she started doing the astrological readings and all the sudden stop in her own surprise, she said, boy here is a miracle that you all are not going to believe, something very special has happen here tonight, you were all called here together to have a very unique experience, I do not know why but there are two groups of you here tonight and you are not going to believe this, but you are all born in almost the same date, in fact several of you are born not only the same date but the same year, now I was thinking to myself this woman is a master liar, no way, this is completely impossible, so I look to the lady sitting on my left and said to her, hey when were you born? boy was I in for a huge surprise, she said my same birth date, to which I said to her bullshit, you are lying, you must have seen my card, let me see some ID, and she said why? I said cause that is the day I was born too, then she said you are a liar, so I said, no I am not, here is my ID, now let me see yours, to which she produced her drivers license, I almost fainted when I saw we were both born on the same date, month and year, now that was not the end, as it turn out there were two groups of people of which most were born a few days from each other, we kept on looking at each others and did not say a word. So she kept on doing her reading and the time came to my friend, to whom she said: ooooo you got two choices in life, one get out of the air force now while you can, or your plane will be shot down in a war the U.S. is going to have and you will lose a leg and be very miserable for the rest of your life for killing so many people. Now I must tell you that my friend was in a secret military mission and almost no one knew about his U.S. military air force activities, nor there was any reason to believe the U.S. government was going to be in any kind of war at the time, since this was back in the eighties well before the Iraq war. She went on telling him that the banking business will fail for him. He worked in a bank at the time. And that there was another path that life was going to provide him which would lead him in a great adventure and learning experience, that this was the path he should take, she also went in quite a bit of details of other areas of his life. Then it was my turn. She looked at me, and paused, then said, oooo you would not care anyhow, and paused again... after all you want proof of my abilities don't you? I said yes I do, so she said I am going to give you enough to convince you, so she started by saying you are a very promiscuous person, and you do not care if I say so, aren't you? To which I answer yes I am, then she said well there is nothing wrong with that, as long as you are always honest with all your partners. She went on describing my career to the t, my life with my parents, my religious experience, on an on, until she said, had enough? I said yes, ok so now let's get on with your future. She said in the following years you will come across a huge amount of secret information, information that you cannot even begin to imagine at this time, but it will come to you from many different sources. I can tell you that to my surprise this has been true, I have met people and been in places that if I tell you, you would simply not believe it, I even have a hard time believing it myself.

From age 22 to the present, I have been on a nonstop quest for answer to the above experiences. The more I searched the more experiences I have had; they just kept and keep on coming. One day for example I had just finished reading chapter one of a small book titled "The Art and Practice of Astral Projection, by OPHIEL first published in 1974, in it the author describes a system he calls "little system" to trigger an astral trip. Now I had heard from my friend the Rosicrucian about his out-of-body experiences and by now I had some believes that this was possible, otherwise I would had not been reading this book. So I went to sleep that night and all the sudden I woke up inside my dream, I became conscious that I was dreaming and more so that I was in the dream, the setting was a party just like any other party were people mingle and talk, this attractive 30 or so year old well dressed lady past in front of me, and as her back was to me on my left side, I decided to tap her on the shoulder to see what would happen, boy was I in for a huge surprise, she turned around looked at me straight in the face and smiled, the experience was so electrifying that it sent me back into my body in a quick rush. I could not go back to sleep, this was more real than anything I had ever experience, it was NO dream, and NO one could ever convince me that it was not real, in fact more so real than being awake. Needless to say this send me on a nonstop study on the out-of-body experiences that so many people have written about, also know as astral travel phenomenon. Now I now that is not such a phenomenon and that in fact that is the real reality and that this is the real dream, also know as the Matrix. I do not expect you to see it that way too for quite some time, it takes having several experiences and a lot of studying to see it as I do.

Since I started exploring the other worlds, (densities and dimensions, as some will use these words to describe it) I have had hundreds of experiences such as the one above. There is literary an unlimited amount of experiences anyone can have if so wanted with a little bit of studying and work, it all starts with meditation, I have dedicated a whole chapter to introduce you to the subject of meditation.

Here is another noteworthy experience I had. One night as I was coming back from an astral trip and was already back in my body but still vibrating at the frequency of the next density (dimension) an entity green lizard type of entity passed by my room at an angle as he was traveling, it gave me a very quick look and kept on going. It was extremely frightening to me to see such powerful being so close and in my room with me. Later on I learned that the more advance beings travel from point to point in this density (dimension) and that they are able to see us, but we are not able to see them. This also triggered me to research further websites I had found on the lizard species and secret government know as the Illuminati's[17]. This opened yet another source of information that I would have normally discarded as science fiction.

On July 1, 2005 I had a shocking experience (no pun intended) a friend brought a few 32 oz water bottles she bought from www.ancienttek.com called "The Spark of Life" Aetheric Charged Water, now this is NO ordinary water by any means, it has what is believe to be a energy charge from the 4th density/dimension, which just about any scientist/engineer will tell you that this is all utterly nonsense lie and probably even becomes furious at you proposing such utterly stupidity; I know it has happen to me already with a few skeptic friends who refuse to even continue the conversation since

---

[17] See David Icke www.davidicke.com many books on this subject.

they are so ingrained in their believe system that there is no space to have this conversation with me. Good for you that you are still reading, cause you are about to learn something new and very important, that is going to change your life and the way you view this reality. So here is what happens with this water, and by the way, I am talking about an ordinary small clear plastic bottle like the ones you can buy a soft drink or water in any common store, no tricks here, it is simply a clear plastic bottle filled with water with a plain and simple label on it. So you take the bottle and open it just like any other bottle, just do not dare take it into your mouth or you will never forget the experience for the rest of your life and probably a few more lives, cause the water contains a huge charge of energy, you can confirm this by holding the bottle in one hand and inserting the tip of a finger from your other hand, when I did this I got a huge shock. Note that I am a hardware electrical engineer, and I have been shocked in the past to the point of passing out and almost dying, I have had shocks leave burn marks and holes going true my fingers more than once, I know quite well what is a high voltage shock and how it fells, that said, I estimate the charge to be the equivalent of 50,000 or so volts, it produces a 1 inch blue spark/arc of energy, but from what I can tell it is not electron based, it is not electricity, it feels similar but not the same, also in other experiments such as a group of people in a circle holding hands and only the last two person closing the circuit touch the water gives everyone the same shock, where if this were electricity as we know it, it will only shock the last two person closing the circuit. So what is this energy in the water? Where does it come from? This and many more pieces of the puzzle will start becoming clear to you as you read this book. They all connect into what is starting to be recognized as Quantum Physics, but wait there, there is more to it, it also connects with what is also referred as spiritual realms, and much more, also gives explanation of such things that one completely dismissed, like water based fuel cells that can run an engine on just water[18], in fact these fuel cells do not even consume the water. You probably ask or worse refute the possibility since it does not fit any of your present believe system, how can this be possible? well it is, and there are good reasons of why this technology is not widely available, since it has one major problem for us to be able to use it, you see this energy acts to the will of the people around it, it is not just another fuel or energy as we know then, this one comes from the same realm our dreams come from and that is the 4th density/dimension therefore it not only requires special equipment to harness it, but it also requires a change in our belief systems for it to work for us, this in part is the main reason of why we are not running all our engines on water. The discovery of this energy is not all that new; there are very well documented scientists who worked with it even a 100 years ago, for example the inventor of alternating current used in every single house and industry in the world, Nikola Tesla[19] also had discovered a revolutionary way, but it was too late, the investors did not want to hear of his ideas, and the US Government made sure all his knowledge was well kept in secret, even till today, more than a hundred years later, some of his inventions are kept by the U.S. Government as national security. Then there was Dr. Wilhelm Reich M.D. who the US Government

---

[18] See www.joecellenergy.com www.cheniere.org Do a web search on Joe Cell, also on Tom Bearden

[19] www.teslatech.info

went as far as imprisoning him and destroying as much information of his as possible, a U.S. Federal Court ordered his books burn and his lab destroyed, in 1954. Dr. Reich died in a U.S. Federal prison in 1957, but luckily for us his work was been preserved and has continued in secret till date from both end, the U.S. and Russian government among others and by a few independent scientist such as James DeMeo, Ph.D. who has written several books on the subject or ORGONE[20] energy.

There are two main reasons why all these technologies have not become widely available, one is the greed of all the people involved in selling, producing etc. the present fuels we use, they simply know that if people had a simple and very economic way of producing energy and of living in perfect health, both energy and medical empires would collapse. Second reason is that this energy can be used easily to cause enormous harm to others, many times worse than a nuclear bomb and many times easier to produce.

Do note that there are many different names used to describe the same source of this energy, perhaps the names used are proper since they describe different uses for the same energy. Here is a brief list of synonymous names used to describe the same energy or source of it: Orgone (organic energy), Oranur, Dor, Indians speak of it as: Prana, Chinese medicine refer to it as: Chi, Aether, Etheric, holy ghost, empty space, bioenergetic energy, auras, in the Western tradition it has also been referred to as élan vital, psychic force,

---

[20] www.orgonics.com www.orgonelab.com

biological energy, life force, animal magnetism, the odic force, the force and so on,,, even sexual energy has been describe by many as an energy not from our dimension.

Mainstream scientists have quietly rediscovered this energy medium too, and it is variously called the Virtual Particle Flux, the Zero-Point Energy Field, the Quantum Physical Vacuum, the Quantum Foam, "Superstrings," "Dark Matter" and "Dark Energy," among other things. They are becoming aware that it must be responsible for the creation of matter. Various spiritual teachers have called it "spiritual energy," "loving energy," "healing energy," "the Holy Spirit," et cetera. All are discussing the same energy field source.

Before you go on to the next section I want to say to you that this books is by no means the answer to all your question, it is simply a guide to get you started quickly in the right direction, and to save you lots of time, since often one finds a books that indeed has valuable information, but it is not in the ideal order one should study. For me it has been like going to a university and getting all the books for an entire career and tossing them up in the air, and ending up studying the last book first, granted you will understand some of it, but it would be much easier if one starts from the begging vs. jumping into an advance book. Even for me after more than twenty years studying these subjects, there are some books in the category of advance, which are still very difficult for me to understand. What I am saying is do not dismiss the information in one of them if you do not understand it, good change that the information is quite valid and that it is you who does not understand it yet, just move on to something easier and more practical for you and later if you fell the need go back to that book.

PART TWO

FROM ATHIEST TO AGNOSTIC

HOW TO GUIDE

Pythagoras, the first philosopher

Take the first step in faith. You don't have to see the whole staircase, just take the first step. **-- Martin Luther King Jr.**

Chapter 3

Benefits of changing from atheist to agnostic

One of the very first things that will happen to you is that you will loose the fear of dying; you will learn that only your body can die, and not who and what you really are which is a soul having a 3rd density/dimension experience/life. Since you really are an eternal spirit of another density altogether.

Another thing that will happen to you in a short period of time is that you will have more financial wealth and much better health, your intellectual wealth will also increase; you will become a much more fun individual, that others will want to associate more with. You will make many less mistakes, therefore earning more money, better health, quality friends and relationships.

You will start knowing what is best for you, in a new fool proof way, that once you perfect it, will lead you to succeed in all your desires.

Your health will improve dramatically, you will find that you will look and fell much younger than others your age. This is hard fact to swallow but it is a very real one. For example often people especially young woman have guess my age more than twenty years less than what it is. Most people will guess my age anywhere from 10 -20 years less. Of course there is more to it than just changing your believe systems and adding to your knowledge, it also takes practicing what you learn.

In time you will also come to the realization that you are also a god and co-creator of this entire universe, with all its ups and downs as you now see them; that you have the power to change all that surrounds you in ways that you cannot even begin to imagine now. That poverty, sickness, lack of, all can be easily changed once we have learned the lesson they are teaching us. You will learn that NO problem ever persist past the lesson learned.

You will even learn that giving time and practice you are able to even change your physical appearance like others have done.

We are all like children's beginning second year of school; completely indiscipline and not knowing which way to go or what to do next, but if we seek to ascend, the information will become available to us in more than one way.

This book provides you a quick and efficient reference of where to start, but it is really up to you to seek the information and put it in practice throughout your life. If you follow trough with it, you will have experiences and pleasures that now you cannot begging to imagine.

Chapter 4

What present scientists are saying

Scientists are becoming aware very S L O W L Y that there is a lot more than meets their five senses and 3rd density/dimension test equipments they presently use, that there are other densities/dimensions and parallel realities. This is extremely difficult and in fact impossible in the mind of most scientists to grasp, they act in the same way of the days when Galilei Galileo[21] was victim of inquisition for writing books that went against the establish norm. Hard to believe that the established norm of teaching as if it where the final fact, on an issue continues till date in almost every schools in the world. The worse thing that formal education has done to everyone is putting in peoples mind the believe system of: "all that cannot be done." vs. saying this is what we know now, perhaps you will figure out a completely different explanation. Teachers have the very bad habit of teaching everything as it where the very final word on the subjects, leaving no room for the student to be creative and explore other possible explanations.

For example when I was 7 years old I started an experiment to make an electrical motor/alternator/battery run for ever, soon after I

---

[21] Galilei Galileo 1564-1642 Philosopher, astronomer, and mathematician who made fundamental contributions to the sciences. Designer of telescopes that revolutionized astronomy.

got it running it did not run more than a few hours at a time, I spent years trying to figure out why it would not continue to run. When I started to research further my ideas, I quickly came to the information that others had already tried the same and had made a Law in science that said it could not be done, therefore I drop my idea and pursue learning from others what they say could only be done. Many years had to pass, before I changed my believe systems from that taught by the school system and ventured again into the true search of the ultimate truth of how it can be done. Now I know that that particular idea can be done and that others have done it. But I have also learned that most who have pursued this ideas of low cost near free energy have been murdered, ridiculed and persecuted by the governments and people in power who do not want this information to come out to the general public.

Something motivated me back then to pursue this avenue of invention, but I was very misguided by the established educational system that seems to know it all at the time, and not provided any information of the much larger reality; I can only assume that this something that motivated me was knowledge from previous life's.

Nikola Tesla was perhaps the first modern time pioneer of the science of harnessing energy from the 4th density/dimension, but his very advance inventions that would have brought the world extremely low near free energy cost where all confiscated by the governments and some is still held as top national security information by the U.S. Government. Same as Albert Einstein[22]

---

[22] Albert Einstein 1879 – 1955 Physicist and Mathematician

Famous equation E=mc2 which we have been lead to believe was not complete, in fact was completed and put to use. Tesla had come to the same conclusion that Einstein did that this technology if developed would not be used for the benefit of mankind.

Fortunately there have been a few true scientists like Dr. Fritjof Capra writer of the book "The TAO of Physics" who have seen further than the established educational norm and government cover-ups and lies. Dr. Capra discovered that what ancient manuscripts said correlates quite well with the latest modern science of physics, in fact that it is quite more accurate and that it fills the gap of what is yet not scientifically known.

Others like James Redfield in his book titled "The Celestine Vision" 1997 has a chapter titled "The New Physics" that give a very good description of how science is slowly evolving into a merger with spiritually, which is no more than clearer explanation of other realms of reality that we are not yet accustomed to. These new scientific discoveries that are now only being propagated through the Internet, will some day very soon surprise us all. Yes there are ways of making an engine run from fuel cells that run from the ether, with no need for conventional fuels, but this will put out of business all the oil mining companies. There are mechanical and electronic circuitry generators that will produce usable energy at no cost, but this technology is not being supported by the governments.

If you think that there is no scientific basis for free energy, you are not current in cutting-edge physics (which is in turn billions of years behind the Universe itself). The work of Myron Evans in O(3) Electrodynamics, Sach's Unified Field Theory, and Michael Leyton's work in higher dimensional symmetry, among others, give plenty of theoretical basis on how it can be done.

The movie titled: What the Bleep Do We Know?[23] Explains that science and spirituality are not different modes of thought, but are in fact describing the same thing, in a very fun and entertaining way. In this movie it demonstrates how to bring the power back to the individual man and woman as it demonstrates creation as the god-like capacity of every individual. Is an informative and fun movie to see, meditate and talk about.

When Dr. Emoto learned that every snowflake is unique, he thought the same thing must apply to frozen water crystals. He developed a way to photograph tiny individual frozen water crystals and learned some amazing things. Water from springs, clean rivers, and holy places around the world creates beautiful crystals when frozen, very similar to snowflakes. Tap water, stagnant, and polluted water does not. Interestingly, tap water that is prayed over or simply has good intentions sent to it makes beautiful water crystals.

See actual pictures of frozen water crystals and learn about Dr. Emoto's work at www.dowsers.com/page52.html

The Ultimate Time Machine: A Remote Viewer's Perception of Time, and Predictions for the New Millennium (Paperback) by Joseph McMoneagle presents a unique philosophical perspective on the nature of the past, present, and future. As a remote viewer with a respected record of accuracy and over **30 years of work with the United States government** and in the

---

[23] More about this movie in Chapter 43

private sector, McMoneagle is one of the most qualified people in the 20th century for predicting what the future may hold. While many readers will initially be attracted to the prophetic aspects of *The Ultimate Time Machine*, the most rewarding aspect of this book is McMoneagle's perception of time. For most of us, time is a tool for marking the events in our lives--what time is that business meeting? how old is he? when was the first wheel made?--but McMoneagle suggests that the future, and even the past, are not necessarily on the fixed, linear path that we think they are, but actually are connected in a flexible web that we continually influence with the ultimate time machines, ourselves. --*Brian Patterson*

It is easier now to talk of multiple realities because many scientists have begun to catch up with the mystics, psychics and others who have been saying all along that this 'physical' world is only one reality within an Infinite Consciousness. These scientists would say other realities are parallel universes and part of a single unified energy field. Quantum physics, which explores reality beyond the 'physical' world of the atom, is saying basically the same as the mystics, and people like me, who talk of different dimensions and frequencies of existence interpenetrating our own.

Spirituality and true science - in its open-minded, open-hearted form – are essentially at one. It is mainstream science and mainstream religion that has caused the apparent rift because they are slaves to arrogance, ignorance and dogma. One is not science and the other is not spiritual. They are two polarities of the same falsehood. The open-minded quantum physicist would have no problem with most of what I am going to say in this book, while the cap-touching, protecting-my-funding, mainstream 'scientist' would roll his eyes in bewilderment.[24]

---

[24] **David Icke,** Infinite Love is the Only Truth, Everything Else is Illusion

Chapter 5

Death, what happens when you die

Not much actually happen, other than the fact that you loose the ability to use the body you are now in and that you loose the ability to interact with the 3rd density/dimension. You continue to think, you continue to have memories, and you continue to have a body. To many it all seems so real that they do not figure out that they are dead or better said that they are NO longer in this plane of existence and have lost their thirds density bodies and are now part of the 4th density/dimension creating their own reality from past memories.

Basically there are two possibilities when you die:

You are aware of what happened and of where you are, in this case you are able to pick and chose where to go and what to do, you

---

[25] Redrawn version of George Ripley's tomb. www.alchemywebsite.com

have a full array of options at your disposal. You are able to use to your advantage all the law of physics of the 4th density/dimension, like almost instant travel, telepathy, levitation, conscious creation, and mush more.

You do not realize that you are dead and you create your own environment very similar to what you were accustomed to when you were alive, this environment is as real as your dreams are, and are of the same source. If you do not want to fall under this category, then it is very important that you learn how to awaken your consciousness, for this I recommend that you start with the free courses provided by the GNOSIS groups, see chapter on GNOSIS.

The fear of death is complete lost once you learn how to astral travel[26]. Death not only no longer a source of fear but in fact becomes something to embraced with excitement and anticipation when the time arrives, and with it a knowing beyond all doubt the true reality of the life of peace, tranquility and harmony awaiting beyond the confines of the physical world.

Death does not go alone without the subject of Rebirth. What is inevitably forgotten in the death process is that the transition -- in any situation -- is in reality, about Death and Rebirth. Death is not the end, but just the closing of one door prior to the next one (or many other doors) being opened. Obviously, the solution is to

---

[26] See chapter 11 on Astral Travel

concentrate more on the fascination of the rebirth (into something inevitably more interesting, exciting, delightful, and just sheer fun), than on the prerequisite of first ending the less delightful portion of a continuous life.

Death is about Life, not about Heaven

Chapter 6

Reincarnation & Past Lives

Reincarnation is an anglicized(do you want to use the American spelling here or use anglicised, wih an 's'?) word of Latin derivation, meaning reinfleshment, the coming again into a human body of an excarnate soul. The repetitive reimbodiment of the reincarnating Human Ego in vehicles of human flesh - this being a special case of the general doctrine of Reimbodiment. This general doctrine of Reimbodiment applies not solely to man, but to all centers of consciousness whatsoever, or to all monads whatsoever; wheresoever they may be on the evolutionary ladder of life, and whatsoever may be their particular developmental grade thereon.

There are eight words used in the theosophical philosophy in connection with Re-embodiment, which are not all synonymous, although some of these eight words have almost the same specific meaning. They are: Pre-existence, Rebirth, Reimbodiment, Palingenesis, Metensomatosis, Transmigration, Reincarnation. Of these eight words, four only may be said to contain the four different basic ideas of the general doctrine of Reimbodiment, and these four are Pre-

existence, Reimbodiment, Metempsychosis, and Transmigration.[27]

We are all intrigued by our past lives, wondering what and who we were in the past. For the evolution of our soul, however, it is really not important "who" we were in the sense of a person (e.g. were we someone famous?), but in the sense of "who" we were as an essence. Therefore, the true questions to ask are "what have I accomplished in a past life", "where lies my connection in this life to my past lives", "what are the lessons I still have to learn, based on my past lives".

In this sense, reincarnation therapy is a valuable tool to help you on your spiritual path. Some people might claim that especially in the New Age, we should live in the "here and now" and not be concerned about our past lives. In my opinion, time is but an illusion, therefore, also your "past" lives are our "here and now".

I also believe, however, that nothing should be forced when it comes to past lives, and that the preferable method to delve into past lives is to stay conscious during the whole process. What you need for this process is a good past life therapist who will help you reach a meditative alpha state meaning that the right, intuitive hemisphere of your brain is more active than the left, logical hemisphere.

---

[27] www.crystalinks.com/reincarn.html

Your therapist will ask you for the picture you see (sometimes you may want to think of a specific difficulty in your present life and concentrate on a picture that will come up to help you resolve this problem). Unlike with hypnosis, you are awake during the whole process and truly experience and remember everything.

According to my experience, the ability of a person to see pictures clearly during their first past life session, has nothing to do with the spiritual background of that person. Sometimes people who meditate regularly (and meditating induces the alpha-state) do no see anything while others who do not practice any exercises and are not spiritually oriented see a whole past life unfolding in their first session. It may, however, take up to three sessions before you see any clear picture. If you don't see or feel anything after three sessions, you are doing yourself a favor by leaving it alone. There are many other ways to take on your spiritual path - regression into past lives is only one of them. And again - you should try this method only with an experienced past life therapist, who will also help you to keep your focus during the session. As this method is not using hypnosis and you are totally conscious, nothing that you cannot handle at this point in your life will come to the surface.

Very often, healing sessions induce spontaneous regressions into past lives. The regressions can happen quite spontaneously and not necessarily while you are meditating, but even while you do grocery shopping, driving home in your car, or something similar. In this case just watch the story that is unfolding in your mind's eye. Most of the times there will be one image that will strike you as having a relevancy to your present life, and many times you will have an immediate understanding of how this image is connected to your past life.

These spontaneous regressions come up as a result of a healing process that has been initiated in your system, and they are important in removing blockages and helping you on your way. Since these images "came to you" rather than "you came looking for them", they will never show up before you are ready for it and they will not do you any harm.

Now let's imagine you are still skeptical about past lives, and you are trying to validate if what are seeing are really past lives? If you do have these concerns you may be constantly blocking yourself throughout the process, making it more difficult. So just take a moment to ask yourself: Why do I see these images? What do they want to tell me? You don't necessarily have to believe that they are "past lives" - as mentioned before, time is an illusion. Just accept these images as part of yourself, accept that they are there and let them assist you on your spiritual path. [28]

It's been said that Reincarnation Is Making a Comeback. Be that as it may, the idea is not nearly as incredible as the average Westernized mind might think it.

Certainly, there are those who would have you believe that, "You only go around once in life, so you have to grab all the gusto you can." For recipients of such sage advice and who find gusto-grabbing to be one of the lesser rewards of heaven, there is an alternative. Perhaps, instead of a single tenure of one life to live on

---

[28] www.ourultimatereality.com by Adrian Cooper

this earth, each of us has (or will have) many lives. As a result, each and every one will have a whole slew of opportunities to reach, grab, or otherwise attempt to acquire the gusto.

Strictly speaking, reincarnation is the belief that a single soul will be incarnated in more than one body. It is the doctrine of the soul incarnating or reappearing after death in other and different bodily forms. This rebirth of the soul can occur numerous times -- in fact, some believe reincarnation can involve hundreds, if not thousands, of different lives.

To the Western mind, reincarnation is often thought of as a product of certain Eastern religions, such as Hinduism or Buddhism. While reincarnation may be considered to be an essential aspect of these religions, it is not necessary to accept any of the other tenets of these religions in order to believe in reincarnation. Reincarnation, for example, has as well a long and honorable history in Christianity, Judaism, and Islam. While the current fad in some religions does not involve reincarnation, suffice it to say that any acceptance of the idea of reincarnation as a realistic or factual possibility carries with it no obligation to accept any established religion, cult, or spiritual standard. Reincarnation is a theory that may be considered separately as an independent and alternative way of thinking about life and death. (Or about Death and Rebirth.)

Reincarnation can be, perhaps, more easily linked with an inherent, universal Justice than can the idea of a single chance at life (and gusto grabbing). It is fundamentally evident, everyone on the planet is not born into equal circumstances or with equal opportunities. If there are multiple lives, however, then there are ample opportunities for everyone to have their shot at being king of the hill. Reincarnation is thus potentially more fair or just.

There is also less drama associated with reincarnation. The first time one rides a roller coaster, it can be quite scary. But after a dozen or so back-to-back, subsequent rides, it becomes pretty matter-of-fact. The same might thus be true of death. Once you get the hang of it, death can become pretty routine. In fact, for anyone who has had a near-death experience, even the close proximity to dying inevitably results in that person no longer fearing death. Kali no longer has any terror associated with her dance. [29]

Reincarnation Is Making a Comeback is a non-fiction book on all things considered to be "New Age". Essentially, it is a Synthesis of all that "stuff", and a discussion of how it all ultimately fits into the grander scheme of things. The book was first published in 1990 by Whitford Press [1] and since revised and updated in 1990 and 2003. As such it remains a worthwhile compilation of a host of ideas and concepts. The book is organized into four sections: Basics, Experiences, Possibilities, and Implications. The basics include discussions of reincarnation, karma, soul-mates, and other topics which seem intrinsically tied to the subject of reincarnation. The second part of the book deals with birth, near-death, and out-of-body experiences as well as regressions to the state between lives and the possibility of "earthbound spirits". The experiences section of the book provides detailed information about the specifics of reincarnation theory, derived from a diverse group of unique and

---

[29] www.halexandria.org/dward425.htm

significant experiences. These experiences may be considered as supporting evidence for reincarnation theory.[30]

---

[30] www.halexandria.org/dward426.htm

Chapter 7

Mental relaxation and meditation

The very first step is to learn the fact that we are like software running in a computer. Same as in a computer more than one thing is running at the same time in parallel. For example you have a part of you that automatically runs your breathing all the time, but if you like you can take over this part by just thinking about it. Same is true about everything else about you; you simple do not know this. For example with a little practice you can easily change your heart rate or your body temperature. With more advance knowledge you can change your weight, appearance, and much more...

Next step is to learn and believe that you are much more than just one piece; even your thoughts are more than one single component running a single task. It even goes further than this: Our brain is just part of the whole we are, yes the brain is just one more component of who and what we are. This may be difficult for you to understand; it will take you sometime to come to this new reality, and it may even be painful to admit to yourself these new facts, but trust me you will be glad you did.

Meditation is yet another word like faith[31] that has taken me a very long time to comprehend. You see meditation is a tool by which you allow (according to Bashar) a 3rd part of a total of 12 DNA parts of which only 2 are in our physical 3rd dimension (the 3rd DNA part is in transition from the 3rd to the 4th dimension) to access the 9 parts that are in the 4th dimension to will what you want and much more; this is the missing link that is referred as the second coming of Christ, an opportunity to connect with our true (higher) self, to enable those who are ready to ascend one level up to the 4th density/dimension.

2012 is when this dimensional door fully opens for those who are ready, and it closes the ability to be here in this planet for those who are not ready. Some will survive it even though they did not prepare, because they had the skills, but most will perish; this is what the book of Revelation, also known as Apocalypses in the bible talks about in a very encoded language that most do not understand. From now to 2012 we all have an opportunity to get ready, cause ready or not, it is going to fully open. The time between now and 2012 is a time of tribulation a time of testing, a time of many challenges, though we get push to the limits we hardly ever get push past our limits; if you think about it, all your problems

---

[31] Faith.- The art of knowing something "**WILL**" happen. For example you know that if you apply a flame to a flammable gas, that the gas will ignite; this is faith, the believe that something WILL happen.

have been survivable, only when one chooses to not survive, is when death comes along to force another opportunity.

We are all powerful, all inclusive and all loving, but we do not know it yet that we are GOD. Via meditation the first thing that happens is that our bodies go through a very quick repair of our 3rd dimensional cells, in addition it opens up the channel of communication to enable: Telepathy, Telepathic Sensing, Remote Visions/Sensing, Psychic Dreams, Precognition, Déjà Vu, Apparitions, Psychokinesis, Psychometrists[32], Clairaudience[33], Clairgustance[34], Clairsentience[35], Clairvoyance[36], Telekinesis,

---

[32] Psychometrists - Those people who can pick up a personal item of an unknown person and uncover what types of emotions that person is feeling. This ability can also be used to find lost objects, calling out to the energy that is already stored in the object to bring about its return.

[33] Clairaudience is perception of messages in thought forms from an entity who exists in another realm. You 'hear' what they are saying in your mind. Clairaudience is a form of channeling. You may actually hear spirits talking or singing in your head but there is no auditory sounds.

[34] Clairgustance is being aware of tastes without putting anything in your mouth. To perceive the essence of a substance through taste from the spiritual or ethereal realms.

[35] Clairsentience - experiencing other realities or entities through the sense of touch: A tickling sensation on the body when connection with spirit. This usually includes the face, hands, neck. Hairs on the back of the neck standing on end when a spirit touches you. A sensation on the left side of the face when talking with spirit.

[36] Clairvoyance is the art of 'seeing' with senses beyond the five we normally use. Clairvoyance is often called the 'sixth sense'. It is related to the images that are

Astral Travel and much more... All of these become enabled the minute we make an effort of using any of them; the minute we ask and allow for it to happen. ORMUS/ORME is the fuel to enable this 3rd DNA. NOTE: This happens at a different pace for each person. For some it has happen so fast that the next day they have been institutionalized in a mental institution and for others it takes many years, for some it even takes many lifetimes, some even take steps backwards to correct and learn lessons better, its like taking a class all over again to understand it better or until being able to perfect it.

Below is an excerpt from Adrian Cooper's Astral Pulse Newsletter on the subject of meditation.

In order to meditate effectively, a sufficient degree of concentration is required, and is one reason why this extremely important ability should be practiced as frequently as possible.

Without adequate powers of concentration it will be very difficult indeed to adequately silence the Mind and therefore to achieve anything worthwhile, and so concentration is an ability well worth practicing.

---

always present in your mind that bring messages from other realms. These images can be shape, colors, still, or animated, remain on a few seconds or last a longer time. You may 'see' them with your eyes open or closed.

It is very important to meditate sitting in a totally upright position with your spine completely straight. Meditation cannot be reclining or even leaning back in a comfortable chair. If sitting on a chair during meditation it is best to sit totally upright, spine absolutely vertical on a hard backed chair, a dining chair for example, with your legs and knees firmly together and your hands palms down on your thighs.

Alternatively sitting cross-legged on the floor, totally upright with spine totally straight is also an excellent position for meditation. It is not necessary however to formally place yourself into an exotic position such as the full or half Lotus, but you may of course do so if you wish.

It is fine in the very early stages to sit on a pillow to make yourself more comfortable, but never sit with your back against the backrest of a chair or indeed against any other support; your back and therefore your spine must be absolutely straight and totally unsupported. Your hands should be positioned with your palms facing downwards and resting lightly on your thighs.

I am often asked whether it is possible to meditate while lying down on a bed. Well the answer is yes; it is possible to meditate while lying on a bed, but not always advisable. The main reason for not meditating while lying on a bed is the risk of falling asleep.

The bed is associated by your subconscious mind with "sleep", and as soon as you lie down the chances are that your subconscious mind will then automatically place you in the sleep state which of course is not conducive to meditation.

It is however quite possible to separate meditation from sleep by telling your subconscious mind that this is a time for meditation rather than sleep. In order to assist this process it is a good idea to do something differently to your regular sleep time that your subconscious mind can associate with meditation. This might for example be removing the pillows so you are lying absolutely flat on the bed. You could light a candle or burn your favorite incense, the emphasis of course being on safety. Do not burn anything that can be knocked over or could otherwise be a safety risk in any way. The important thing here is to separate meditation time from sleep time in your subconscious Mind. If you can do this then lying down is fine.

Of course you need not lie on a bed. To separate meditation from sleep you can place something on the floor or better still lie down on the hard floor.

I am also asked why it is necessary to keep the spine erect while meditating. There are various reasons for this. The reason most frequently given is to aid the Energy flow. While this might be true to a point; specifically within the energy meridians of your Energy body itself, we must also dispel one common misunderstanding in that Energy somehow comes down from "above", enters through the crown of the head, sometimes known as the "crown chakra", and then travels down through the body eventually leaving at the feet.

It is of course quite possible, using the powers of the mind, to guide Energy in this way, but it is certainly not "natural". The Source of all Energy is The Source in absolute terms, and The Source is within us and not external to us either above or below or anywhere else. We are all an integral aspect and therefore extension of The Source, and the Source is within, not without.

So when we are drawing Energy into ourselves as for example for healing, we imagine the Energy being provided from The Source which is within. That said, Energy is all around us physically as well, and we can therefore concentrate Energy from around us, and "breath" that Energy into ourselves, thereby accumulating it.

It is a good idea to meditate in the same place and at the same time of day where you will not be disturbed. Although such items as candles, incense and other materials are not at all strictly required, you might very well find them, as with meditation while lying down, to be useful in setting the specific meditative mood and focusing of your Mind on the state of meditation. By using for example certain scented candles or incense, these will become associated with your meditation time and might therefore assist you in reaching the required level of Consciousness and relaxation more quickly and effectively. This is a matter of personal choice entirely.

The next stage in the meditation process is to perform some deep breathing exercises, in order to help you to achieve the required level of relaxation, and to help you to focus your Mind away from mundane matters. Breathing in for a slow count of five, holding your breath for a slow count of five, and breathing out for a further slow count of five is excellent for helping to achieve a good level of relaxation before commencing meditation. Repeat this five times initially, and more if you feel it is beneficial.

While performing the breathing exercises you can also imagine inhaling pure, glowing or sparkling white light, and exhaling through your nose grey light containing any tension or negativity stored in your body.

When you are totally relaxed and use all of your powers of concentration to empty your Mind of all thoughts; only a complete vacancy of Mind should prevail. Should you have difficulty in achieving this immediately at first, you can reach this state of concentration and state of Consciousness in stages over time. It really does not matter how many sessions it takes to achieve the total vacancy of Mind state, but reach it you must in order to be able to meditate effectively, and the sooner the better. The previously discussed concentration exercises are an excellent way of achieving complete vacancy of Mind, and I strongly recommended that you complete the concentration exercises before commencing the formal practice of meditation.

To commence with your meditation assume your chosen meditation position, attain the necessary degree of deep physical relaxation by performing the breathing exercises and then begin to observe your thoughts as they pass through your Mind. It is very important not to participate in these thoughts, tempting though it might be, but to merely be a passive observer, acknowledging the thoughts as they occur but then allowing them to simply drift by without further involvement. Again, it is most important not to attach yourself to any thought and become involved with it. Continue this exercise for as long as you can, but ideally for at least ten minutes each day; at least thirty minutes each day being your ideal objective. When you first commence this exercise you might be besieged with thoughts, particularly if you have not practiced the concentration exercises first, and it is strongly suggested that you do, however from session to session the number of thoughts will diminish until they finally become few and far between.

This might well only take a week or might take several weeks or even months depending on your individual circumstances and levels of relaxation, concentration and focus. You can reinforce this process throughout the day by pursuing the same procedure as suggested for part of the concentration exercises, only thinking about what you are doing at any particular moment in time. Do not allow any extraneous thoughts to enter your head and interfere with your current task. For example, if you are driving your car, think only about driving your car and do not allow your Mind to wander to other unrelated matters. The same applies for any activity whether it be shopping, your job of work, cooking a meal and so on. Always focus exclusively on the task in hand to the total exclusion of all other thoughts. This will assist greatly in thought control and strengthen your powers of concentration.

The next stage in our process of learning to meditate is to select a single thought or object of your own choice and to hold the thought or image of it in your Mind for as long as possible.

This might for example be a memory of a place you enjoy visiting, a memorable holiday or any other happy memory. It might be easier at first to visualize a familiar object such as a favorite picture or an item of household furniture, or the image of a loved one. It does not need to be something you are actively involved with or interested in, any object will do as the object of your visualization such as a fruit, candle, cup or other such familiar item.

Having decided on the object of your thought, assume your chosen meditation posture by sitting in your chair or on the floor with back totally straight, and, after any relaxation and breathing exercises, bring the thought or image firmly into your Mind as realistically and with as much presence as possible. Ideally your thought or image should fill your entire Mind. If any other thoughts attempt to intrude then with all the will power you can summon reject that extraneous thought immediately and bring your Mind firmly back to your intended thought or image.

It is very important indeed to immediately reject any intruding thought the very moment it tries to join your chosen thought or image. You will find this exercise will become progressively easier over time, with your thought or image becoming stronger, and with less and less intruding thoughts which will become easier to reject.

When you can hold your thought or image vividly and solidly in your Mind for ten minutes without wavering, or any intruding thoughts, the final stage is to be able to dismiss that thought or image at will right at the end of your meditation session, leaving you with a full vacancy of Mind where the image once existed. Hold you Mind empty of your chosen thought or image for a few moments before gently raising your Consciousness back to the physical level.

After this has been fully accomplished, for future sessions you can proceed to the full meditation stage; full vacancy of Mind.

This step involves assuming your meditation posture and rather than holding a thought or image in your Mind, hold your Mind totally devoid of all thoughts not allowing any thought to intrude. In the beginning you might find the occasional thought attempts to intrude into your silence; if it does simply use all of you willpower to reject it immediately. When you can achieve this stage you are now ready to meditate effectively.

As an interim stage in your meditation learning process, you can commence your meditations with a single chosen thought or image, and then after a couple of minutes or so remove the thought or image and proceed with a complete vacancy of Mind. After a time you will find it will be possible to omit the thought or image of the scene or object altogether and proceed immediately with a complete vacancy of Mind from the outset of the meditation session.

Having achieved this level of concentration and emptiness of Mind you can now proceed to meditate effectively. A meditation session should ideally be at least twenty minutes, but less will suffice initially. This however is only the beginning as you will discover naturally as you progress; each meditation session will progressively deepen your inner awareness.

Remember you are focusing inwards towards The Source and not to some "higher" level relative to The Source. As previously mentioned, when we refer to the "higher" worlds and states of life and being, these are actually inner states relative to the physical world and physical body, with the highest vibration of The Source, The First Cause of God at the very center, and the lowest vibration of Energy at the outermost level, the physical, material level from where meditation commences. Your focus should therefore be inwards towards the Astral and Spiritual worlds, your Higher-Self, and ultimately with the highest and most Divine, God.

With time and dedicated daily practice meditation will come progressively deeper and with more profound levels of inner awareness, soon becoming a very blissful experience, bringing with it the potential for the profound benefits described earlier.

Ideally while meditating you should reach a stage where you completely lose contact with the feeling of your physical senses body and surroundings, being totally focused on the inner states of Consciousness. This is an ideal state to reach and should be your immediate objective.

Meditation should become a daily habit, and one that you should always look forward to. There is no fixed duration of time for meditation; some people meditate for up to thirty minutes each day, while others might meditate for several hours at a time or even for a full day, completely absorbed in their inner Consciousness.

During the process of deep meditation situations might occur that you should be aware of. These situations often involve imagery to varying degrees and intensity. One of these is often known as the "TV screen", or "cinema screen" effect. This is exactly the same effect as frequently occurs during the Astral Projection process.

This "screen" is actually a "window" into the Astral planes. Should this situation occur you have two choices; either to observe the screen and to simply learn from these visions and what they mean to you, or you can alternatively convert the meditation into a full Astral Projection by imagining yourself moving towards the screen as it becomes larger and larger, eventually passing straight through the image in the screen into the Astral worlds.

It is also quite possible, and quite often occurs with some people in particular that the meditation can become a full out of body experience. The first signs of this would usually be the ability to "see" through your closed eyelids. This means that your Etheric body has already moved out of phase with your physical body as happens during a normal sleep cycle. You are actually viewing your surroundings with your inner senses rather then through your actual physical eyes. Should this occur you can maintain an absolute concentration and remain in a state of meditation, or you can simply decide to leave your body in order to enjoy the out of body experience. If you do decide on the OBE, then proceed as for an OBE. If you decide to remain concentrating on your meditation, then your Etheric vision might either remain, it might fade, or very often, as your vibrations rise it will give way to the "viewing" of the Astral worlds, in which case you might proceed as described above.

As this is a meditation session it is preferable to choose the "viewing" option rather than converting to a full Astral Projection or an OBE, but the choice is always yours. It is always the best to follow your inner guidance, which can be much more powerful during meditation, being much more closely in touch with your Higher, or more accurately Inner-Self. Much can be learned by simply observing the Astral images displayed before you, and in particular any associated symbolism.

While meditating and focusing on your inner awareness your Mind is also tuned into the inner worlds of the Astral and Spiritual planes; this can be at any level depending on your level of vibration that will always correspond to the level of the Universe your Consciousness is focused within. This focus and awareness can frequently result in communications with beings such as Spirit guides, deceased relatives or even your Higher-Self. These possibilities are one of the most valuable aspects of meditation.

Should you make contact with these Beings you will clearly "hear" their voices in your head, often just as clearly as if they were speaking to you in the physical world.

You might also "see" the beings you are communicating with by means of clairvoyance. It is most useful to engage in two-way communication when these opportunities arise; much can be learned about the inner realities and in particular about yourself and your life situations, but always depending on the precise nature of the Being you are communicating with. Communication is performed mentally by telepathy, either in the form of words, images or both. You can ask questions simply by thinking or imagining your questions as clearly as possible, and the answers will arrive back in a similar way.

As you progressively absorb yourself into your meditation your brainwave frequencies will progressively slow down. This also happens quite naturally from time to time during the day according to the type of activity you are engaged in at the time, but more usually occurs before going to sleep at night where the brain passes through all of the decreasing frequencies until you go to sleep completely. The highest brainwave frequencies occur in the normal waking state; this is known as the "beta" state characterized by very fast frequencies of between 13Hz and 40Hz. Brainwaves slow down somewhat, as often happens while daydreaming during the day, and which will usually happen as meditation progresses, the "alpha" brainwave state is reached. This alpha state is characterized by brainwave frequencies in the order of between 7Hz and 13Hz.

During meditation or trance work, after sufficient practice and experience, brainwaves can slow down even further to the "theta" state, characterized by brainwaves of a frequency of 3.5Hz to 7Hz.

Theta level is the most profoundly clear and focused state; many people experience profound inspiration, intuition, ideas and other thoughts while in the theta state, originating both from beings of the inner spheres and from the Higher-Self. Theta is also the state of vivid imagery where the powers of imagination and visualization are particularly profound.

There have been famous scientists in the past who would place themselves into such a deep state of concentration and depth of thought that they would reach the theta state. Indeed, many such famous scientists have intentionally invoked the theta state for maximum inspiration and creativity. This has resulted in many important inventions and theories, a notable example being the "special theory of relativity" which was postulated by Albert Einstein while in a deep thinking theta state of Mind.

Meditation in general, and in particular deep, highly focused meditation with a high degree of concentration is an excellent way to achieve answers to almost anything at all. These answers will often originate from your Higher-Self, or more accurately your Inner-self, that part of you that is in the most direct contact with God, and these are all messages that are totally reliable. The Higher-Self is sublime, it knows everything that "Is", and is mostly concerned with your evolution.

Any inspiration, intuition or message from the Higher-Self is unmistakable for what it is, and must always be acted upon without question, always. Failure to act on inspiration from the Higher-Self will either lead to no result, or sometimes, worse, suffering.

These are just a few of the numerous possibilities and benefits resulting from deep meditation. For many people, particularly of the Far Eastern cultures, the ultimate objective of true meditation is to achieve such a profound level of inner Consciousness as to become one with the very highest of the Spiritual planes, a state mystically known as "Samadhi". Those who achieve this state of extreme bliss, approaching the innermost levels of Energy and vibration know beyond any doubts that everything in the Universe is indeed one, and that everything and everyone is an integral part of "everything that Is", The Source, God.

One of the most important aspects of the practice of meditation is to remain totally focused with maximum possible concentration, while maintaining your Mind free of all thoughts and external influences, and to accept and to learn from any inner situation arising. These include all of the possibilities previously discussed, but there are indeed many other possibilities. Maintain clarity of Mind and be prepared for any experience occurring during meditation from which valuable lessons can be learned and information or intuition gained. You will very soon find that your daily meditation is something you look forward to, and your meditation sessions will become progressively longer and more profound with practice. Dedication, commitment, and daily practice are keys to the practice of successful meditation.

The important thing to keep in mind is that meditation is not, or at least should not be perceived as some sort of mystical and/or oriental process while in some obscure, contorted position, but rather a profoundly beneficial experience that everyone can and should practice.

Meditation can help you to achieve anything, but most of all it places us in communication with the true source of our Being, and therefore of who we really are; infinite, immortal, unlimited aspects of The Source, The First Cause, "God", with exactly the same Divine potential, powers and capabilities.

Just as "God" is the creator the Macrocosm, Everything that "Is", as Divine, individuated but integral aspects of The Divine we have unlimited potential to achieve anything; all we have to do is to realize that potential meditation is an excellent way of helping to achieve that.

For further information see Adrian Cooper's websites and books:

Our Ultimate Reality Book: www.ourultimatereality.com

Binaural Mind Power www.binauralmindpower.com

Mind Power Studio: www.mindpowerstudio.com

Mind Power Books: www.mindpowerbooks.com

Astral Pulse Newsletter: www.astralpulse.com

There are many excellent sources on the subject of meditation, among them www.crystalinks.com/meditation.html

Basically, science's rejection of astrology is based on ignorance. Science's ignorance. When the astronomer Edmond Halley asked Sir Isaac Newton (essentially the "patron science of physics") how he could possibly believe in astrology, Sir Isaac answered, "Because I have studied the matter, Sir. You have not." And therein lies the crux of the matter. When Shakespeare made the comment of the "stars influencing our lives", he too was mis- or un-informed. Astrology is about the planets of our solar system, not the stars![37]

---

[37] www.halexandria.org/dward330.htm

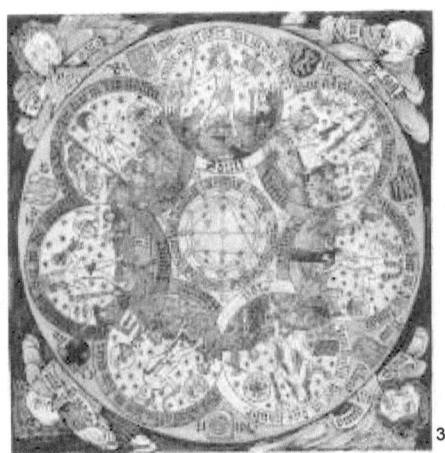

Chapter 8

Astrology

Astrology is the art of foretelling a person's possible future via the position of the planets in our galaxy, something that at first seems quite childish, bizarre and even stupid, but I can assure you that there is lots of truth to it, especially if done correctly. Note that to properly chart a person's astrological chart it is necessary to take in to account, not just the day and month of birth, but also, the year, time and place of birth, without this additional information the astrological chart is incomplete. Another issue often misunderstood is that the sun sign (the main sign) The sun sign is where one is going towards too, therefore the younger and/or less progress a

---

[38] 15th century astrological woodcut www.alchemywebsite.com

person has made, the less the astrological sun sign will make sense. For example lets say your sign says that you are good at music, but you do not know how to play any instruments and never have even though about it, what is saying is that if you do, you will be good at it, that it will be much easier for you than for others that do not have this in their astral chart. This is one of the main reasons why I recommend you become familiar with your astral sign, it will give you tips about yourself that you have not even though of. Then there is the aspect of the constant changes for each of the signs, these are energies that constantly change, persuading you to act in a certain new way, usually felt as a desire to do something different, such as a new food, physical activity, education, travel, business, it even affect your sexual mood and appetite. Often puts you in challenging situations with others. Signs interact with each others in many ways throughout the day; in fact astrology is so accurate that it can predict ones moods even by the hour. Here is an example that I personally experienced and found quite fascinating: My astrology ones says that woman from the Gemini sign were going to be extremely attracted to me for a period of a few weeks, that this was once in a lifetime opportunity to interact with woman from this sign, to enjoy it, but gave warnings, this was very temporary, that as quick as they would be in love and all over me, they will not give me the time of day past this astrological influence; was this true? You bet it was, in just one day I had three Gemini woman almost beg me to go out with them, it was just amazing how true this was, in fact I fell for one a lot, had a great time and wanted it to go into a long-term relationship, but sure enough, a few weeks went by and she would not even give me the courtesy of a simply hello, it was exactly how my astrology said. Knowing well ahead what to expect made it all fun and reduce my heart being broken. This is a good example of how to use astrology to your benefit; it simply helps you to know ahead of time what to expect.

But astrology goes much further, it also gives you a very good insight of what to expect from others, for example going back to Gemini's. Gemini's are very interesting and fun people to be friend with, BUT just not all the time, so if you have Gemini friend like I do, I know when to quickly back off and give them their space, I know quite well to NEVER plan a date more than a few minutes (not even hours) ahead of time with a Gemini, they simply change their mind about everything way too often to be able to commit to doing something with you. On the other hand, this same energy that keeps them changing all the time makes them quite interesting people, since they would have delved into all sorts of subjects.

If you want to know how to make someone happy, or what gift to make for someone, or how to get along better with someone, most important learn more about yourself, astrology is the tool to use. For example never give any imitational (fake) jewelry to a Capricorn, they will simply be insulted, Capricorns only appreciate the finer expensive things, like fine jewelry, top choice clothing and perfumes, on the other hand, do not waste your time for the most part on expecting them to be good travel companions, or to have a technical conversation, it simply not in their interest. Capricorns are very clean and tidy in their appearance, with their surrounding throughout their homes, but very disorganized with keeping document in order, do not expect a Capricorn to quickly know where they left a document. I predict that the Capricorn sign one day will be divided in two, since this sign has several opposite features that no other sign has; this subject is way out of the scope of this book.

By the way, it gets a bit more complicated, because everyone has the ultimate free will to change as they see it fit, and the environment they were raised has an influence on whom they are. But overall you will find that knowing the basic trades of a sign will give you a huge insight of who a person is and why they act the way they do. It will help you tremendously in not only knowing yourself much better but in also knowing how to deal with others, regardless if it is at home, school or work.

The way it works is that there are 300+ subtle energies radiating from the entire universe all the time, and going true our bodies. A very good explanation of these energies can be found on the personification of the Greek gods (archetype) mythology. The Greeks were quite elaborate in the creation of all sorts of stories that personify these energies as gods. The strongest ones are from the planets in our galaxy and are the ones identified and used mostly to chart a person's or an event in astrology.

Most ancient civilizations watched the heavens as patterns in the sky that allowed them to know when the seasons changed - among other things. They built great stone monuments called celestial observatories - such as Stonehenge as celestial clocks to mark these events and the passage of time.

They believed their gods lived in the skies and named them and the constellations after them. This is the reason astrology, astrology and mythology all follow the same patterns. In the end - the answers are in the sky - as they come from above. In metaphysics we call this moving into higher frequency than what we experience in our third dimensional bodies. Our creators are from higher realms. They have powers that are lost to us in the physical body.

Astrology is a large and extended subject. As such it does not lend itself to quick and precise answers, mathematical equations and other succinct descriptions, and especially the quick and dirty prognostications found in the local newspaper's daily horoscopes. (Virtually all professional astrologers abhor these types of horoscopes!) Instead, one sees many astrological influences -- sometimes contradictory -- operating in a subject's life, and it then becomes a matter of weighing the potential influences to grasp where the individual is going. Science, by contrast, likes to eliminate all of the side effects or distracting annoyances, and limit itself to only the most blatant effect, the "active ingredient". But it is in the side-effects and asides that the really part of life resides. Such is astrology.

Any study of astrology must ultimately be an extensive one. Thus, this very brief treatise on the subject is really only sufficient to whet the reader's appetite.

I highly recommend these two websites for beginners:

www.astro.com and www.astrologyzone.com

Zodiac According to the Doctrine of Correspondences in the Emerald Tablet [39] ("As Above, so Below"), the stars must find

---

[39] The Emerald Tablet is an ancient artifact that reveals a profound spiritual technology, which has survived to this day despite centuries of effort to suppress it. Encoded within the tablet's mysterious wording is a powerful formula that works in

expression on earth and in mankind. In alchemy, it was essential to consult the zodiac before commencing any of the major operations.

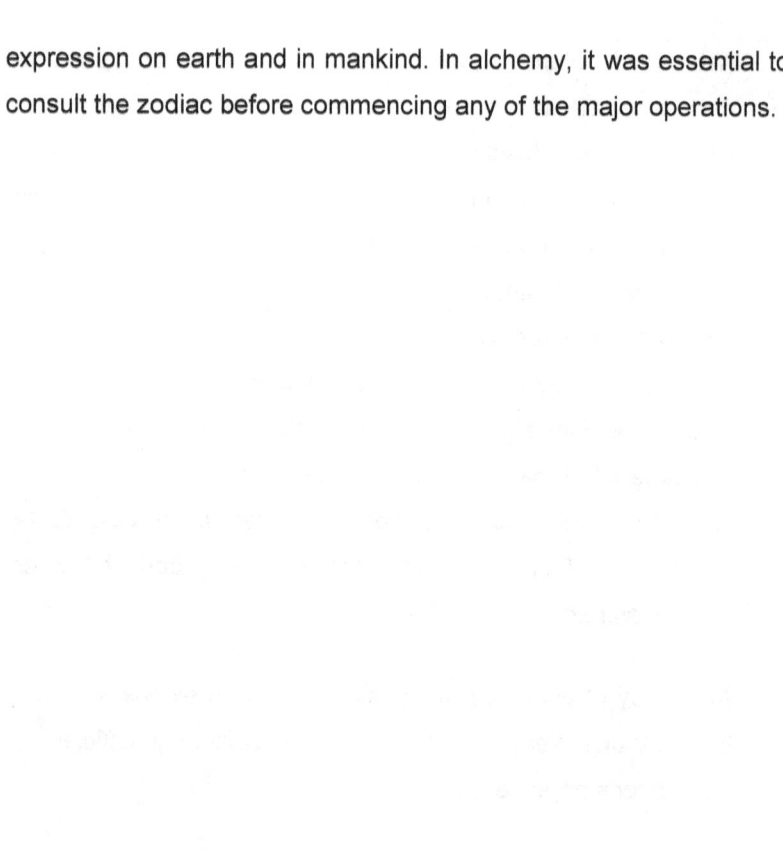

very specific and comprehensible steps on all levels of reality at once -- the physical, the mental, and the spiritual -- and shows us how to achieve personal transformation and even accelerate the evolution of our species. The source of alchemy and the Hermetic sciences, the tablet's universal approach made it forbidden knowledge, condemned by patriarchal powers for thousands of years, from the Egyptian priesthood, to the medieval Church, to our modern politicians and religious leaders. To ensure the survival of such "dangerous" principles, which guide people to higher states of consciousness, the ancients concealed their knowledge in a succinct declaration that has become a time capsule of wisdom for future generations.

Imagine there's no heaven,

It's easy if you try,

No hell below us,

Above us only sky,

Imagine all the people

living for today...

Imagine there's no countries,

It isn't hard to do,

Nothing to kill or die for,

No religion too,

Imagine all the people

living life in peace...

~ John Lennon

Chapter 9

The Art and Practice of Conscious Creation and our Believe System

There is a very large variety of books covering this subject in just about every imaginable way, with many different titles to entice a new audience. Same as this book has a title geared towards the atheist audience, you may find many books for beginners to advance audience, all leading to the same basic knowledge with a different angle of explanation, some target earning money via business practices, which are no more than spiritual guide books targeted to business practices.

For me reading a variety of them has helped me clarify a subject that has been most difficult to understand. Even the bible (in its very obscure parable ways of explaining) in many ways says the same thing; unfortunately the Bible was not for me and I am sure it is not for you either; otherwise you would not have the need to read this book nor others. Fortunately for you and me there have been other writers who used words easier for us to grasp.

Below I am going to explain how I understand how to consciously create what we want and I am going to give you reference to other books to read, combined they will open the door for you to create the quality of life you most desire.

First it is important to understand that learning a new complex subject such as this one is no different that learning some other complex subject, almost no one is able to master a subject in just one day or by reading one book, it takes time and lots of practice to become even a low proficiency apprentice student of any art. Even the simpler tasks in life such as eating without making a mess, walking, flying a kite, riding a bike, cooking, etc. take time and effort, they do not come without your conscious desire and personal participation. Conscious creation is no different, and same as any profession, it has rewards which make it worth while, in fact little you have ever done or will ever do, will have as much rewards as learning the true mysteries of getting out of life all you want thru the art of consciously creating what you want, when and where you want it.

First of all, lets agree that anything and everything starts with a though. No building, no vehicle, no clothing, no education, no knowledge starts without a thought. Things become reality because of a though. For example pick any item you posses, before it came to your possession, you or someone had to think about it, otherwise it would not exist. From the smallest to the largest thing we posses, started with a thought. The problem is that most people do not realize how powerful their thoughts can be. The art of conscious creation is about learning how powerful our though can be. Way more than what you imagine, yes, a LOT more...

Conscious creation is intertwined and tied very closely with faith. Not only do you need to have a very clear though of what it is that you want, but you must also have (I hate to say it) faith. So what is faith? Faith is the ability to know that something will happen before it does. You need to know it as a fact, and not just a vague hope or desire.

Same as any skill or profession, it takes time to master faith. Faith does not tend to work well the first few times we consciously use it. It takes practice and time to master faith to ones full advantage. Same as a painter or musician can benefit of some small amount of knowledge/skills and from time to time even see spikes of good results; you will also see your faith grow and your conscious creation improve. Faith, same as any other skill must deliver some results for you to want to continue. At first the results may not be much, but with time, same as with other skills, you will eventually call yourself a master in the art of conscious creation (a magician/witch). As any master can attest, it takes time and lots of practice before you can call yourself a master, in fact before you can even call yourself an apprentice it has already taken you lots of time and effort. You will only come to master faith as you experience results; therefore the day you entrust something big/difficult to your higher-self you will know that even though it may be taking time, that in the end, you will get what you want, and more so, what it is best for you.

Remember as a child when you wanted something and you did not get it? Something that was dangerous and not good for you, aren't you glad you did not get it? I remember this gal I wanted so bad to have sex with, I remember complaining that I did not get her; now I am quite glad I was not the unlucky one... Part of conscious creation is trusting you will get what is best for you, no mater how long it takes.

We all have a huge list of failures throughout our lives, therefore we can easily agree that we should not trust our ideas and desires as being good for us, except for the fact that they will teach us what we should not be doing.

There is a way to eliminate all mistakes from our lives, and that is to trust our higher-self to make the ideal choice for us, but for this we must allow it to do so, we must have faith that it can and that it will. All we need to do is guide it in the direction of our desires and let it make the final choice details for us. If we do, we will find out that it has more and better in storage for us that what we ask for in the first place. Same as parents know best for a small child, so does our higher-self.

The Law of Attraction.- The law of attraction is quite simple, think that you have abundance around you and you will have even more, think that you lack and even that that you have will be taken away from you.

You need to learn to think big and in abundance, regardless of how little you think you have. You not only need to think in abundance but you also must act as you have abundance.

For example, lets say that you go to the store to buy some groceries, and you have enough just for the weekly groceries, vs. buying all items of the lowest possible cost, buy at least one item just for the joy of it, something that you would only buy if you really had abundance; this tells the Cosmos. Universal Subconscious Mind, Higher-self, God or whatever you wish to call it, that you know how to deal with abundance; it will listen and provide you with lots more.

The only way to have abundance is to think in abundance, no one who ever though of poverty even became rich. Make it a point to treat yourself as if you were the riches person on earth. Always think big. If there has been space and abundance to create the universe with all its vast richness, surely you request can be filled.

Remember that at the same time there is mass poorness there is also mass richness. All you need to do is change the way you think and have faith!

The important thing to keep in mind, and of course to practice, is to never allow thoughts into your Mind that are contrary to your wishes, including those particularly destructive thoughts; fears, doubts and uncertainty; thoughts that ensure that many people who might have succeeded with The Law of Attraction never do! Any negative thought should be immediately cancelled by saying to yourself, either aloud or in your Mind; "cancel!, cancel!, cancel!", until the negative thought dissipates.[40]

There is nothing wrong in having negative thoughts, what is wrong is to align (participate) with the negative thoughts.

There are many books and websites on the subject of conscious creation, among them one of the best is The Nature of Personal Reality[41] it is a book that covers in details how we can and should

---

[40] http://www.ourultimatereality.com Adrian Cooper's Astral Pulse weekly newsletter

[41] The Nature of Personal Reality: Specific, Practical Techniques for Solving Everyday Problems and Enriching the Life You Know by Jane Roberts. Seth teaches us that we are not at the mercy of the subconscious; the conscious mind directs unconscious activity and has at its command all the powers of the inner-self. These are activated according to the ideas about reality. The words of Seth show readers that they possess hidden powers within themselves that have the potential to transform their lives. This book shows readers how to improve health, create material

change our believe system from one of Seth[42] many books. So vast is the subjects covered by Seth that I have dedicated a whole chapter about Seth' books.

www.consciouscreation.com has over 250 articles from many authors.

Have You Ever Wondered How The "Privileged" Few Can Become So Wealthy While Everyone Else "Works" So Hard For So Much Less? Now You Too Can Discover The Secret!

It is no coincidence that a few people become very wealthy, often without seeming to "work" very hard or in some cases "work" at all, while the majority of people struggle through life, working hard for 40 years or more, only just making enough to get by, often not enjoying life or even making enough to retire comfortably.

Does this sound all too familiar?

---

success, and make relationships more satisfying. By learning to control their own experiences, they can create a new, fulfilling reality. A reader writes: "Do you know how there are some moments that are so magical in your life, you wish you could go back and live them over? That's how I feel about *The Nature of Personal Reality*. Honestly I don't know how many times I have read this book through from cover to cover. Such is the amazing impact it has had on me and my view of the world. It has influenced everything from how I interact with others to why I became an author."

---

[42] For a good description of Seth books go to www.jonasridgeway.com/seth.html

It should do; it is happening to millions of people around the world today.

But life need not be like this. If people can become very wealthy, and they can, why shouldn't it be you?

Question: How do the wealthiest people enjoy such a seemingly endless stream of wealth beyond the wildest dreams of most people with so much ease? Clue: it is most certainly not just by hard work!

Answer: The wealthiest people throughout history understand that The Secret of infinite wealth, health and happiness is not a factor of how hard you "work" or indeed whether you "work" at all, but rather in applying The Secret Universal Laws that have been used for centuries by the privileged few.

Fact: Absolutely anyone can become very wealthy, totally regardless of your current circumstances.

Let's dispel some of the more common myths and excuses right away:

It simply does not matter how your life has been to this moment

It simply does not matter who you "know" or what you "know"

It simply does not matter that you do not have any spare cash available to invest

And let's dispel another common myth: there is no such thing as "bad luck", "chance" or "misfortune".

Absolutely everyone, without exception creates their own reality. Those who fail to create the reality they desire usually find it easier to blame everyone and everything but themselves.

The truth is, you can create any alternative reality, including unlimited wealth, health and happiness if only you could have access to The Secret of success as other wealthy people over the centuries.

See www.charleshaanelbooks.com for a whole set of books that teach you how.

www.scienceofgettingrich.net provides a fun informative way of learning these secrets. "The ownership of money and property comes as a result of doing things in a certain way. Those who do things in this certain way, whether on purpose or accidentally, get rich. Those who do not do things in this certain way, no matter how hard they work or how able they are, remain poor.

"It is a natural law that like causes always produce like effects. Therefore, any man or woman who learns to do things in this certain way will infallibly get rich." Start by getting their free books.

www.ImagesOfOne.com has one of the best books I have ever read on the subject of conscious creation, its title is quite misleading of its spiritual content, and ideal book for the atheist... it is titled "A happy pocket full of money." Buy it; read it is a few times, it is worth more than its weight in gold.

www.lazywayebook.com Often we think that all come via hard work and only hard work, but there is no truth to this. When you consciously create what you want, there is magic in it, no matter if you work hard or not.

In an average day there are 86,400 seconds. Out of that 86,400 seconds we have approximately 65,000 waking thoughts. Out of those 65,000 thoughts how many are positive, uplifting, wonder filled thoughts? How many are negative thoughts that are ruled by your past, your environment, and the mass consciousness? Most people have an average of 15,000 seconds of positive uplifting joyful thoughts a day. That leaves 50,000 seconds of dense, negative down in the mouth energies. Now imagine those 50,000 negative (or rather not exactly positive) thoughts as people tromping through your living room. Day after day you allow 50,000 negative people to just walk through your sacred space. Apply that same thought to 50,000 negative vibrations/thoughts leaving dirty little puppy prints all over your auric field, your hopes and your dreams!! Are you ready to yell "STOP" yet?

You are Commander-in-Chief of your world your thoughts your creations. You say stop, you say go! Your life is not a runaway train, and you are not Momma being thrown from it! You and only you have control over your life, your feelings, your wants and your desires. Do you want to continue to rent property in "victim-hood" or move to a shiny new neighborhood?

Your past (in what ever form it takes) lives in the past. It cannot reside in the Now (present) unless you ask it to become a roommate and move in with you. The past sits patiently as old blue the hound dog waiting for you to call it forward into the Now. You do that by thought. Only thought can escort your incarcerated past into the holding cell of the Now. Look at the energy you are having tea and crumpets with on a daily basis.

Every moment of every day you have the option to create anew. The old recipes of self from the past no longer serve you unless that is what you want for dinner. Thoughts are living breathing energies. They have a life of their own and an electromagnetic charge. At first birth they are singular in nature, yet very magnetic. They seek like vibrations as they travel encircling you throughput the day. Imagine them as a single Dalmatian puppy in first morning light, but at the end of the day you feel like Cruella De'ville surrounded by 101 Dalmatians. Each one displaying an energetic encyclopedia from A to Z of all of your thoughts in the last 24 hours, good, bad and ugly.

Everyone complains that it takes too long to manifest. The time between manifestation and thought has shortened greatly since the beginning of 2000, but still there exists a time line, which is very necessary. Imagine everyone on the planet capable of instant (just add water) manifestation. What would the world look like if that were a truth? As much as humanity likes to grossly over express themselves through animated 4 letter words, the planet would look a lot like a cow patty palace to put it mildly. The earth is only a hair away from instant manifestation. As CEO of your time/space continuum it is your responsibility to focus/create/know/ what you want, and what you don't want and then let your words and your world reflect that knowledge.

Most people leave it up to spirit to do the thinking and go about their merry way without any focus on what they as co-creators would like to create. Everyone on earth is/was an Ascended Master. That was a prerequisite for Earth School 101. Everyone on earth has been instantaneously manifesting for eons of time, so why the dumb blond act?? (Forgive me all you beautiful blondes.) Stop asking the universe to do your homework. Get busy and study what your soul desires and earth wants are. Then focus, intend, know and create!

Manifestation follows thought. Both are neutral and free of opinion. Your energy is what fuels all thought and all manifestations. Focus on what you don't want and you will get it easily (or even easier) than what you do want. The Universe/aka Spirit does not feel the need to censor your experience. You get what you put energy into, focus upon, and think about. The good, the bad, the ugly all have front row seating. Which one will you look eye to eye and invite into your world? Think only upon that which you want! Do not dwell one moment upon that which you do not want![43]

Simply put, "The best way to predict the future is to create it." Our thoughts determine the present and future of what is contained within our lives. It's all about our choices. How and what we choose, upon what we focus, concentrate, or direct our attention, and where we spend our mental and emotional energies -- this is precisely what we will attract or draw to ourselves. And the universe always provides.[44]

Affirmations

One of the tools that goes together with conscious creation is affirmations. The most important thing to remember about affirmations is that they must be done in present tense, in other words, lie, lie, lie, yes lie and never tell the truth yourself. For example you wake us felling sick, say to yourself "WOW amazing how good I fell today" or "Never felt this good before" you will be surprised a short while later to find out that you actually end up having a very healthy day. I know I done it and I can attest that it really works. Same goes for anything you want, if you want wealth,

---

[43] *A Singular Molecule of Doubt Can Become a Lethal Toxic Weapon*! Created and Channeled by Gillian MacBeth-Louthan The "Awakening-Healing News" is Free and so are You! To Subscribe send Subject: Subscribe News@Awakening-Healing.com

[44] www.halexandria.org/dward003.htm

then act like wealthy individual do, never ever talk about poverty or sickness or lack, do not allow others to do in your presences. Do not associate with individual that make it a habit of complaining.

"One secret about affirmations is that it MUST have an emotion attached to it." So when you say I feel great, attaché the emotion of felling great. It helps to recall times when you actually felt great, remember the emotion? Well recall that emotion while you say "I fell great."

One final word on consciously creating and attracting to you what you want. Quite often we also unknowingly attract bad situations to ourselves. For example when I was in school I hated writing, I did not want to do what I was told by my teachers, I constantly devised ways of not attending school, of not writing, of not doing any physical activities, so far it went that I started to ask myself (higher conscience) how to device the ultimate way of not writing or being involved in sports at school, I visualized that I did not write, that I spent my time reading what I wanted to read, this went on and on... So one day I got my wish to come true, out of the blue my body developed a most bizarre tumor inside a vain on my hand, it grew twice its size every week for a few weeks, until I had a surgery to take remove it. Luckily for me it was not a malignant tumor. So you see I got my wish come true, I almost never wrote again nor got involved in physical education and sports until my last day in school. Needless to say, this is not a good way to get what you want.

I could give you thousands of examples of all the things that go wrong to almost everyone for unknowingly applying the conscious creation laws in a negative non-productive beneficial way. Once I had a car accident with two very drunk kids in a motorcycle who decided to have a head-on collision with the car I was driving; All day I had been wishing for a way out of the following few days; you know what? I got my wish! I spent a whole week in jail; which by the way turned out to be a rewarding fun experience, which was what I wanted for that week. Some for example do not want a job or a relationship and end up developing all sorts of diseases which unknowingly make their wishes come true. Does honey I have a headache sounds familiar? or that just in time cold? that makes you stay home... Think about it... the next time you wish for something, cause it may just come true...

Chapter 10

Drugs

The first thing about drugs is to: "Forget everything you have been told so far." The fact is that if you are in a rush to find out if all what this book says is true or not, you can find our in less than 5 minutes with the use of some drugs. For example the drug named DMT[45] within seconds will convert the leader of the most atheist movement into a spiritual person, yes the experience is SO STRONG and powerful that NO one will argue that it was spiritual in nature and out-of-this-world. Ketamine[46] a drug that has been used by millions as a general anesthesia (perhaps even including you) is guarantee to change anyone's concept of reality in less than one hour when used in small dosage. Then there are the long used drugs by shamans such as hallucinogenic mushrooms and cactuses. These drugs have been used by shamans throughout history. There are huge websites dedicated to these types of drugs.

---

[45] DMT.- The Spirit Molecule by Rich Strassman, M.D.

[46] Ketamine.- Dreams and Realities by Karl Jansen M.D., Ph.D.

Now I am not telling you to go try any of these drugs, I am just letting you know that it is yet one more way of finding the truth.

In order to short-circuit the process, Carlos Castañeda went through a brutal initiation using hardcore psychedelic compounds discovered by the shamans, such as peyote, psilocybin mushrooms and Jimson weed. Don Juan would use these compounds to guide Carlos through an initiation into these higher worlds, with the idea that eventually the compounds would no longer be necessary for the access. Carlos was especially resilient to his training and thus he "tripped out" many times before he got the message.

Yet there are plenty of none drug ways of accomplishing the same such as Binaural Synchronization techniques of the Monroe Institute represent a drugless way to induce out-of-body and mystical experiences using the properties of sound.

The Natural Mind: A New Way of Looking at Drugs and the Higher Consciousness by Dr. Andrew Weil, M.D. Is yet another book by a professional on how to use your mind to consciously create your health.

Chapter 11

Astral Travel, Out-of-Body experience and Near Death Experiences

Astral travel, Out-of-Body and near death experiences are all synonymous for the same thing. Basically one (your sole, YOU) leaves the body for a while and goes any where it wants. For those who have had this experience there is no longer any doubt that there is a lot more than meets the bodies five senses. Astral travel to me is the highest aspiration that you should have. There is nothing more valuable than the ability to astral travel at will.

In order to fully enter into a higher plane, we have to do it in a body that is essentially less physical, and more of a direct form of conscious energy. In fact, the Hindu cosmology associates the seven chakras[47] with seven different energy bodies, and thus in a sense we have seven different bodies, of which we could use those above the third density for travel in higher realms. This is essentially what happens when we have a dream or an out-of-body experience. We leave our physical bodies where they belong in the third density, and use a higher form of body.

---

[47] Chakra means Wheel in Sanskrit

The benefits of Astral Projection and OBE are profound, and well worth pursuing.

Astral projection (or etheric projection) is the ability to separate one's consciousness from the confines of the physical body, enabling one to travel vast distances through time and space and then return safely.

Once separated, the possibilities in this spirit-like form are endless, as there are no restrictions in the means of locomotion as are present in the physical body. You may choose to walk, glide, fly or even think yourself to a location simply by imagining the place you want to be.

Perhaps you wish to visit someone on the other side of the planet - you only have to think of that person and you'll be there, in an instant. Being a non-solid form, the astral body (body of consciousness) is able to pass through walls and other solid matter with ease and could even make physical contact with another projector.

Although there are some people out there practicing astral projection, it is not commonly known in the western world and most people in the street would scoff at the idea.

Well, little do they know, but every time we sleep at night our astral-selves rise slightly out of line from the physical body the very moment we lose consciousness, and stays in this position until we awake. The purpose of this is to regain the energy lost during our waking hours and is thought to be a form of recharging.

You may have experienced the sensation of falling, followed by a jolt, just at the point of falling asleep. This is caused by the sudden return of the astral body as it attempted to leave the physical before unconsciousness took place. In other words, the beginning of a projection occurred... [48]

Many Astral locales including entire cities are inhabited by very large numbers of Astral residents, all continuously influencing the same creative Energy, and thus giving these Astral locales their permanency. As mentioned previously, the mid-Astral worlds to which people are attracted after the transition from the physical world in accordance with the Energy characteristic of the individual Astral and Mental body, the Soul and Spirit, are almost identical to the physical world, so much so that many people do not immediately know they have actually passed on. This is because the people of the Astral worlds model the Astral worlds based upon their own specific experiences and perception of the physical world they have just left, and how they "imagine" it should be. People at that level of evolution on the path often believe that "reality" is represented by material things just as they did on Earth, and accordingly use their powers of the imagination to reproduce that same habitat and perception within the Astral worlds, thereby creating that reality for themselves with which they feel the most comfortable. [49]

---

[48] www.astraldynamics.com

[49] www.ourultimatereality.com

The Astral worlds are vast, varied and complex, consisting of an infinite number of realms from the earthly equivalent of past present and future, many of which have been created by beings not of the Earth, but all of which have been created by the very same vibrations, creative Energy of the power of thought, the creative power of the imagination.

There are many excellent highly informative sources of information on this subject, from very good books to very good websites.

Astral Dynamics : A NEW Approach to Out-Of-Body Experiences by Robert Bruce The author provides an advanced guide to achieving and maintaining out-of-body states, and explores the hows, whys, and ways of nonphysical exploration, from projection techniques and energy manipulation to psychic self-defense and astral sex.  Robert Bruce has drawn on his lifetime's experience of traveling in the astral dimension. This book provides, all in one package, a personal narrative, techniques, a troubleshooting guide, and a theoretical perspective. Whether you are a skeptic, a veteran astral projector, a novice, or an armchair traveler -- there is a treasure here. Astral Dynamics provides the intelligent and motivated reader with everything needed to put theory into practice. www.astraldynamics.com This site will help you reconnect with your spiritual psychic nature and higher self. Content focuses on energy work, astral projection, healing, auras, psychic self-defense, and on increasing your understanding of the greater reality. Lots of information for beginners.

The Art and Practice of Astral Projection by Ophiel This is a practical book that provides you with all the theory necessary to understand the art of astral projection. Offered in an easy step-by-step method so you can safely enter and function in the Astral Plane, and return with all the memories of your experience. This book offers you  the opportunity to learn four different methods of dealing with the Inner Planes; How to return to the physical plane, at will; How to remember the trip; and much more. This is a great book for beginning students. Ophiel was one of America's best known occult writers. His "Art and Practice" series is probably the finest ever written for beginner and intermediate students and has gotten rave reviews from serious beginning students. This book is a classic and the first one I read.

www.astralpulse.com/forums/index.php will have by the time this books is printer well over 10,000 subscribed members and 200,000+ messages. The numbers speak for themselves...

www.astralsociety.com/Forums/index.php will have by the time this books is printer well over 5000 subscribed members and 100,000+ messages. The numbers speak for themselves...

www.jonasridgeway.com for a more comprehensive list of recommended books on astral travel visit this website among them Jonas favorite:

Seth, Dreams and Projections Of Consciousness by Jane Roberts This is my all-time favorite book on out-of-the-body experiences! I love all the Seth books and this is a must-have for any Seth junkie. An incredibly exciting book, which provides essential instructions and information for those interested in working with dreams and out-of-body experiences. Seth is the real deal.  Everytime I read any Seth book I have to put it down periodically and breathe deeply and stare off into space -- his words hit the deepest part of your Self and they always ring true. I challenge anyone to read ANY of the Seth books and not be changed by it, altered in some wonderfully fantastic way. You will view yourself and everyone around you differently. Nothing is random -- everything happens for a reason. You are in control of your life and every aspect of it. You create your own reality. There is nothing to worry about. Life is fun! Get out there and enjoy it, both in and out of body.

Chapter 12

Akashic Hall of Records

Akashic Records is a place in the 4th dimension where one can find information on just about any subject you can thing of and then some.

My first venture into the Akashic Records was an exploratory one to verify its existence. I was in an out-of-body state and I requested to be taken to the Akashic Records, once there I automatically met a young female attendant, I proceeded to ask her to see a record, to which she use a very advanced computer terminal, something that I would place in at least 100 years from present day technology. To my surprise it took it sometime for it to fetch the information, by no means it was instant, there was a short delay, same as our present computer systems. Now I realize that the interface was just something created by my subconscious mind for my convenience and amusement.

With the proper meditation anyone can reach the Akashic Records and fetch any information going back for approximately one million years and going forward for approximately one thousand years. Time and space is only relevant to our 3rd density experience.

Every religion describes God through metaphor, allegory, and exaggeration, from the early Egyptians through modern Sunday school. Metaphors are a way to help our minds process the unprocessible. The problems arise when we begin to believe literally in our own metaphors." Those who truly understand their faiths understand the stories are metaphorical."

When did I realize I was God? Well, I was praying and I suddenly realized I was talking to myself. ~ **Peter O'Toole**

Chapter 13

Who? What? Where? Is God

The ancient god moniker has nothing to do with divinity per se. The word god is from ancient Scandinavian language meaning a powerful person, a leader, a superior, and a ruler over the people. Anybody who was a political, military, or theological leader would be a god or lord person.

The word God is a very misunderstood and misused word, for example in Spanish is used always in the plural form, vs. English which uses it only in the singular form, the contradiction between the two languages is quite amusing and proves that neither uses it correctly. Both languages need further improvement on they way they use the word god.

So Who? What? Where? Is God. For the answer of Who? I have a simple answer, NO one, since it is not a single being that we can give singularity nor name to. What then is it? It is everything that we know; it is you and everything that surround us, including the entire universe. Where? It is simply everywhere, since it is everything, it is like saying all, the all, the all knowing.

The word God is simply a poor explanation for the all encompassing existence of everything there is. Some have attempted to modernize this word with a better description, such as The Primal Force, The Universal Subconscious Mind, The Cosmos, Divine Cosmic Spirit, Tao and many others... And of course some have made the terrible mistake of giving it a name such as Jehovah, which totally misleading, since Jehovah is the name of a common god.

God is also a title for a status after Angel, same as Doctor in some professions is a title given after Master. When a being just like you or me attains total control, in other words becomes almighty, meaning that has learned all there is to learn about the laws of the universe, this being becomes a god on its own rights. The titled god has also been used to describe deities, such as in the Greek mythology, which personifies most if not all the human traits as gods, not that these gods exists, it is just that some do, or we/are known by these traits.

But most important of all, keep in mind that you are a god in the making, that you posses all the potential of the mightiest of the gods. You yourself are as much god as any other god.

When you hear or read the word God, simply translated in your mind to something like "Universal Subconscious Mind" which to me and hopefully to you to, will make a lot more sense.

Father is other words very much misunderstood, since both are commonly used with no explanation at all. Lets start with Father, Father is the same as saying Universal Subconscious Mind, God, ALL, it means everything, from the this ALL comes everything, you, me and everything else, so when you say Father help us/me, or may the will of the Father, you are referring to the Universal Collective Mind, that means you me and everyone else in the Cosmos/Universe.

Mother is yet another very misunderstood word. Mother refers to a subpart of you; it is your subconscious, your soul, the part of you behind the scene (3rd density/dimension,) the one that knows all about you, the one that knows your REAL needs, the one that knows all your past and future. So when you ask the mother to help you, you are asking a part of you that knows best, yes it knows better than your egos and your conscious mind. Kundalini is yet another synonymous word for Mother; it is often used as Mother Kundalini.

Jesus Christ is also another very misunderstood name. Christ is a level of accomplishment such as doctor or engineer know as Christ Consciousness. Jesus is a name of a man who knew a lot and made an effort to teach the people of his time. Christ is not his last name.

It is wise to learn how to invoke these forces properly, to enable you to get what you want and most important what you really need, much quicker and effortlessly.

Below is a reprint of chapter 1 from "Reclaiming Your Divinity[50]" A book that gives a very clear and concise explanation of the god we all really are. It is written by two followers of Sathia Sai Baba's teachings; they lived with Baba for over 20 years, in which they learn quite well how to explain a complex subject with simple words and songs that we all can relate too.

---

[50] Reclaiming Your Divinity, exposing the ultimate deception by Lightstrorm Published by SHANTI Publishing and Child's Sunvillage, Inc. USA 208-634-8335 Canada 250-380-3760 lightstrorm@ctcweb.net www.ctcweb.net/~lightstrorm $5.00 USD Feb. 2005

What came first, the chicken or the egg?

Dearest Reader, if you are truly and earnestly searching for some truth about questions like, "Who am I? Why am I here? Who or what is God? Where is God?" and basically, what the heck is my life or this creation all about? Then please read on!

Then this small book, in which we will be sharing some of our own experiences, might be of some help in your quest. But understand right now that everyone must inevitably walk through their own personal experiences to fully comprehend and finally know the Truth.' Truth, like Love and God, will soon start to make perfect sense, and is usually the simplest thing to understand, when the mind gets out of the way of the heart.

All right then dear inquiring Self, let's get to it. Shall we look at some of the following questions that require some deep inquiry and contemplation?

In the beginning there was God, and God created all of Creation!

So, if everything originated from God, by God, through God, then what single thing in all of Creation is not God? "So, who is God? What is God?" "Where is God?" "Or for that matter, does God have one particular name or form?" "... And what is the real idea of religion?" On the other hand, what part of the separate feeling EGO-MIND concocted the various organized religions?

Well, what do you think? Is God a Divine personality living in some heavenly existence? Is He, She or It a "Burning Bush" or "The Light"? And, if everything originated from God, by God, through God, what would that make us, hmm?

Some say, God separated Himself so He could love Himself. Yeah could be, but God is Love ... and God is complete, so why would God need Love? Especially when God is everything? ... Or nothing?' Oh boy, here we go again, this stuff is beyond the mind.

So, we double dog dare you to tell us: "What, in all of this manifested creation isn't GOD!" (And don't say Bush.) Come on, we dare you! You can't, can you? Because, in the beginning, what was there? Come on, you know. God, Heavenly Father, Divine Mother, Allah, En-Sof, The Formless, all pervading, all Loving, all Inclusive, and all Powerful, YOU!

Or, if all of this is just too much to handle, let's just have some fun with it, and think of it this way, "God was just bored! So He divided Himself in order to Love Himself!" Don't we get lonely sometimes and just want some company, to share with, make love to, or just have a loving conversation? We can relate to that idea can't we? Haven't you ever been bored?

So, let us take a look at the idea of God, and how Creation came to be, shall we.

Let us start with a bit of research into the last question, "What is the real understanding of religion and why are there so many different ones!" and so many names for God. My goodness, for something so basic and simple, why does the ego-mind make everything so complicated, why? Could it be because the mind can only identify with an object or idea like a name and form? How boring ...

Ohhh ...Yeah, maybe that's it, the mind also became bored with the idea of just one religion and one name for GOD. One must wonder how many more the mind will create. (Oops, that's future ... fantasy ... "Mind into the tool box!)"

All religions declare that in the beginning there was God! They either depict this God idea or conceptual God as a name or a form, or as a formless Eternal Divine Energy Consciousness beyond our human experience, beyond the mind's ability to comprehend. Look at that statement, beyond the mind! God simply IS ... always ... without beginning or end! And if you hold on to this thought, there is no mind. Ooooh, how scary! (Ha ha)

The Christian Bible states: In the beginning there was God, From GOD the FATHER came the WORD, and the word became flesh, thus Adam was created and from Adam came Eve and so proliferation of Creation started.

In the ancient Hebrew religion of the Holy book Kabbalah. It states:

In the beginning there was the En-Sof, God, which translates into, limitless or boundless (E=without, Sof=end). To them this symbolized total unity beyond the mind, beyond our comprehension. It simply can not be explained in words or even understood by the mind. Because it is beyond the mind!

The Kabbalists played on this difficulty ol expressing the inexpressible by pointing out thai the En-Sof, by all definition, should be nonexistent. All the words of any language cannol explain HIM. The Hebrew Kabbalah furthei explains that God (En-Sof) by the power of the secret 'WORD' created the first Sefiroth (like the Christian Adam). This idea of the Sefiroth agair represents the Cosmic Mind or the Creative Principle. The ancient Kabbalists also realized that the only way to perceive God (En-Sof) was to control the mind and then go beyond it. They state, "Silence the mind and you will know yourself as GOD."

In the Islamic religion the un-definable God principle is simply called, Allah.

In metaphysical terms (as we perceive it) the idea of Creation could be expressed in this way: Now before we play with clear intellect, let us state here that it is not possible to explain God, since we are still using words, ideas, concepts (the mind) and God is beyond the mind. But maybe this simplistic perception can serve to give a fraction of clarity to this idea of Oneness! Just feel the underlying energy behind the words or between the lines of, ALL LOVING, ALL INCLUSIVE, AND ALL POWERFUL, and this might help you understand its origin, or shall we say our origin. It is truly quite simple and easy, but the mind's job is to complicate the idea of GOD far beyond our reach, and that is how it seems to stay in control. So right now, let's reclaim our control over the mind.

First there is Eternal Consciousness ... Self-Awareness ... Perfect, Luminous Intelligence. Then by reflecting (just like an object in a mirror) or projecting Consciousness on its own luminous Intelligence, which is also the Self, an inner reflection of the Self appears like an EMANATION that seems separate from the Self. Thus Consciousness perceives itself as, "Oh, I am also that!" This is the first illusion, the idea that there are two Selves, Maya. This inner mirrored reflection of the Self then becomes the womb of Creation, an imagined silent inner elliptical Space which (due to consciousness) is endless. Think of it as an eternal imagination with no limits. (As you think it, so it shall be.)

This Womb then becomes the source of all life, of all name and form, as we know it. This emanation continues to reflect itself in the mirror of that Self-Aware Intelligence and in turn causes an oscillation or movement in this inner Space (or shall we say womb) which causes a frequency pattern, or a sound which then, rises up out of the Silence. This we call the 'Word of God' or the primal Sound, the "AUM" or "OM" sound, the first VIBRATION. This vibration is the energy stream of Love or Life-force, Chi or Prana. Then this ever expanding movement of vibration becomes a variable sea of different vibratory patterns, which speed up or slow down, change-re-arrange, merge-separate, collide-explode and so on; and with this process, of ever changing and interacting electro-magnetic cyclic impulse patterns, the MIND with its creative powers, creates all DREAM MANIFESTATIONS. This includes all creations, on all the levels and dimensions of Creation (universes, heavenly realms, nether or hell regions etc..). This fundamental energy stream of Love, Life-force or Chi is the flow of what we often call God's Divine Love. It is a benevolent omnipresent, all knowing, all loving, all inclusive, all powerful and ever expanding vibration, which is the foundation of EVERYTHING, of ALL.

So by following this metaphysical explanation of Creation, we must inevitably come to the following conclusion that (by using our pure intellect and discrimination), since all of Creation is only Consciousness of constantly moving energy to begin with, and representing itself in different forms or stages of movement, nothing can ever really die, it can only change states (or transmute itself) by re-arranging patterns or changing frequencies or speeding up or slowing down. (Einstein also came to the same conclusion.)

When energy slows down it seems to appear as solid matter to us, at least to the naked eye. Under a high powered microscope this is of course not true. Then as the movement of energy speeds up, it becomes less and less solid or dense until it is space or ether again. Maybe you can think of it like this: An ice-cube represents solid matter, heat it a little and it will melt and become water, heat it some more and it becomes steam. Yet all the while it is the same conscious energy (atomic essence) but in different stages of movement. That is why wise people know that there is really no "death" for our Consciousness, only change!

In Hindu philosophy, in regards to the most ancient Hindu text called the Vedas it states: In the beginning there was Paramatma (the Primal Source God principle).

The Vedas describe The Paramatma as "Not this - Not that" because this Primal Source of all can not be explained or conceived of through the mind or intellect. The Vedas continue to explain that the sound that started Creation, is the 'AUM' or 'OM' sound. Centuries later this' 'AUM' sound became 'HUM' for the Buddhists, 'AMIN' for the Hebrews and Muslims, and 'AMEN' for the Christians. This 'WORD' or 'AUM' sound originated from the Primal Source, God, and consequently the form of Narayana came into being to give a beginning concept to the human mind. Then Brahma the Creator grew out of Narayana's navel. (Same idea as the Sefiroth or Adam). Brahma again represents the Cosmic Mind or the Creative Principle, the Architect (so to speak, of the mind) of this Creation of name and form, of separation Brahma could also be described as a single point of God's projected form of our Divine Consciousness.

Consequently this point of projected Consciousness (Brahma, the MTND) became the first created illusion of separation from God, or the first mirage of an imagined DUALITY. Brahma then, by His mental projection, His imagination, His dreaming ability (which inherently has the exact same power as the Primal Source Consciousness - God) created this diverse and multi-dimensional Divine Dream Creation of endless names and forms. All the ancient Spiritual Adepts, Masters, Rishis, Yogis and Teachers, Saints and Sages realized the Truth, that there was nothing else but 'GOD,' through painstaking investigation and self-disciplined effort of certain practices (mostly by trial and error), and that it was the uncontrolled MIND'S imagination which was the root cause of feeling separate from God.

They realized that the way to re-connect with our God-Self was to meditate and practice silencing the mind. They practiced, and became masters of the mind, by letting go of, or controlling, all thoughts dealing with the past, because they saw it only dredged up the illusion of old feelings and emotions.

They also saw how important it was to control all thoughts that ventured into the future, dreaming of some unreal imagined fantasy, because that created more desires and attachments to this ever-changing momentary illusion of Creation. Then they reasoned correctly that there is only the present moment, 'the NOW,' which we can truly experience and interact with. Eventually with practice the mind became their tool as they walked through this dream called life in the 'NOW.'

So we can plainly see that every Spiritual Master, along with all major religions of the world, tend to agree on and have declared, "In the beginning there was God and God created all of Creation!"

Here we should question, "Are we God or are we His Creation?" It's as simple as this: If you believe yourself to be only the body, the mind and senses, then... Yes! ... you are separate; you are His mind creation. Sefiroth, Adam, Brahma, Manu, Harry, Ronesa, Joe, Mary, Irene, Jane, Cassidy, Jaydon, Trent, or whoever, and then when you DIE, you are DEAD and gone, that consciousness is deleted from Creation, you and nothing of you exists, and that's it! Kaput... Fini!

But, if you know your Self as Divine-Consciousness, (the soul) which is forever, eternal, that can never be harmed in any way or die, all powerful, all loving, and all inclusive, YOU ARE GOD! You ... yes, you who have always been and will always be, eternally and forever. So choose! Choose to be Divine, or if you like, you can believe the mind and eventually be food for worms. Which one sounds better? Pick one ... Your Divinity, or worm food, the mind's creation. And then stick with your decision, make it your Truth. You will have to fight for it, because it is a battle!

However, right along with this Truth comes the great responsibility of living your life in accordance with it. So if you are God, then your thoughts, words and deeds must reflect or express this Truth in your daily life as all loving, all inclusive, and all powerful (and that power must be based in selfless pure love or you will reap bad karma). We will come back to this and discuss it further.

Mankind has given a thousand and one names and ascribed many forms to this mental and emotional concept of God. The Creator, Heavenly Father, Divine Mother, Paramatma, Christ, Narayana, Jehovah, En-Sof, Allah, Ahura Mazda, The Light, The Burning Bush, Naugual, Nirvana, Sat-Chit-Ananda, Self-luminous Divine Consciousness, The Eternal Absolute, Tripura Ma, The Primal Source, The Almighty, Divine-Self, Life-force, The Force, The First Cause, Creative Love Force, The Nameless One or Energy and so on...

Still, no matter how many different names or forms the mind has given to this idea or concept of God, the common theme voiced by all religions and spiritual Masters is, that there is only the ONE single underlying 'Reality' or Truth (God), which manifested all of Creation. They further declare that God is Love.

So the answer to the question about religion would be that religion should BE and always represent Divine LOVE I As Sai Baba tells us, "There is only one religion, the religion of Love!"

If any religion does not express itself on the stage of the world as pure Love in thought word and deed, then it must be a man made, mind created dogma of concepts and rules for some other purpose.

(Mmm, maybe ego you think?)

And so the mind created its child called the ego in order to feel special, important, and separate.

It stands to reason, if everything originated from God, by God, within God, through God, Consciousness and Love, then we and all of this Creation must be God.

That is the reason why we are forever, personally and consciously perfecting ourselves. We want to be so good at everything, and we are forever searching for love all around us, not realizing, (because the mind tricks us) that the love we are searching for, is within us and has always been within us. Everyone and everything in this Creation is the 'Embodiment of Love,' God, or this underlying Life-force or Conscious Energy stream of Divine Love.

Here is something to contemplate. When you feel or perceive that deep, clear, love in your heart or around you, it is always only your own Love reflected back to you, because somehow you are aware that you are that Love. This is a reflective Creation and you can only experience what you are and what you project! When this Love is for God, it is always a perfect reflection, like a clear undistorted reflection from a bright spotless mirror. The same reflective idea goes for everything else, like beauty, joy, inner peace, or anger, resentment, worry and fear. So you can see that exactly what you send out or project will return to you. As you sow, so shall you reap!

Christ like the Buddha, Rama, Krishna and Sai Baba as well as all the other Spiritual Masters and Teachers, Saints and Sages realized and shared with us that God's nature is pure Love. That God is Love, Peace and Bliss, and that all of Creation is really an illusion or a dream created by the Mind principle.

The Buddha explained the Primal Source, God principle, the Divine Consciousness (which is everything as well as 'no thing') in another way. He declared that there is only Nirvana, Self-aware Bliss. He realized that there is nothing anywhere that is not inherently Divine, and that in the final analysis and experience, there is no personalized separate entity or God figure of name and form. He realized that the idea of a separate God was a mind created illusion; and that this Creation was a mind created dream.

The 'Being state of Self,' the state of Nirvana, the Immortal Absolute (the En-Sof, Paramatma, Allah, God or the 'I AM' God-Self if you like), only that is real, and that is everywhere! We are all connected, that is why his philosophy was to do no harm to even the smallest creature.

He also explained this BEING state as a 'Great Emptiness' (like endless space without any stars) that is totally filled with the Light of Self Aware Eternal Consciousness and therefore can never be empty as we understand it. The Buddha, like many others, realized that all of Creation is really a constantly changing, momentary illusion or a dream created by the Cosmic Mind Principle. His personal experience taught Him that it was the uncontrolled mind, with its many attachments and desires, which causes this feeling of separation from the Creator and in turn creates all human misery.

God's nature is LOVE or "God is Love." This stream of Love is the underlying ONENESS which all the Divine Teachers, Avatars (conscious Divine personalities in human form), Saints and Sages have told us about. But remember Love does not always have to be just obliging smiles and outer gentleness or softness. It can take on many outer expressions and be very disciplining, correcting and forceful.

Example:

When Jesus the Christ was throwing out the money lenders, upturned tables and freeing the animals that were being sold for slaughter in the Temple, He was definitely physical and forceful.

Yet, the underlying selflessness of Love, in every case, the total care for all, is always the clear, underlying, unchanging reality.

The Eternal Consciousness, the Divine-Self or God Principle is the root cause of All and Everything, and in the same breath it must be said that it is beyond everything, beyond even the mind, it is really 'no thing,' because, God cannot be described as a 'thing' which can only be name and form.

The reason why we say that 'everything is God' is because God is the only underlying reality. God is inherent or the root cause of this Mind Creation, yet God is beyond Creation, beyond the Mind. But for our body consciousness self to identify with anything, or everything, our mind has to have a name or form identification so that we can try to conceive, understand or FEEL it.

Thus the mind created a system we call religion, in order to represent a belief in the idea that there is an Immortal, Absolute, Primal Source, Eternal, Unchanging, Omnipresent, Perfect, Creative Consciousness, Energy, Vibration, Force, God, which is the Creator of everything!

The rest, of what we label as religion in this world, is a manmade, mind created system of various dogmas, spiritual interpretations, personal opinions and rituals of elite secret societies or fanatic ego personalities, a pretense of specialty (of some imagined higher awareness of God) by self-serving individuals, brotherhoods or institutions.

We are presuming here that these religions were originally created to help us find some sort of reconnection to our True Self.' But as always, if we allow the mind and ego to run amuck, then religion becomes egotistical and self serving. Just look at what the catholic religion did with Jesus' simple teachings of Love! They created a fearful God full of wrath, one that would condemn you to Hell if you did not adhere to their rules.

So you see, as long as we propagate some ritualistic practice of placing Religion first and a Loving God second, we are creating a separation above and beyond our human reach, and we will always feel separate, less than or unworthy. (Even the concept of true spirituality will seem beyond our reach.)

Or on the other side of the spectrum some will rebel and fight against anything to do with religion or God and become an atheist.

Heck, today we even make idols out of words and ideas. We put the idea of Liberation, Moksha, Salvation, Self-realization, unconditional Love and even the Light on a separate almost unattainable pedestal in front of which we mentally worship, by hoping that, someday in the future, we can acquire it by the Grace of God. (This is the mind's way to control our life by giving us the false idea of endless time in some future that does not exist.)

For each idol the mind creates, we start a separate religion or ideology, a secret society or brotherhood, a new church or building, a political governing party or cooperation, a New Age trend or what have you, and heaven knows what else we dream up in order to appear special to the world around us.

The original idea to create a personalized God (one that has a form and or a name), was to allow us to have a closer relationship with God. And eventually merge or feel connected with God, It is extremely hard for people to identify with nothing, or 'no thing,' since the mind can not create a feeling of closeness or intimate connection without some sort of reference.

So if individuals would fully identify with this God form/name and constantly think of God in a closer and more intimate fashion, then sooner or later the separation between God and the individual will become blurred and before too long they will merge into each other by losing their separate mind identity, due to this constant feeling of closeness, this all inclusive togetherness. This intense love or bhakti for, and devotion to, this God form/name will eventually dissolve the ego-mind-personality identification and in turn take them beyond the mind, into the state of ever existing Oneness of all. This has been the experience of many of our religious Saints and Sages.

If we look closely, we can see that same premise (of the underlying ONENESS) is represented in all the world religions. All of Creation is willed, fashioned or originates from the ONE Primal Source of Consciousness, God, En-Sof, Jehovah,

Allah, Paramatma etc ... It is, All LOVING, ALL INCLUSIVE, ALL POWERFUL!

Now one of the best or easiest ways to correctly utilize this 'tool' called 'the mind' is to let the mind become completely immersed and attached to any chosen name or form of God and thereby let go of all other worldly attachments and desires. In other words, GOD becomes your first love, your only desire.

This will at first show itself as worship, which we all must walk through, one lifetime or another, and if we are earnest, it will quickly blossom into one-pointed devotion, (another way to focus and discipline the mind) which in turn will soon mature into unconditional LOVE for God and all of God's Creation, since they are always one and the same. The result of this complete Love identification, and immersion with God and God's Creation (everywhere in everyone and underlying everything) you will eventually lose your false ego separate self identification. And this will automatically result in the personal experience of being one with God. Then by this personal experience, YOU will know your True SELF as the ALL, the ONE, as GOD!

This then, is the simple and ultimate shortcut to Knowing God, the 'SELF.'

When Christ told His disciples, "Love thy neighbor as thy self!" or "Love ye one another as I have loved you!" He was expressing the Divine Principle of Unconditional Love, that they should follow, and that He Himself was living.

Krishna (a Hindu Avatar) explained in the Bhagavad Gita (part of the Hindu scriptures) to simply surrender your mind and heart, every thought, feeling, word and deed in love and devotion to God. To only see God as the doer, as the underlying reality in all. To think only of God at at all times. In that way, Krishna explained, the false illusion of the mind-created ego-personality self will no longer function as the dominant controlling aspect of your life. God will then become the charioteer, captain, guru or guiding energy of your life. By becoming the watcher, by surrendering, or letting go of this 'false you' (mind) as the controller, doer, sufferer or enjoyer of anything, you (Your Divine-Self) will thus allow God's energy (a higher Consciousness energy) to guide you through the maze of life. This full love and devotion to God will result in the final Oneness, the complete merger with God.

The Buddha, Christ and all the other Avatars like Rama, Krishna, Sai Baba etc... along with all the Saints and Sages of Creation, shared with us that the one unchanging 'Reality' or Truth' is that there is ONLY GOD! That God is within you and all around you, and is our Divine Consciousness-Self which is all loving, all inclusive, and all powerful. All the rest was, is and will be, simply an ever changing cycle of mind created illusion, a diverse emanation of momentary or temporary dream like experiences, created by our attachment and desire that the mind tricked us into believing we needed in order to survive.

When Christ said, "Split any piece of wood or lift up any stone, look close, because there you will find me, there I AM!" He was telling us again that God is everywhere and in everything.

Or when Christ said, "Whosoever sees me, also sees the Father!" What does this statement suggest? Does it not say, "I and the Father are One? I am God?" all else is a projection of the MIND.

***

Here are a couple of simple practices that you could work with.

a) Mind created thoughts from the past, are history! They no longer apply in the moment, they were only lessons learned. So when, or if, these sneaky little thoughts creep in, YOU your Divine-Self, take charge, and tell the mind, "Get into the tool box. I will call you when I need you. I choose to live in the moment"

b) Mind created thoughts of the future, are fantasy! They do not exist in the moment. It is the mind trying to create a false existence, and draw you away from the NOW.

c) In order to go beyond the mind you must let go of all mind concepts, preconceived ideas, judgments, prejudices and coveted perceptions, because they are your prison bars that will not let you be free. To have perceptions is perfect, but the moment you believe the perception to be true and more valid than any other, it becomes a judgment due to your ego or emotional input. Have the perception and then let it go. It only means you are aware, which is perfect, but do not believe it to be 'real,' true, more important or lasting.

d) You may be doing this for as long as the body is breathing, but once the mind realizes that you, Your Divine-Self, means business, the mind (like the naughty child) will listen and it gets easier.

e) NOW is Eternity, all else is the mind illusion. Life only happens in the moment.

f) When you wake up in the morning, become consciously aware of any thoughts or feelings that are present. See if there is any sort of mood that just seems to be present.

g) Then purposely decide that you will be joyful and energetic all day, just because you like it that way! In the beginning your mind may try to tell you, "I can't just decide to be happy, it does not work like that! There are just too many unpleasant issues to deal with in my life to be happy." Think a moment! Then if you do not discipline the mind it will instantly drag up a past left over anger or frustration situation or create a non existent future scenario of how you must worry and stress about something that might come up. So remember, the mind is now YOUR TOOL! Be vigilant and every time you catch the mind dictating your thoughts and feelings by indulging into the past or in some non-existent future, you must immediately discipline it. "I am here in this moment; in the now and I choose to be happy! How dare you try to deprive me of that! You're my tool now, so get into the tool box!"

***

AUM

Chapter 14

How to become immortal and /or improve your health

Parts of your body are dyeing and others are being born as your read these lines, some are just seconds old and some just died. A mother is able to create a new body for her new born, so can you create one for yourself. Even after you have died there are still new cells in your body being born. You can consciously decide how these new parts that are replacing old ones get created, they can be with the old way of thinking, that we grow old and die or you can make a paradigm shift and create a new healthy immortal body for yourself, one that is disease free, full of vigor and good health. Is this possible? Yes it is! All it takes is for you to change the way you think.

The only reason you are not immortal is because you have not consciously chosen to be so, you have not yet realized the god within you. The day that you (same as did Jesus and many others) figured it out, you will also become immortal. In the meanwhile before you and I completely figure how to do it; there is a lot we can do to help us out in improving our present body conditions and to get one step closer to immortality.

Here are some excerpts from others who explain it with different words:

The physical structure of our bodies is a holographic projection of our consciousness, each of us is responsible for our own health. What we now view as miraculous remissions of disease may actually be due to changes in consciousness which in turn effect changes in the hologram of the body. Similarly, controversial new healing techniques such as visualization may work so well because in the holographic domain of thought images are ultimately as real as "reality". [51]

There is nothing in Universal Subconscious Mind that desires our bodies to be warped away from the purposeful functioning for which they were intended. It is our conception of ourselves that this visits disease upon us, and when we have conceived ourselves to be spiritually perfect, we become physically perfect. The real you is not your body. Your body is but an infinitesimal extension in time in space. The real you is mental and spiritual, free of the confines of space and time, limitless in power and the capacity to understand and create. When you have recognized your true spiritual self you have become identified with immortal Self, and disease cannot exist in your body, for there is no limitation in Universal Subconscious Mind. [52]

Start by taking responsibility for your own health, your health, even your looks are your own creation. Aging is a programming fact you have created and not a real fact of life, you can change it, if you

---

[51] Library of Halexandria www.halexandria.org

[52] Three Magic Words by U.S. Andersen 1979 Edition Wilshire Book Company

want too. Even a broken bone can be placed back in its place in a instance with the power of your mind, I know it can be done, cause I did it once with a broken bone on my leg; I felt it brake and hear the sound of it braking in three places, the pain was so much that my consciousness left my body, when I notice I was out of the body I quick went on the business of repairing it and it worked.

More on chapter 38.- Tips and tools for improving your life and health.

Chapter 15

The Law of KARMA and DARMA

KARMA - Finally a word of caution; all your thoughts, imaginations and creative visualizations must only be for the purposes of good, either for yourself or for other people. Never, ever be tempted to use these powers to harm another person. If you do, the Universal law of Cause and Effect, of which karma is an integral aspect will most surely operate against you, and either in this or a future life you will have to pay the price. This is not intended to be a system of punishment as such as with a court of law. The simple fact of the matter is that every cause has its corresponding effect, positive, negative or neutral, and karma is no more than the causation of the Law of Attraction that ensure that no being can be the cause of anything negative without experiencing the corresponding effect. Note that we use the word "experiencing" rather than "suffering". Everyone is here to experience and to evolve and not to suffer which is a human construct based on a perception relative to self and the ego. The Universe operates under the influence of the most powerful force in the Universe, Unconditional Love, and that applies to every aspect of human evolution, and indeed the evolution of the entire Universe and all Beings, all expressions of God.

www.ourultimatereality.com

All prophecy are fluid and changeable. The future is not set in stone. The reason is simple: We create our own reality through our collective thinking (mass consciousness). **What a prophet "sees" is one of the probable outcomes of our future. If we don't like** *what the prophet has to say, we have the power to change it.*

Chapter 16

What is really going on with our planet? 2012

I am not the originator of the information that follows. I have simply gathered together several sources for your perusal. I did not discriminate from where I obtained the information. Part of my motivation is to get you directly involved in looking inward to your own gut feelings and doing your own research. Many already sense something is wrong big time with Earth but can't put their finger on it. Be careful how you view this material. Some have a tendency to ignore all the sources in a body of information that causes great consternation if they determine just one or more are not acceptable. This kind of thinking is illogical. The utmost seriousness has gone into putting together this work of warning. A myriad of sources from the sciences, government, history, politics, legend and spirit is combined here.

You will do yourself and loved ones a great disservice if your mind set is to discount all you consider credible when presented side by side with sources your cultural experience and educational programming have not deemed worthy of consideration. Before the time of the greatest events, the overwhelmingly vast majority will see, hear and experience enough to know that our earth is about to change dramatically again. By the time your awareness peaks into realization, it may be too late to repair it if you don't begin to get up to speed on the situation now.

I've spent my time researching, accumulating, organizing, discussing, and weeding out side agendas. I present this subject in such a way as to bring a quick clarity to the layman or someone who is completely unfamiliar with it. If you've never read anything about the when and why of earth changes before, this work may be all you'll ever need. Reading up on endless conspiracies, for the most part, will not help you with your life. Understanding only this one may be important for your survival. Nailing down the science that shows the regularity of these events is important to see clearly how close to the end of this cycle we are.

Questions will come to mind when the acceptance of what is about to happen does sets in. Will I have time to make it to a safe area? Am I there already? Will I have resources enough to sustain myself over an extended period of time, or the ability to create needed sustenance on an ongoing basis? Do I care to leave all which I hold dear to start anew? Am I just too married to or fearful of leaving my things, lifestyle and community, even at the expense of my life, if I can't take them with me?

Watch your thinking carefully as you read. Your mind may make up unsound reasons for ignoring the obvious to avoid the discomfort of having to prepare. It is an honor to be a vehicle or messenger of this information. I'm one of the many that have chosen or have been chosen or some combination thereof, to do this work. I'm sure I'll meet some people in the aftertimes that acknowledge me for warning and helping them survive one of the most severe physical calamities Earth has gone through.

On the other hand, others may wish they never learned or prepared because of the difficulties presented then compared to their lifestyle before. At that time I would simply say that YOU were primarily responsible for drawing the information toward yourself and determined your level of personal preparation. I'm not fishing now for your future thanks, but am trying to avoid you berating the messenger. Just learning now and not being able to prepare because of family ties or financial binds could end up causing needless worry, prior to your passing on. So, be careful before you jump in too deep here. It's not always better to know.

My focus is to find people who want this information, or who have been drawn to it by whatever means to make their right choice. Staying alive might be a good one. The fact that you're reading this perhaps means that your gut instinct is telling you something is not quite right with the world, and the reasons you've run across thus far have been less than adequate.

There's no doom in being made aware that you live on the railroad tracks, the train is approaching and what time it will arrive, so you can pull up your roots to get the hell out of the way. It's ignorance that will put you in harm's way during the up and coming cataclysms. There will be many places that have a good chance of being safe. I'm now going to paint a word portrait using some of my words and mostly those of others. In order to view the mosaic, look at it in its entirety. Focusing too closely on one part or another might result in your missing the big picture

This work could have been 10,000 pages or more. There is much more than that volume of material confirming all that is presented here. Studying the data and the myriad of different sources becomes very repetitious. I strongly urge you to do your own research if you need more information. Much more related truth is out there. Since I've outlined where to look and what to look for, it will be easy to obtain more sources for this subject matter. If you're like me, once you've seen enough of it, you'll quit looking for more, even though you've come to the understanding so much more exists. You'll then make your plans and go back to living your daily life. On the back burner of your mind you'll know there are some wild times and big changes just around the corner. Plus, you'll know, more than likely, that you'll survive them because of your ace in the hole of being informed. Are you getting my drift here? These events are going to be exhilarating, adventurous and monumental. Doom, gloom and fear shouldn't be your mind-set whatsoever. The most exciting, serious, unbelievably dramatic scenes you've ever viewed at the movies will be played out in your real life from day to day shortly, whether you watch the previews of this book or not.

Since 1995-6, Earth's weather has changed dramatically. This is how it starts every time! To understand what the current effects of X are now, weather and seismic activity should be closely monitored throughout the globe. Watching and listening closely to the intentional and unintentional warnings from the world's government officials will add clarity to the picture. Studying legend, folklore and prophecy might finally grab your heart and seal your knowing.

Taking a little vacation time to reserve some time at a small observatory with coordinates and dates to find X, that I'll show you how to get later, might just shock you into action once you've seen it with your own eyes. Now, if you've some extra money, you could pay others to do your footwork for you in terms of further research and observatory time. I do caution you that there is as much disinformation as correct information. Much of the same truth I present here is intentionally mixed with skepticism and fabrications elsewhere.

If you don't do your own research, how do you know which is which is being reported back to you? At some point you'll have to get used to doing things for yourself and possibly for others in the aftertimes.

The monetary playing field will be equalized after X's passage. For the first few years, cash will be worthless. Even right preceding to the events, cash could devalue severely. The longer you wait to prepare, the greater the price you'll have to pay. If you wait too long, you'll pay the ultimate price.

In the aftertimes, barter and co-operation will be king if you luckily end up in the right community. Mad Max scenarios will reign elsewhere for a while, until they play themselves out. At a certain point you will have learned enough to make a prudent decision to leave unsafe areas. Starting with just a search of Pole Shift or Earth Changes information will land you in the middle of a mountain of evidence confirming Earth's surface changes regularly and quickly.[53]

The biggest question that is starting to go through many peoples mind is: What is really going on with our planet? Why so many earthquakes? Why climate changes? Why there is a planet warming problem? Is it related to our fossil fuel burning? And most important: How bad is it really going to get? Is it truly the end of the world as many prophecies say?

The Mayan calendar[54] ends in December 21, 2012 and there is a good reason why it does. The Mayan's where a very advanced

---

[53] Foreword by Mark Hazlewood www.crawford2000.co.uk/mark1.htm

[54] Mayan Calendar, a complex instrument for measuring the passage of time in roughly 5,125-year increments.

civilization, so advanced that they did not need many of the so called modern tools and technology we have, since they had more advanced technology than we do. In fact they had technology that our scientists are not even dreaming of yet. Just imagine if as a society we were able to teleport ourselves, would we use automobiles? Or imagine if we were harnessing free energy from the 4th density/dimension, would we go through such difficult effort to mine oil from the earth? Raising heavy object would be something of team mental effort and not that of a machine, as it has already been demonstrated. Now if you use a little bit more imagination, you can see that many things in earth would be quite different than what they are now, if we already new how to use the 4th density/dimension at will.

Back to the main question, how bad it is really going to get? One way to answer that is by reviewing many of the prophesies made by individuals such as Edgar Cayce, Cayce and others went at length describing what are the step towards the big changes. Can Cayce and other be trusted? My answer after many years of studying this information is YES. These prophets had information of what has happen in the past and had the ability of projecting what most likely will happen in the future. It is like you or I seeing a car speeding out of control and predicting what it will look like in the very near future, once it impacts with another car, we can predict quite accurately what the impact will look like and the outcome of the cars. The prophets knew quite well that the Earth's rotation axis is not fixed in space and what happens when our galaxy visits once more the part of space that causes the changes, therefore they were able to predict what will happen this time, which though it is different than last times it is quite similar. This is called the Precession of the Equinox[55], it is a 25,920 year precession period, which is a period of 25,920 years for our entire planetary body to travel around the sun, a trip of 360 degrees. In this trip there are also cycles of 2100 years that takes our galaxy through all the 12 signs of the zodiac. What is misunderstood about the astrology is the fact that our planet's position related to other planets and the entire galaxy influences our behavior, due to the fact that all these planetary object radiate energy that affects our body and mind. In this precession trip our galaxy also encounters a part of space that is now known as the Photon Belt[56], it takes 2000 years to cross this energy belt. We are very close to entering it, in fact it is estimated that we will enter it in or around 2012. The proximity to this energy belt is the cause of all our planetary changes. Until the time that we are fully immersed in it, we will continue to experience earth changes. Once fully immersed in it, earth will change its vibration rate, which will be the cause of the shift from the 3rd density/dimension to the 4th.

In summary, it all starts with mayor climate changes, some that we already are starting to see such as category 5 hurricanes, and category 9+ earthquakes, soon the categories are going to go past their original scale. Planet warming (which we all are quite familiar

---

[55] www.crystalinks.com/precession.html has a detailed explanation.

[56] www.crystalinks.com/photonbelt.html

with) is yet another change. Eventually this all leads to a major rise on the ocean level, preceded by huge earthquakes, tsunami, rapid meltdowns of the polar icecaps, hurricanes, cyclones, and volcanoes, which may very quickly be followed by a new ice age, magnetic pole shift and 20 degree shift in the planet's position. Will all human race become extinct like the dinosaurs? NO, this will not happen, but those caught in the danger zones, most definitely will. In the past cycles complete civilizations where destroyed, but did not become extinct nor will we. Our race will survive, but not intact. In fact there are prediction maps that display what our planet may look like after all the changes take place. Future Map of the World.

32 Names for Planet X

Ancient history, astronomy, folklore and prophecy record many names for Planet X. The Sumerians called it the "12th planet" or "Nibiru" (translation; planet of passing). Bet ween the Babylonians and Mesopotamians there were at least three names: "Marduk," "The King of The Heavens," and The "Great Heavenly Body." The ancient Hebrews referred to it as the "Winged Globe" because of its long orbit high among the stars. The Egyptians had two names "Apep" or "Seth." The Greeks called it "Typhon" after a feared leader and "Nemesis" (one of its most telling names). Other ancient peoples have given it labels such as; "The Celestial Lord Shiva" and "God of Destruction." To the ancient Chinese, it was known as "Gung-gung," "The Great Black," or "Red Dragon." The Phoenicians said it was "The Great Phoenix." The Hebrews called it "Yahweh." The Mayans called it "Celestial Quetzalcoatl." The celestial body was known to the Latins as "Lucifer." Revelation (8:10-12). The name of the star is "Wormwood." From works of prophecy, there are other names for X. The "Red or Blue Star" is of the Hopi Indian and

Gordan Michael Scallion designation. The "Fiery Messenger" is in the Ramala prophecy. The "Great Star" is from the Book Revelation. "His Star" is how it is referred to in Edgar Cayce Readings. The "Great Comet" and "The Comet of Doom" is right out of the Grail Message. From an early English prophet named "Mother Shipton," "The Fiery Dragon" was the name she gave, as seen from her second sight. Our solar system's "10th Planet" is "X. "There's also "The Intruder" and "The Perturber" from astronomy.

Apparently 25% of all observed comet orbits are being measurably perturbed by the magnetic or gravitational pull of this planet. The largest of our planets' orbits are being perturbed toward Orion.

No matter what the name used, it's the same object that has the same effects before and during its passage of earth. The Sumerians also had a name for its approximate 3600 year orbit, "A Shar." The ancient Hindu astronomers gave the name "Treta Yuga" for its 3600 year orbit. The destruction X causes even had a label "Kali Yuga." Some of the names given by the ancients are akin to names for god. These people viewed the power and destruction that this planet brings with it to be so significant as to believe it could only come from the hand of god. It's not that they worshipped the planet, rather they just had great respect for the sweeping changes it brought with each passing.

Akakor

Akakor[57] is an ancient set of history records/books written throughout the past 15,000+ years. These books clearly describe two past catastrophes and predicted another one sometime around the year 1981. These books have been kept in South America underground caves; they describe a rich ancient indigenous civilization that guarded this knowledge.

Ice Ages -- Grade School Science

Earth truly is one of the most dangerous planets in the Universe. Remember back in grade school when you were first told about Ice Ages? This was your first big hint that something goes wrong with your home planet Earth on a regular basis. Most of the researchers, who all agreed this phenomenon was real through the science of archaeology, just didn't figure out the correct reason for it, or exactly how often it happens and why. Plus, they really mislabeled it. The poles and ice shifting to different parts of the globe are certainly not the only thing that happens. Different areas of the planet would show varying times for the last event when looking for only the effects of ice and cold. Yes, they discovered something absolutely

---

[57] The Chronicle of Akakor by Karl Brugger

real. No, most of them didn't know the correct why for the phenomenon.

The so-called Ice Ages are thought to have happened over a period of many years. In fact, the great mammoths found with tropical food in their stomachs that were flash frozen is just one fact from the tip of the iceberg of evidence that shows changes happen very quickly. A little later I'll bore you to tears with Earth Science to show this. There are no so called ice ages. Earth's crust slips over its molten core periodically as Planet X passes.

This shifts the poles to different areas of the world periodically. Glaciers don't just magically start moving up or down from Earth's current poles on a regular basis. The poles themselves shift to different parts of the globe in a matter of hours. All life where the new poles settle flash freezes instantaneously. A few thousand years ago Greenland was a polar ice cap of Earth. There's still way too much ice there for its latitude relative to the current poles.

You are solely responsible for determining for yourself what is proof or evidence. Even though this is very simple, most do not possess the mental capacity to piece together the varied disciplines to see what's right around the corner, even when laid out as concisely as I do in this short work. If they do see it easily, there's a shorter supply of people that are type "A" individuals that take action in their lives. Most will not want to leave obvious unsafe areas until Planet X is squarely in their view. In this case that will be fatal for the majority. This is just the sort of realization that gets to me. Even at my best I can only expect to awaken a small minority. For those who read, grasp the situation and prepare, you are in a very exclusive club.

I don't like being correct on this issue. Warnings will not be broadcast by public officials over the TV, radio, or newspapers. Warnings will not be broadcast by public officials over the TV or newspapers. Warnings will not be broadcast by public officials over the TV. A knock on the door from government workers of your city or state, saying it is time to evacuate, will not be forthcoming. There are just too many people to deal with. Don't you understand?

There would be no place prepared to evacuate to, or resources available to sustain the many over any length of time. Consequently the call to leave will not come. It's just too huge. You are alone in determining your fate. For those of you who tend to ignore important issues or can't handle the truth, this is one truth that will find you. Will it be when you look over your shoulder and see a tidal wave or a building collapsing down on you or in time enough to reach a safe area?

Remember this if you choose not to move from unsafe areas such as within 100-200+ miles of any coast line. This includes all of California and Florida. Please pay attention to everyone around you as the time approaches if you haven't made your move. You will see families silently moving away with talk of just a vacation, covering up that they are scurrying away to their shelters. Now for those who think God will give you a warning and take care of you. Hold that thought and consider this written work may be your warning.[58]

---

[58] Mark Hazlewood www.crawford2000.co.uk/mark1.htm

It gets a bit more interesting... Not only is this Planet X going to come by earth sometime between 2009-2015, but it is quite inhabited, in fact they are our creators/parents.

WE ARE NOT ALONE -- that there is one more planet in our own solar system from which intelligent beings (Nefilim, Elohim, Anunnaki in Sumerian) had come here some 450,000 – 600,000 years ago for their own reasons, and who some 300,000 years ago engaged in genetic engineering to bring about Homo-sapiens by mixing their genes with those of the evolved hominids. Their home planet, which has an elongated orbit around our sun lasting some 3,600 years, was called NIBIRU: "Planet of the Crossing."[59]

Zecharia Sitchin suggest that a race of 'flesh and blood' gods who were capable of space flight visited Earth from their home planet, which the Ancients called 'Nibiru', nearly half a million years ago. He goes on to speculate that they came in order to mine precious minerals which were abundant on our planet; that they created modern Homo sapiens by genetic engineering, mixing their own genes with those of the primitive hominids they encountered ('in their own image'); that they did this in order to create a slave race to take over the mining and refining work; and that they lived for sometimes thousands of years, were capable of good, evil, compassion and brutality, and warred with each other and their human offspring"

---

[59] Zecharia Sitchin www.sitchin.com

There is much evidence throughout history of a cataclysms taking place due to some planetary event. Here is an excerpt from Dr. Immanuel Velikovsky in his book Worlds in Collision:

There is a Mexican tradition, recorded in the Nahua-Indian in the Annals of Cuauhtitlan, that once in the remote past the night did not end for a long time. Friar Bernardino de Sahagun, a Spanish scholar who came to the New World a generation after Columbus, wrote that the American aborigines told of a great catastrophe, in which the sun had risen only a little way above the horizon, and then stood still. These are but two of the many traditions from all parts of the world which refer to a disturbance in the earth's orderly rotation.

Dr. Velikovsky's work crosses so many of the jurisdictional boundaries of learning that few experts could check it against their own competence. The main body of evidence in Worlds in Collision is historical, and the details are drawn from - among other sources - the Old Testament, the Talmud, the Egyptian papyri, the historical texts, traditions, and the legends of Rome, Greece, Babylonia, Arabia, Persia, India, Tibet, Finland, Iceland, West Africa, Siberia, China, Japan, the Pacific Islands, Mexico, and Peru. Dr. Velikovsky describes the area of his investigations as "anthropology in the broadest sense," concerning itself with "the nature of the cosmos and its history."

The comet, at the first of the two meetings reconstructed in Worlds in Collision, touched the earth with its gaseous tail, and one of the first signs of the encounter was a rain of fine, rusty pigment. The world turned red. "All the waters that were in the river," reads the Book of Exodus, "were turned to blood." The Manuscript Quiche' of the Mayas tells of the rivers turning to blood, and so does the

Papyrus Ipuwer of the Egyptians. Then, as the story continues in the Visuddhi-Magga of the Buddhists, the fine dust turned to coarse dust, "and then fine sand, and then coarse sand, and then grit, stones, up to boulders as large... as mighty trees on the hilltops."

And with the shower of meteorites the earth stopped turning.

It came to rest so faced to the sun that a long night, darkened by the cosmic refuse sweeping in from interplanetary space, fell on Europe, Africa, the Americas, and the valleys of the Euphrates and the Indus. The Babylonians, the tribes of the Sudan, the Finns, the Greeks, the Peruvians, and the American Indians all have traditions of a long night accompanying a catastrophe which the earth did not survive. Further east, the Iranians saw the sun suspended several days in the sky. In china, it is said that in the reign of the Emperor Yahou the sun did not set for a number of days and all the forests burned. We suppose that if the earth stopped turning it would destroy itself, as HG Wells imagined it would when his "man who could work miracles" commanded the same act. Our idea of momentum - and the Law of Gravitation, about which Dr. Velikovsky has much to say - leads us to assume that the earth's surface would fly onward in the direction of its rotation and be torn apart. A great global catastrophe, with seas and continents changing their places, is in fact described in the traditions of mankind. The world gave every sign to its inhabitants of being on the brink of destruction.

Approached by the body of the comet, the earth was forced out of its regular motion; a major shock convulsed its entire surface. The major shift in the atmosphere caused by the approach of the comet and the stasis of the planet, itself produced hurricanes of enormous velocity and force. "The face of the earth changed," writes Dr.

Velikovsky, summarizing the Mayan account from the Manuscript Troano, "mountains collapsed, other mountains grew and rose over the onrushing cataract of water driven from the oceanic spaces, numberless rivers lost their beds, and a wild tornado moved through the debris descending from the sky."

The human population was decimated and many species of animals perished entirely. The surface of the earth burst. Three Mexican manuscripts tell how everywhere in the Western hemisphere new mountains came into being. New volcanoes opened and fissures in the flat land threw forth fire and smoke and liquid basalt. The rivers steamed and the sea boiled. The Zendi-Avesta of the Persians says that a star made the sea boil. The Polynesians say that a star caused new islands to appear.

It was the tenth plague of Egypt, the night of Passover, when the Lord passed over the huts of the Israelites and struck the mansions of the Egyptians (the light rush houses would survive and earthquake more easily than heavy stone ones). "There was not a house where there was not one dead," says the Book of Exodus, and St. Jerome wrote that "in the night in which Exodus took place, all the temples of Egypt were destroyed either by an earth shock or by the thunderbolt." The head of the comet cam close to the earth, breaking through the darkness of the dust cloud, and the Hebrew tradition tells that the last night of the Jews in Egypt was as bright as the noon of the summer solstice.

The blow fell at midnight. Dr. Velikovsky observes in passing that as the israelites counted the days from sunset it was for them the 14th Aviv; and, ever since, the Passover has been celebrated on the fourteenth day of the first month of spring. The Egyptians counted from sunrise, as we do, and for them it was the 13th Thout, a day forever after unlucky. As for the thirteenth of any month, said the Egyptians, "thou shalt not do anything on this day." The Aztecs also counted the day from sunrise, and in their calendar it was noted that on the 13th Olin, a month called "earthquake," a new world age had come into being.

When a comet encounters a planet, it may become entangled and drawn from its path, then forced into a new orbit, and finally liberated. This is what happened to Lexell's comet, which was captured by Jupiter and its moons in 1767 and did not free itself until 1779. Some form of balance between attraction and inertia was maintained for twelve years; Jupiter and the comet did not crash together. Neither, according to Dr. Velikovsky's thesis, did the earth and the comet that came near it in 1500 BC. They exchanged discharges of electrical potential.

The action of the sun and the moon on the earth produces the ocean tides. If the earth were to slow down, the seas would first recede toward the poles; but the attraction of a large comet close to the earth would draw them back toward itself and heap them high in the air. The story of the seas divided and then rising to break over the land is widespread. The Choctaw Indians say that when the land was in darkness a bright light appeared in the north, "but it was mountain-high waves, coming nearer"; the Peruvians say that the ocean left the shore and inundated the continent; the Chinese annals say that in the reign of the Emperor Yahou a great tidal wave broke over the mountains into the Chinese Empire and flooded the land for decades.

The tides carried huge rocks along them. For instance, the Madison Boulder, near Conway, New Hampshire, is a ten-thousand-ton piece of granite quite different from the bedrock beneath it. An early nineteenth century explanation of this and other "erratic" boulders was that great tidal waves, originating in the north, must have swept the rocks and geologic till (clay, mud and gravel) across the land. According to the calculations based on the amount erosion under them, the boulders were deposited in their places less than six thousand years ago. It has been assumed that the stones were drawn along by the glacial ice sheet, but the disquieting fact is that accumulations of rock were moved from lower latitudes to higher latitudes - and even uphill toward the Himalaya, through the existing glaciers push stones down, not up, the slopes.

At the Sea of the Passage the Israelite tribes saw the water drawn aside and heaped up in a double tide; and, after they crossed, the waters of the Mediterranean fell and broke into the Red Sea in a great wave. "It was an unusual event," writes Dr. Velikovsky, "and because it was unusual it became the most impressive recollection in the long history of this people. All peoples and nations were blasted by the same fire and shattered in the same fury. The tribes of Israel on the shore of a sea found in this annihilation their salvation from bondage. They escaped destruction but their oppressors perished before their eyes. They extolled their Creator, took upon themselves the burden of moral rules, and considered themselves chosen for a great destiny."[60]

---

[60] Harper's MAGAZINE The Day the Sun Stood Still by Eric Larrabee

My summary:

After reading hundreds of books, I have come up with some understandings; perhaps predictions of what will happen in the very near future (2007-2012-2025). Yes I could point you to the many books I have read, it would take you years to read them, but let's see instead if I can briefly give you a short summary of my findings.

There are two energies in the universe, one positive the other negative. Apparently a collective mind has had some control over it, at one point it was to darn positive and NO change ever took place, nothing really happen, so the collective decided on inputting some negative energy, maybe they went a bit to far with it and/or maybe they lost control of if. But do note: It is 100% up to the receiver (us) to accept either one, it's like choosing a TV channel. At the time, almost everyone liked the negative energy, therefore they picked the negative channel, so much that we became a very negative planet, it was the new fad; so negative that only the very brave and/or stupid dare get close to our planet. Many came to help us, but ended up caught in the negativity too. This negative energy feeds on itself and gets stronger. It affects our entire galaxy. Once every 25,960 years our galaxy goes through a belt of energy for 2,000 of those years, this energy belt forces a balance between both energies, regardless of which way it is tilted. Same as a balance, if it is way too tilted in one direction, then the force to put it balance will be strong, if it is near balance then the force is minimal. Previous times it was so negative that it ended up destroying one entire planet of our solar system, and the last time (25,960 years ago,) it tore open our planet, which caused and enormous amount of water to be release from the planet all the way up to the clouds, creating a huge deluge of water. This time is expected to be much less, but nonetheless there will be large if not huge problems.

So where are we now? Well we are much better than 20, 50, 100, 500, 1,000, 10,000, and even the last 2 cycles of 25,960 years ago. In other words we are not at the very far end of the negative scale, but we are most definitely in the negative portion of the scale. Assuming a scale of 1-10 where 5 where perfect balance, I would say we are at a 2-3 towards the negative side. So what does this translates too? Two things, one keep in mind that this energy that is starting to hit us IS to tilt the scale towards the center, do not forget this, everything is going to get a lot better, but, but, but, this balancing energy is a very forceful one and by NO means a welcomed one by those who have aligned themselves with the negative energy, the negative aligned individual will resist and fight back, this means wars, political and economic collapses, earthquakes, volcanoes, hurricanes, viruses, etc. We collectively, consciously and sub-consciously create everything, therefore those who resist and align with the negative energy, trigger the earth change problems themselves. Most of these earth changes would not be a problem IF they were taken into account, for example by moving away from coastal and northern areas of the planet, by eating property, by not eating meat (which is a negative aligned need of the mind), by not aligning with negative thoughts, by service to others vs. service to self, by allowing alternative energy and health technologies, by openly resisting all negative established paradigms such as religion and corrupt governments, etc.

A good example on how one should deal with this new energy can be found with menopauses women. A woman going through these changes has the option of being aware of them and ignoring her bodies' moods, by setting her will over her body, otherwise you know -- shit hits the fan... Same is true of astrological energies, if one is aware of them one can override the automatic body responses with an awaken conscience. Allover us we can find examples of the negative and positive energies, it is really up to us individually to align with one of the other.

In summary, my view of the coming changes boil down to one, "Stay out of harms way" The following few years is a time to be as far away from main civilization as possible, in the safest places on earth. Let the changes take place, without being caught in them. Let those who subscribe to the negative energy perish, that is their choice, why be part of it? If you consciously chose not to be, then the opportunity to not be will come to you, but first you will have to start by not aligning yourself with the negative and align yourself with the positive, this you do by not being part of it as much as you can, move away from the core of it.

One more note: I believe/speculate that the positive energy started taking effect much more this past November 20, 2006 with the new planetary alignments. It seems to me that the luck of those aligned with the negative energy is starting to run out. For example, there was recently an apparent attempt at detonating one of those Russians lost portable nuclear bombs, but according to well assumed theories, everyone involved is now dead, it simply did not happen. Lots of similar negative plans from those in governments and against governments are starting to fail. Part of it can be seen with the failed attempt of the present most negative fashion of government loosing the election in many parts of the world, this may very well foil many war plans, including WWIII. By no means let's not assume everything is honky-dory now, but I think it has been a noticeable move towards the positive energy vs. the negative.

Yet another note: So what may be the first wave of problems? I think it is going to be severe weather changes. That just started the first month of 2007. I cannot tell you if this is it or not, but I can tell you that the weather theories and prediction seem to be happening now. What I believe has happen is that the North Pole is or maybe even already has completely melted; I just got Encarta 2007 and it no longer shows ice in the north pole at all, did I missed that it was once all covered with ice? So this sweat water mixes with the salt water, causing a TEMPORARY acceleration of the hot water current going from the Equator to all northern shores such as USA/Canada/Europe. This is why all the sudden it is much warmer than it should be. This causes all sort of weather problems like hurricanes, monsoon rains, draughts, etc. But this is not the real problem to be worried about; the theorized real serious problem is that once all that sweat water mixes with the salt water it may/will stop the warm water current from flowing north from the equator, therefore bringing in a new ice age. Science has been telling us for many years that past ice ages were very sudden; this can only lead us to assume that the same thing may happen again, leaving millions dead in a very short period of time. Parallel with this there maybe some massive earthquakes and volcanoes. There is a recent movie on this subject, what is scary is not the movie, but the links that are found on the movies website. I forgot the title of the movie.

The sun has a 14 year solar cycle, on Jan 1, 2008 it is estimated that a low cycle ended and a high cycle started. This high energy cycle will bring lots more weather, earthquake and volcanoes activity. The PHOENIX FIVE EARTH CHANGES BULLETIN[61] is an excellent source of information.

So where are the best places to survive?

No where near a coastal area and NO more than 15-20 degrees north or south, and way up, at least 1200 meters above sea level on as hard solid rock as you can find. Do I need to tell you that E C U A D O R Andes Mountain ridge, is one of the very few choices. O and do not forget clean drinking water, low population too.

The last time this happen there were very few survivors, even though every single one could have been saved. Same as us now, everyone was on a dream thinking that nothing was going to happen until all the sudden it was upon them.

Southern California probably will be an early stage victim of this process, I just can't see it surviving for very long into the process, it is on about the sixth most unstable piece of real estate on the planet (Sumatra - Fiji plate margin, New Zealand, Carib, Japan, and Alaska beat it and will also take early heavy hits) THE GOOD NEWS HERE IS THAT MOST OF THIS IS GOING TO HAPPEN WITH A LOT OF PRECURSORS WHICH POINT TO THE INEVITABLE. Those who want to ride out the storm and follow the Galilean's advice, "watch", will survive quite well in an orderly fashion. I do NOT EXPECT THAT ANY OF THIS HAS ANYTHING TO DO WITH THE 2012 CALENDAR CLICKS ON THE MAYAN CALENDAR, NOR WITH

---

[61] http://groups.yahoo.com/group/earthchange-bulletins

THE PURELY IMAGINED NEBIRU OR PLANET X. Nor does it have anything to do with mass Ascension or Rapture fantasies nor how well we all "stink" with positive thoughts. All this is the slow and evitable grinding of the vast cosmic mill in the endless cycles of our solar system. It MAY have quite a bit to do with the electrogravitics of the Sun, as it turns out...[62]

Y2K vs. 2012 A.D.

December 21, 2012 A.D. has a lot more evidence of it being a cause to be concerned than Y2K, since Y2K only had as reference the information provided by the experts. On the other hand, 2012 has scientific evidence that is foolish to ignore. Did you know that two planets in our galaxy have recently experienced pole shifts? Pole shift is no small laughing matter; pole-shift spells massive catastrophes. Just one quick search in Google for 2012 yields 32 million hits; this fact on it is own should give you some food for thoughts...

Not up-to-date on what is the big deal about the year 2012? Read this 192 page FREE book, it will give you plenty of scientific facts to ponder. http://www.soulsofdistortion.nl/ What I found most valuable of all this book is that it has plenty of references to real quantum physics science, the references are not just what someone says, they actually explains in more than enough details necessary to convince any scientist of all the facts of how it works; they are not

---

[62] Michael Mandeville

blind predictions, but predictions based on scientific evidence. After reading the above FREE book go read another 3 free books at www.ascension2000.com now www.divinecosmos.com in the order they appear below; they are a MUST read, these books have the answer to what is happening and will happen in the coming to 2012; they explain it in lots of easy to understand scientific details, the how and why of the huge increase in earthquakes, hurricanes, tornadoes, volcanic activity, weather changes, earth changes, and much more... I found this entire website so educational that I spent close to 40 hours nonstop reading it.

Here is the list of the books and the order you should read them, I suggest you skip the rest of the website and just jump in and read the books first.

THE CONVERGENCE SERIES: A SCIENTIFIC CASE FOR "ASCENSION"

1. The Shift of the Ages

2. The Science of Oneness

3. The Divine Cosmos

All the prophecies are starting to make sense now, aren't they?

Some say, "It's the end of the world" and think they've got it figured out. Others say that a Golden Age of humanity is dawning, heralded by an event known as "Ascension" where there is a spontaneous transformation of matter, energy and consciousness. (We believe this to be the case, and that this is not a "doom" situation at all.) Most who espouse such concepts do so because a certain religion, prophet, indigenous teaching and / or alleged "channeled" ET group said it is so.

However, if such an incredible event were indeed "real," then there should be a massive amount of straightforward scientific evidence to support it. Many say that this website arguably contains the penultimate collection of that evidence, which forms a completely new paradigm for understanding the Cosmos as well as a sound and advanced body of spiritual teachings to support it.[63]

Are you concerned now? Do you have stock investments? If so, this site is a must read for you. www.cycle-trader.com

www.michaelmandeville.com If you want just the predictions, go here...

2012 is a two sided sword. On one side there is the fact that our planet is going through a very rough transition, and yes there will be plenty more catastrophes, especially for those who live in big cities and in coastal areas. On the other hand it is a time of spiritual awakening, a new opportunity for human kind to make a quantum leap improvement in all areas, not just spiritually, but technologically too. It is the beginning of a new era of peace and plenitude, but first we must manage to survive till the magic date arrives, and not just survive but thrive in new knowledge, and not just learning but putting into practice what we learn. As we get closer and closer to 2012, you will notice the stress level people experience increases.

---

[63] www.ascension2000.com

There will be more wars and all sorts of problems. The challenge is to learn better ways to deal with it and not become involved. The next step is to do your best to help in preventing these problems; yes you can help alleviate them, and even help prevent them. We do have the power to change the outcome If we all were to work together. The problem is that we are not working together, which leaves only one option -- "save yourself." This you can do by studying a lot and by relocating out of the danger zones.

What are the danger zones? In my view they are all areas of the planet where one has to depend on advanced systems to survive. If you need fuel and/or energy to heat your home, if you are under ice for 6 months out of the year, if you depend on elaborated systems for your food supply and water or if you are in anything less than a thousand meters above sea level, you should rethink about living there If you wish to be among the survivors.

Besides picking an obviously safer place to live, it is as important to pick who you will be with. No sense in picking the best place in the world, only to find someone pointing a gun at you. You will need to be with people who fully understand consensus making decision methods and that are willing to respect it, people who are smart enough to know who among their group should and must be trusted to make a quick decision in an emergency situation. There will come times when acting quickly and wisely will make the difference of surviving or not. We have received many letters from people who are basing all their decisions in fear. Fear is not the way to make a choice in life; fear should not be your only way of making your choices. You must learn how to use your intuition, your higher self vs. fear. This is where a non-stop continuous education is essential. When situations get difficult, it is important and essential to have a well tuned higher-self to help out making decisions vs. letting your ego decide for you and get you in plenty of trouble.

Our galaxy is part of 8 other suns' systems and that our galaxy has an orbit around one of these sun systems. BTW: This information has been around for thousands and thousands of years, but only to a few that where able to comprehend it. Our solar system goes through a 25,920 year cycle, 2000 year of this cycle are inside an energy belt. When earth is inside this energy belt, it moves up the scale a bit from the 3rd density/dimension into the 4th density/dimension. The physics laws of the 4th are different from the laws of the 3rd. For someone who knows how to enter the 4th at will, all this makes sense and would not argue.

Sometime at or around 2012 earth/we will enter the energy belt. The effects of getting close to the belt are already being felt by all the planets in our galaxy, including earth. I do not know if the entry is gradual or sudden, but it seems that it is gradual. The fact is that the laws of physics are about to change on earth for a period of 2000 years.

If you take the time to study many old books, you will realize that all this is true and that the Mayan calendar ends December 24, 2012 for this reason, cause the law of physics will change that exact date or around that day and a new era of 2000 years will begin. The bible and many other books talk about this, but not in clear terms. They were clear for those who wrote them; it is like us talking about computers without giving a thorough explanation of what a computer is.

Things to expect:

In the 4th density/dimension there is light everywhere, no need for either natural or artificial light. This is the answer for how people travel hundreds of miles into tunnels in the past.[64]

There may be a few days with a second sun in the sky. Basically this is a sun that is inside earth and it comes out for a few days. Note: The new scientific model of how earth was created, believes that the earth core is the same as the Sun, therefore works in sync with the Sun.

Lots and lots of natural catastrophes will occur as we get closer to 2012 as well as the changes we are already seeing on our planets.

People, you, me, all of us, being pushed to their limits, tested, and improved. If you improve yourself you may be among the few that will survive. I suspect there will only be 5-8% of the population left alive, the rest will die and move on to another 3rd density/dimension suited to their needs.

If I recall correctly, according to Samael Aun Weor, there are 48 differences in the laws of physics from one dimension to the other, many have to do with mental abilities, those so called powers, such as telepathy, reading peoples minds & moving objects. Aging will stop and one will be able to fix/improve ones body, etc. Those that

---

[64] See the book: "The chronicle of AKAKOR by Kark Brugger.

cannot handle them will perish and move on (born again) to another planet with similar circumstances as earth. Only the best will be able to remain here.

We will be able to see with ease parts of the 4th dimension. Such as hidden cities, animals, fairies, angels, etc. This you can do now, but with a lot of effort. I have done it, therefore I know for myself this to be a real fact.

The proceeding two thousand years will be heaven on earth. Then earth drops again to the 3rd density/dimension.

For more detailed information and to learn how to improve yourself, sign up for the free courses at www.mysticweb.com There are hundreds of lessons and hundreds of books that detail all the above information. Step by step teachings on how to enter the 4th density/dimension at will.

To me December 21, 2012 is the day we hit bottom in all respect of our evolution. It is the final day of this epoch where we are all given an opportunity to wake up our consciousness and be prepared to live in the 4th density/dimension. Those who are not ready will have perished by this date or will shortly thereafter, since they will not be able to cope with the new rules (laws of physics) of the 4th. Once in the 4th everything will improve at a dramatic fast pace. Things such as the perfection of our DNA will quickly start taking place.

Prophesies are warnings of what will happen if the present course of action is not changed. Prophesies give us a choice of changing our course of action, prophesies are not fixed, they are just indicator of what will happen if one proceeds on a certain course of actions. In our case we need a change of consciousness, a complete change of the way most people do things now, which is Service To Self, vs. Service To Others. If we were to change to Service To Others, reality would change too and we would not meet the negative outcome of the prophesies. In the end is all an individual matter, some will lose their lives and start allover again in a planet suited to their level of evolvement, others will evolve here, in the midst of all the problems and will take the quantum leap into the 4th density/dimension.

The Secret Coded information allegedly found in the bible provides a possible view of things to happen in our very near future if we do NOT change our course of actions.[65]

The Bible Code was made famous by Michael Drosnin's book (of the same name), but the discovery of the apparent code predated him by two or more decades. As such, it is reputed to be a code embedded primarily in the first five books of the Bible (the Jewish Torah) -- but theoretically elsewhere in the Bible as well. Allegedly, the Bible Code is able to predict all manner of events, ranging from the Nazi holocaust to Hiroshima to the assassination of presidents and prime ministers, and several near-term future events. The Code has, according to http://www.diagnosis2012.co.uk/1.htm, been verified by both mathematicians and code-breakers to be quite real. Furthermore, the last encoded date (thus far established) is the seventh month of 2126 A.D., when comet Swift-Tuttle is expected to return to the vicinity of earth. In the interim, however, is the

---

[65] www.halexandria.org/dward415.htm

prediction of another comet due in 2012 A.D., which is expected to crumble into pieces or "annihilate" the Earth.

The End of the Mayan Calendar is scheduled for December 21, 2012 (give or take a year). The possibilities of what this "end" might mean is an increasingly hot topic on the Internet, in conferences, printed articles, and in discussions all over the globe. This is because it just might be an incredibly important moment in history -- e.g., the end of history! [66]

The Mayan Calendar is not necessarily your average, run-of-the-mill calendar. It is, among other things, reputed to be the most accurate in the world. This is due in part to the fact it is also a relatively complicated calendar, using cycles of 13 and 20 (weird!), relating to the cycles of other planets (e.g. Venus), and in general incorporating some 22 (at last count) different sub-calendars, such that every contingency can be accounted for.

The Mayans did not elaborate in great detail about what would happen in 2012 A.D., just which their calendar would end. However, there has been no end (pardon the pun) to the possibilities being forecast by modern day interpreters of what the Mayans might have meant. These possibilities include 2012 A.D. as a time for:

- major changes in human DNA (as in Indigo Children),
- an enormous leap in Consciousness,

---

[66] www.halexandria.org/dward420.htm

- dimensional shifts (as in Hyperdimensional Physics and/or Superstrings),
- the cessation of linear Time,
- an evolutionary human pinnacle,
- a huge surge and multiple breakthroughs in technology,
- the end of Money [Shirley, you jest!],
- massive genetic mutations [the good news!],
- a serious, altogether-too-close encounter with a Near-Earth Objects member,
- and a cosmic alignment of our solar system with the plane of our Galaxy, the Milky Way. The latter represents the end of a 25,920 year cycle -- a cycle based on the Precession of the Equinoxes).

"Prepare physically? Physically means finding a place that feels safe and storing food and necessary equipment for up to a two year period. This may or may not be right for you. Understand the situation. First of all, this period of time you would be preparing for is before the change, not after. The idea that we are to prepare and wait, and then after to come out of the shelter and resume life after the change is misleading. Once the change has happened, the next world will not be visible to the old one. We will ascend into a new world on a different wave length where any physical preparation made on earth will be useless there. Just as in death, you cannot bring it with you. [emphasis added]

"So the reason for physical preparation is to give one a safe place to make the transition without violence and struggle -- A calm place and time to meditate during the outer changes going on. If, however, you do not feel it is necessary that is all right also. Spirit is forever. No matter what happens, you will survive. What is truly important here is your state of consciousness during this transition. Your consciousness can overcome any of the physical problems." [67]

Another piece of the puzzle, is what is now called planet X, which coincidentally all takes place at the same time, and perhaps maybe the real cause of what is happening and will continue to happen to Earth.

A book called The 12th Planet written in 1976 by Zechariah Sitchin tells of the ancient Sumerian legends of a planet with a comet-like orbit that came into our area of the solar system every 3600 years. The inhabitants of this planet were like gods to the earth natives. They shuttled from their planet to earth with rockets and mined gold to take back to their home planet, Nibiru. He contends they were the ones the Bible in Genesis refers to as the Nefilim, and as giants.

Could this same Planet X or 12th Planet be the source of the many myths and legends that describe comets as portents of doom, and speak of battling planets? Could it be the cause of the periodic destruction's of great civilizations of the past by earthquakes, volcanoes, tidal waves, as described in many ancient texts, including the Bible, and by Velikovsky?

---

[67] www.halexandria.org/dward415.htm has a good description ABOUT 2012 A.D. along with many links.

Can Planet X cause a pole shift on earth as it passes by?

In January 1981 several daily newspapers stated that Pluto's orbit indicates that Planet X exists. The report stated that an astronomer from the U.S Naval Observatory told a meeting of the American Astronomical Society that irregularities in the orbit of Pluto indicates that the solar system contains a 10th planet. He also noted that this came to no surprise to Zechariah Sitchin, whose book about this planet came out three years prior.

The Sumerian's called it the 12th planet or Nibiru (translates into; planet of passing). The Babylonians and Mesopotamians called it Marduk, The King of The Heavens and The Great Heavenly Body. The ancient Hebrews referred to it as the Winged Globe because of its long orbit high among the stars. The Greeks called it Nemesis. (Its most telling name) Prophets have named it The Blue Star, The Red Star, The Fiery Messenger, and The Comet of Doom among others. No matter what the name used, it's the same object that has the same effects before and during its passage of earth. The Sumerians also had a name for it's approximate 3600-year orbit (A Shar). The ancient Hindu astronomers named Treta Yuga (3600 years) and the destruction it causes Kali Yuga.

Each time it approaches it starts a chain of events that culminates with it passing by and causing our earth's surface to change. These changes are the cause of massive death and destruction. History is rich with these stories. Many people from the past didn't draw the connection between what looked to be a large comet overhead and what they were experiencing at the time (volcanoes erupting, earthquakes, land masses sinking and rising, tidal waves, severe weather and floods). Some of these writers from the distant past simply noted what they thought was a foreboding sign or messenger of the prophets, instead of the cause for their woes.

The records of this approximate 7 years of turmoil prior to passing are part of biblical record from at least the last time it came by earth. With correct scientific and historical information you don't need to be a prophet to predict the same cycle of events are happening again during Planet X's approach. These events are just a minor taste of what will come when it goes by this time. And yet even these relatively minor events can cause much destruction.

I sincerely hope that Zitchin, the Hopi and others are proved wrong, otherwise we are all in for an extremely rough ride in the next few years...

Chapter 17

The mechanism of a prayer

A prayer can be compared to riding on a bus, car, train or plane. One can sure ride in one, even if you do not where the destination is, or if it is going to be a safe ride. One does not need to know how it works, how fast it is going, when or where is it going to stop in order to take the ride, not even how much is it going to cost. Remember the story of Gandi, when he got thrown out of the train, he knew he had a first class ticket, he was dress for the occasion, but none the less he got thrown out of the train. Something similar can happen with a prayer, it may just be thrown away, never heard and never answered. A prayer is a mechanism of communication similar to an auto, train, plane, skates, being a mechanism to transport oneself. <u>A prayer is a mechanism to access the higher realms of reality of the other densities/dimensions and same as a transport system, it is very useful and important to understand the intricate functionality in order for it to work in your best interest.</u> What good is a bus if you did not know what a bus stop was? If you did not know, then most of the time you would get off in the wrong place, and maybe a few times you get lucky and get off in the right place. A prayer is the same; you need to know how it works.

Often people pray to God in general, and say things that do not make any sense whatsoever to themselves, but somehow expect that something out there somewhere called God will respond. Needless to say these prayers more so than not, are never answered. They simply were made in the incorrect format or asked for something that cannot be granted. Even worse, the prayer may be answered but at a much later date than expected, such as in the next incarnation/life.

Often you have heard the saying: "Be careful what you ask for, you just might get it." And in deed it often happens that people get exactly what they asked for, but are so asleep that do not even notice they got it. Often because they got what they specifically asked for, which was not what they really thought they wanted.

But the real question is: Do prayer really work? The very short answer is yes "if" done in the correct format. But what is the correct format? A good place to search for answer is surprisingly in the Occult art of Magic, Wishcraft, Pagan and Wicca practices. These practices often use a form of prayer that go by the name of ritual, a ritual is an elaborate form of prayer, that when done properly uses this tools of communication properly and often with excellent results.

A properly done prayer is like a contract; you specify from whom to whom, the petitioner makes itself responsible for the outcome.

PART THREE

WHERE TO FIND MORE INFORMATION

PREFACE

As a logical person you probably are, you want useful, practical and to the point information that you can put to use in a reasonable amount of time. Part three of this book will give you some of the most valuable pieces of information that have made my life much easier and better to live. Putting in practice the advice giving in the following chapter will enhance your quality of life substantially. In the following pages you will find a brief introduction to some masters. By no means is this list complete or exhaustive in any way whatsoever, it is simply a place to start. There have been many masters available throughout history for each and every language and epoch, but never has there been so much opportunity to get translated and condensed and improved information at so much ease. My advice to you is: read from many masters, but DO yourself a favor, do not just read, do put in practice what you read. The last chapter of this book will give you a clear explanation on how to get started. You will find that all good masters (yes there is a lot of incorrect information out there, especially the one brought to you by religions) will in one way or another lead you in the same direction, some slower and some faster, some starting from one directions and other starting from another, but ALL roads lead to the same ultimate truth. The same as when traveling any road, if you have been on it for a long time and something does not fell correct, ask for further directions, in this case, move on to the next master. A sign that you are with a good master is that he/she will never tell you that his/hers is the only way, all good master will tell you to follow your heart (your higher-self knows best) and to take what fells right for you at the time. For example some master tell their pupils to abstain from sex, even from sexual thoughts, while others have very emphatically and clearly told them to go have plenty of sex, in fact have told them to go to an orgy, and in fact even provided a place for orgies, furthermore they were told to only come back to him once they were fully sexually satisfied, he went on telling them that there was no sense on trying to concentrate on his teaching if there thoughts were on sex, food or anything else. For example many schools of the so called secrets arts, (there are NO secrets) tell their student that they have to become vegetarians, but this does not work when you crave meat. Only YOU will know when it is the time for you to become vegetarian or to stop eating cooked food, or to have or not have sex. And it is quite easy to know, just follow your heart. How do you do this? Simple, just do what gives you the most joy, though here comes a paradox, I said you do what gives you the most joy, not what gives your ego the most joy.

There is a very long list of masters[68] who have lived on Earth to teach us, among them we can find: Confuscius, Djwhal Khul, El Morya, Ganesh, Gautma Buddha, Hilarion, Jesus / Sanada, John the Baptist, Kuthumi, Maitreya, Mary, Melchizedek, Metatron, Milarepa, Nada, Paul the Venetian, Quan-Yin, Saint Germaine, Sanat Kumara, Serapis Bey, Zoroaster to name just a few. It is really up to us to seek the information they left behind. In the following chapters I will guide you to the ones that I believe will be

---

[68] You may find a description of each of them at: www.crystalinks.com

the easiest for you to understand, and that I believe to be of most value to our present time needs as a society. In addition to the many masters there have also been several mystery schools that have very closely guarded this information; I will also point you to a few of them that I have found most valuable.

Chapter 18

Deepak Chopra

The Seven Spiritual Laws of Success

Dr. Deepak Chopra, M.D. is the author of more than 20 books on subjects ranging from medicine to business management. Dr. Chopra has a splendid ability to explain a complex subject is the easiest words to understand. Dr. Chopra is a true master on several different subjects and ALL his books reflect it, you will be hard pressed to find more than just a few words repeated in any of his books. Each of his books and videos are a true work of art, rated on my view as one of the best modern masters of medicine and much more...

If you have not read a book from him yet, I recommend you put it first on your list for your next book to read.

The Seven Spiritual Laws by Dr. Chopra are nothing new, what is new is his eloquent ability to explain them. These laws have been said time after time by many master in many languages, what is really distinguishes Dr. Chopra is the ease with which he describes them. By no means these are all the laws that once should put into a new believe systems, there are many more, but these are most definitely a great start, together with some more that I will give your from a few other masters.

The Law of Pure Potentiality

The source of all creation is pure consciousness . . . pure potentiality seeking expression from the unmanifest to the manifest. And when we realize that our true Self is one of pure potentiality, we align with the power that manifests everything in the universe.

I will put the Law of Pure Potentiality into effect by making a commitment to take the following steps:

1. I will get in touch with the field of pure potentiality by taking time each day to be silent, to just Be. I will also sit alone in silent meditation at least twice a day for approximately thirty minutes in the morning and thirty minutes in the evening.

2. I will take time each day to commune with nature and to silently witness the intelligence within every living thing. I will sit silently and watch a sunset, or listen to the sound of the ocean or a stream, or simply smell the scent of a flower. In the ecstasy of my own silence, and by communing with nature, I will enjoy the life throb of ages, the field of pure potentiality and unbounded creativity.

3. I will practice non-judgment. I will begin my day with the statement, "Today, I shall judge nothing that occurs," and throughout the day I will remind myself not to judge.

The Law of Living

The universe operates through dynamic exchange . . . giving and receiving are different aspects of the flow of energy in the universe. And in our willingness to give that which we seek, we keep the abundance of the universe circulating in our lives.

I will put the Law of Giving into effect by making a commitment to take the following steps:

1. Wherever I go, and whomever I encounter, I will bring them a gift. The gift may be a compliment, a flower, or a prayer. Today I will give something to everyone I come into contact with, and so I will begin the process of circulating joy, wealth and affluence in my life and in the lives of others.

2. Today I will gratefully receive all the gifts that life has to offer me. I will receive the gifts of nature: sunlight and the sound of birds singing, or spring showers or the first snow of winter. I will also be open to receiving from others, whether it be in the form of a material gift, money, a compliment or a prayer.

3. I will make a commitment to keep wealth circulating in my life by giving and receiving life's most precious gifts: the gift of caring, affection, appreciation, and love. Each time I meet someone, I will silently wish them happiness, joy, and laughter.

The Law of "Karma[69]" or Cause and Effect

Every action generates a force of energy that returns to us in like kind . . . what we sow is what we reap. And when we choose actions that bring happiness and success to others, the fruit of our karma is happiness and success.

I will put the Law of Karma into effect by making a commitment to take the following steps:

1. Today I will witness the choices I make each moment. And in the mere witnessing of these choices, I will bring them to my conscious awareness. I will know that the best way to prepare for any moment in the future is to be fully conscious in the present.

2. Whenever I make a choice, I will ask myself two questions: "What are the consequences of this choice that I'm making?" and "Will this choice bring fulfillment and happiness to me and also to those who are affected by this choice?"

3. I will then ask my heart for guidance and be guided by its message of comfort or discomfort. If the choice feels comfortable, I will plunge ahead with abandon. If the choice feel uncomfortable, I

---

[69] "Karma" is both action and the consequence of that action; it is cause and effect simultaneously, because every action generates a force of energy that returns to us in like kind.

will pause and see the consequences of my action with my inner vision. This guidance will enable me to make spontaneously correct choices for myself and for all those around me.

The Law of Least Effort

Nature's intelligence functions with effortless ease . . . with carefreeness, harmony and love. And when we harness the forces of joy and love, we create success and good fortune with effortless ease.

I will put the Law of Least Effort into effect by making a commitment to take the following steps:

1. I will practice Acceptance. Today I will accept people, situations, circumstances, and events as they occur. I will know that this moment is as it should be, because the whole universe is as it should be. I will not struggle against the whole universe by struggling against this moment. My acceptance is total and complete. I accept things, as they are this moment, not as I wish they were.

2. Having accepted things as they are, I will take Responsibility for my situation and for all those events I see as problems. I know that taking responsibility means not blaming anyone or anything for my situation (and this includes myself). I also know that every problem is an opportunity in disguise, and this alertness to opportunities allows me to take this moment and transform it into a greater benefit.

3. Today my awareness will remain established in Defenselessness. I will relinquish the need to defend my point of view. I will feel no need to convince or persuade others to accept my point of view. I

will remain open to all points of view and not rigidly attached to any one of them.

The Law of Intention and Desire

Inherent in every intention and desire is the mechanics for its fulfillment . . . intention and desire in the field of pure potentiality have infinite organizing power. And when we introduce intention in the fertile ground of pure potentiality, we put this infinite organizing power to work for us.

I will put the Law of Intention and Desire into effect by making a commitment to take the following steps:

1. I will make a list of all my desires. I will care this list with me wherever I go. I will look at this list before I go into my silence and meditation. I will look at it before I go to sleep at night. I will look at it when I wake up in the morning.

2. I will release this list of my desires and surrender it to the womb of creation, trusting that when things don't seem to go my way, there is a reason, and that the cosmic plan has designs for me much grander than eve those that I have conceived.

3. I will remind myself to practice present-moment awareness in all my actions. I will refuse to allow obstacles to consume and dissipate the quality of my attention in the present moment. I will accept the present as it is, and manifest the future through my deepest, most cherished intentions and desires.

The Law of Detachment

In detachment lies the wisdom of uncertainty . . . in the wisdom of *uncertainty* lies the freedom from our past, from the known, which is the prison of past conditioning. And in our willingness to step into the unknown, the field of all possibilities, we surrender ourselves to the creative mind that orchestrates the dance of the universe.

I will put the Law of Detachment into effect by making a commitment to take the following steps:

1. Today I will commit myself to detachment. I will allow myself, and those around me, the freedom to be as they are. I will not rigidly impose my idea of how things should be. I will not force solutions on problems, thereby creating new problems. I will participate in everything with detached involvement.

2. Today I will factor in uncertainty as an essential ingredient of my experience. In my willingness to accept uncertainty, solutions will spontaneously emerge out of the problem, out of the confusion, disorder, and chaos. The more uncertain things seem to be, the more secure I will feel, because uncertainty is my path to freedom. Through the wisdom of uncertainty, I will find my security.

3. I will step into the field of all possibilities and anticipate the excitement that can occur when I remain open to an infinity of choices. When I step into the filed of all possibilities, I will experience all the fun, adventure, magic, and mystery of life.

The Law of "Dharma[70]" or Purpose in Life

Everyone has a purpose in life . . . a unique gift or special talent to give others. And when we blend this unique talent with service to others, we experience the ecstasy and exultation of our own spirit, which is the ultimate goal of all goals.

I will put the Law of Dharma into effect by making a commitment to take the following steps:

1. Today I will lovingly nurture the god or goddess in embryo that lies deep within my soul. I will pay attention to the spirit within me that animates both my body and my mind. I will awaken myself to this deep stillness within my heart. I will carry the consciousness of timeless, eternal being in the midst of time-bound experience.

2. I will make a list of my unique talents. Then I will list all the things that I love to do while expressing my unique talents. When I express my unique talents and use them in the service of humanity, I lose track of time and create abundance in my life as well as in the lives of others.

3. I will asks myself daily, "How can I serve?" and "How can I help?" The answer to these questions will allow me to help and serve my fellow human beings with love.

---

[70] Dharma is a Sanskrit word that means "purpose in life."

Chapter 19

GNOSIS

To me the master of modern GNOSIS[71] is Samael Aun Weor[72]

Samael Aun Weor wrote and talked mostly about two subjects: The first one and most important is the elimination of your EGOS. Almost no chapter of his extensive library of spiritual books does not talk about how to and the importance of the elimination of all the egos.

The process of the elimination of an ego starts by self-evaluation of one's thoughts. For example, some one insults you. If instead of quickly and automatically responding, you should stop for a few seconds and observed your feelings and thoughts; you will notice that there is something there that is not really quite you ready to respond, you may feel and array of feelings going along with your ready to speak response. Now your automatic and quick response most likely is not on your best interest and not really how you feel and would respond if you give yourself time to think about all the consequences of what you were about to say.

Here are a few drastic examples to demonstrate how egos work.

---

[71] GNOSIS.-

[72] Samael Aun Weor.- Spriritual leader and master.

The next step is to judge the ego. Only you can be the judge of a part of you. If you find this ego to be guilty of running your life for you and you pass the sentence of wanting to get rid of it, then and only then you can proceed to the next step which is the elimination of the ego.

Master Samael Aun Weor divides the inner part of ourselves into two, one he reefers to it as the Father and the other as the Mother. In order to eliminate and ego you must ask your inner being to do it for you, this is also called the subconscious, in fact it goes by many different names, depending on the source of this information. Lets simply use master Weor's method.

Ask in a respectful way as if you were talking to yourself: Mother Kundalini please eliminate this ego "...", I have found it and I have judge it and I have passed sentence. It serves me no good and I do not want it anymore.

Surprisingly and amazingly something miraculous happens after a while of one doing this. This egos s l o w l y start to disappear. In other words you no longer get an automated response being generated for you under the same or very similar circumstances.

Notice my underline and bold emphasis above. First of all it is slow process; do not expect to see results overnight. One has hundreds of egos and hundreds of variations of the same ego. Unfortunately it is a process of identifying each and every one of the egos and their variations.

It is not the same variation of an ego if some stranger you just met a few seconds ago calls you an idiot, that if a close relatives does. One may have a simply quick response like you are and idiot too, while the other one may have a considerably more complex response that may involve one or more feelings and thoughts.

Master Samael Aun Weor and many other masters such as Ramalu have written thousands of pages of the subject of ego elimination. I do not pretend to cover this subject in detail here since not only I would be repeating what they have written so well about, but it would not fit on this book. What I do want to stress to you in the fact that this is one of the most important things you should learn.

One more thing I want to point out to you, self-improvement is an uphill lifetime job that gives lots of satisfaction, but none the less it is an internal battle/war. DO NOT underestimate the egos, they DO NOT want to die, they DO NOT want you to get rid of them. They are living parts of you, very much like any bacteria, virus, parasite that depends on you for its existence, they are something even worse, since they do posses a level of intelligence and will put up a fight. For example:

I though of myself as a well balanced peaceful individual. Thoughts about killing someone or of finding malicious ways of hurting someone never had entered my mind prior to delving into the elimination of the egos. At the time I started to do so, I was living in quite an ideal situation, I had most everything anyone desires, wealthy enough to not had to worry about earning a daily living, plenty of food, plenty of tranquility, awesome weather, good relationship at home, in short not much nor anyone to bother me. So I decided to start with the ego that I though to be the least challenging of them all. The ego of ANGER. Was I in for a huge surprise. The minute I started to think about the ego, it was like waking an internal dragon. Shortly someone said something I did not like and all sort of angry feelings came out of no where. I do not mean a little angry I mean a lot. So I noticed right away that it was an ego doing it for me and I did not let it act. I quickly proceeded to ask my Mother-KUNDALINI to please eliminate this ego. I thought to myself, o that was not all that bad, I got it under control, but NO, I was in for a bigger surprise. This went on for weeks. It got to the point that I was angry all day for no reason, I was so angry that I could not even sleep. All this for no reason other than this ego not wanting to die peacefully. None the less after a few weeks of this internal battle, it started to go away.

I even did a few experiments like letting it ack to me, to see how far it would go. VERY BAD IDEA! NEVER LET YOUR EGOS CONTROL YOU. I got close to being out of control, it wanted to take it to the next step of being violent. Have you heard of people killing others and then saying "I do not know what got into me," well this is how it happens AND why it is SO important to eliminate your egos.

One good example of an ego in American's society is jealousy. I never have experienced this ego since I believe I eliminated it in a pass live. But none the less I have seen it in action on many man and women. People let this monster (ego) take control and all sorts of bad things come their way. From the lost of a love one to body pains ranging from a head ache to a heart attack or brain seizure.

Never in my life have I experienced jealousy, be it from others or in a intimate relationship. What has this brought me in this life is peace of mind, good health and plenty of more time to enjoy life to its fullest. Now almost nothing can make me angry and most definitely no one can make me jealous. If you experience the ego of jealousy, do yourself a favor, get rid of it. It is just an ego. You can get rid of it.

You may think for example that you do not have the ego of a thief, but in fact most likely you do have it. For example, if you are a very young child and all is given to you, the ego of theft is in hibernation, there is no opportunity for it to come out. If you are an young person or an adult with financial abundance, that ego is most likely in hibernation and much more difficult to find its way out for you to detect it. This is where egos come out in dreams. Yes another thing you should learn is how to remember your dreams. Once you find an ego in your dream, proceed to the judgment and elimination steps.

Egos do NOT need to be part of what and who you are;

You can get rid of them.

If you have access to the internet, I highly recommend that you visit www.mysticweb.com and take their FREE online courses. The courses are improved version of all the information that Master Samael Aun Weor left in more than 80 books. If you know Spanish I highly recommend you visit www.samaelgnosis.net and take their free online courses.

Chapter 20

Sathya Sai Baba[73]

What first caught my attention about Sai Baba was a book titled: "Sai Baba and Physiatrist"

What convince me the most about Sai Baba was meeting Johnima and Kalassu, two followers of Sai Baba who lived with him for over 20 years. They recently wrote a book titled "Reclaiming Your Divinity[74];" this books is perhaps the best description ever written on the subject of who we are, what we are, where we came from

---

[73] Sathya Sai Baba is a living Avatar who presently lives in India. He is world known for his abilities to manifest many things such as food, candies, jewelry and even micro weather storms with lightning and rain. There are accounts of these facts from peasants to kings. I have personally heard of some of them first hand from very credibly mature and psychological stable people.

[74] Reclaiming Your Divinity, exposing the ultimate deception by Lightstrorm Published by SHANTI Publishing and Child's Sunvillage, Inc. USA 208-634-8335 Canada 250-380-3703 lightstrorm@ctcweb.net www.ctcweb.net/~lightstrorm $5.00 USD Feb. 2005

and most important where are we going to. It is a very practical book on how to live life moment by moment. Best of all it is written in very clear to understandable English.

How to spend your time

Sai Baba gives a very simply advice on how one should spend each day, he says: Spend 30% on your personal task, such as: work and personal needs, such as cooking, buying food, earning a living etc. 30% improving yourself, this can be meditation, studying, attending spiritual group activities, etc. And 30% helping others, this can be by teaching, helping children or elders, or even writing a book such as this one. I for once have rearranged my life to follow this rule and it has help my quality of life tremendously, I once more have done what other consider impossible, yet I have accomplished it.

The best book I have found so far about Sai Baba's teachings is titled: "A Compendium of the Teachings of Sathya Sai Baba[75]" the books is 700+ pages and has 1100 subjects.

---

[75] www.saitowers.com ISBN 81-86822-19-4

Chapter 21

Bashar

Bashar is a multi-dimensional being who speaks through channel Darryl Anka from what we perceive as the future. Bashar explores a wide-range of subjects with great insight, humor and a profound understanding of how reality creation occurs.

Channeling on topics such as reincarnation, karma, ascension, psychic predictions, spiritual healing, higher self, metaphysics, extraterrestrials, UFOs, alien abduction, holistic health, financial success, relationships, and much more. Bashar speaks with insight, personal understanding and phenomenal accuracy!

Bashar has brought through a wave of new information that clearly explains in detail how the universe works and how each person creates the reality they experience. Over the years, thousands of individuals have had the opportunity to apply these principles and see if they really work to change their lives and create the reality that they desire.

WHY DOES IT WORK?

Bashar would be the first to say that it's because this information is based on the laws of physics and is not just a "nice New Age philosophy". Perhaps this is a more advanced version of physics than you may have encountered in the past — but nevertheless, it is based on physics. Hence, when you apply these principles and techniques to your day to day life, you can see dramatic results, both in what you experience and how you feel!

Bashar describes the importance of belief systems and explains how to change what you believe about yourself and your world to dramatically change what you experience in your life. The new perspectives he shares can change the way you view "reality" and help you get in touch with the beliefs and ideas that are presently guiding your life so that you can change them if you decide to. Bashar's message emphasizes your self empowerment and your ability to use your conscious free choice to create the life and the world that you prefer.

SELF EMPOWERMENT IS KEY

Bashar describes the planet as going through a major transformation— an evolutionary leap to the next level of consciousness. Bashar's message simply acts as a reminder of what you already know but may have forgotten, and can help you experience this transition smoothly and joyfully, by expanding your awareness of the unlimited possibilities that are truly available to you. The message emphasizes increasing your self empowerment and your connection to your Higher Self as being key to consciously creating the kind of reality you desire.

ECSTACY IS YOUR BIRTHRIGHT

Bashar's message helps to expand your capacity for learning and change. It re-awakens your ability to use your imagination and express yourself creatively... so that you can experience the ecstasy that is your birthright. The techniques that are contained in the Bashar material are fun, challenging and interesting to work with and Bashar's uniquely humorous and direct approach enhances the entire experience!

A WIDE RANGE OF TOPICS

Bashar also provides cutting-edge information on a wide range of topics:

History of the Universe	Earth Changes
Extraterrestrials & UFO's	Healing Methods
Crop Circles	Life after Death
Psychic Phenomenon	Future Technology
Spiritual Ascension	Sacred Geometry

Chapter 22

Seth channel by Jane Roberts

BOOKS:

The Seth Material by Jane Roberts Seth is the acclaimed non-physical teacher whose collected works are the most dynamic, brilliant and undistorted map of inner reality and human potential available today. His articulation of the furthest reaches of human potential, the eternal validity of the soul, and the concept that we  create our own reality according to our beliefs, has been presented in books that have sold over 8 million copies and been translated into over a dozen languages. Seth's empowering voice clearly stands out as one of the major forces which led to the current New Age philosophical movement. This book chronicles Seth's first contact with author and medium Jane Roberts. It is a mixture of great Seth excerpts, selected by topic, and further explained by Jane. Topics covered include: afterdeath & between lives, reincarnation, how to get rid of Illness, why people are born into different circumstances, God, All That Is, Dreams, exercises to develop the inner senses, and much more.

The Nature of Personal Reality: Specific, Practical Techniques for Solving Everyday Problems and Enriching the Life You Know by Jane Roberts This is one of my very favorite Seth books. Seth teaches us that we are not at the mercy of the subconscious; the conscious mind directs unconscious activity and has at its command all the powers of the inner self. These are activated according to the ideas about reality. The words of Seth show  readers that they possess hidden powers within themselves that have the potential to transform their lives. This book shows readers how to improve health, create material success, and make relationships more satisfying. By learning to control their own experiences, they can create a new, fulfilling reality. A reader writes: "Do you know how there are some moments that are so magical in your life, you wish you could go back and live them over? That's how I feel about The Nature of Personal Reality. Honestly I don't know how many times I have read this book through from cover to cover. Such is the amazing impact it has had on me and my view of the world. It has influenced everything from how I interact with others to why I became an author."

Seth, Dreams and Projections Of Consciousness by Jane Roberts This is my all-time favorite book on out-of-the-body experiences! I love all the Seth books and this is a must-have for any Seth junkie. An incredibly exciting book, which provides essential instructions and information for those interested in working with dreams and out-of-body experiences. Seth is the real deal. Everytime I read any Seth book I have to put it down periodically and breathe deeply and stare off into space -- his

words hit the deepest part of your Self and they always ring true. I challenge anyone to read ANY of the Seth books and not be changed by it, altered in some wonderfully fantastic way. You will view yourself and everyone around you differently. Nothing is random -- everything happens for a reason. You are in control of your life and every aspect of it. You create your own reality. There is nothing to worry about. Life is fun! Get out there and enjoy it, both in and out of body. Fear -- what's that?

Seth Speaks: The Eternal Validity of the Soul by Jane Roberts One of the most powerful of the Seth Books, this essential guide to conscious living clearly and powerfully articulates the furthest reaches of human potential, and the concept that we all create our own reality according to our individual beliefs. Having withstood the test of time, it is still considered one of the most dynamic and  brilliant maps of inner reality available today. From a reader: "The title of this book should be renamed to The Bible of Metaphysics. It is, without a doubt, that good. Out of all the channeled books I've read, this one (and all by Seth) far exceed them all."

The Nature of the Psyche: Its Human Expression by Jane Roberts In this book Seth outlines a new concept of self and tells about the secret language of love, the inner reality that exists apart from time, and how people choose their own physical death -- sometimes years in advance. This book also covers human sexuality as it relates to the private and mass psyche and explains how distorted

beliefs about sexuality can hold back spiritual progress. From a reader: "... this book explains the 'nature of sexuality' more completely than any before. I am euphoric Seth shared his opinion because it is a very important subject. Many, many people may be shocked at Seth's view of sexuality, homosexuality, or lesbianism. Seth helped me understand this hot topic much better. Anyone interested in this area should read. In addition, Seth can explain how we create our reality like no one else."

A Seth Reader by Jane Roberts In 1963, Jane Roberts, an intelligent and somewhat skeptical writer and college graduate, began to receive a series of communications from "an energy essence personality" who called himself Seth. Psychic investigator Richard Roberts has chosen from some 3,000 pages the most thought-provoking and helpful of Seth words from eight Seth books ranging from  The Seth Material (1970) to the last book Dreams, "Evolution," and Value Fulfillment (1986). Among the topics are the nine "families of consciousness, the evolution of Earth and its creatures, how thoughts form reality, how we create our lives from the dream state, the illusion of time, simultaneous incarnations, "probable" alternate selves, unknown realities, the three "Christs," and the eternal validity of the soul. Introduction: "A Brief History of Channeling."

The "Unknown" Reality, Volume 1: A Seth Book by Jane Roberts In Volume One of The "Unknown" Reality, Seth initiates a journey in which it seems that the familiar is left behind. Where do the events of our lives begin or end?

Where do we fit into them, individually and as members of the species? These questions, with Seth's explanations, are the heart of Volume One. From a reader: "Brain food for the advanced Seth reader. Seth adds depth to some of the concepts introduced in Seth Speaks (Reincarnation, Probabilities) and adds new flavors (Counterparts, Families of Consciousness). Excellent and intriguing as usual ..."

The "Unknown" Reality, Volume 2: A Seth Book by Jane Roberts In Volume Two of The "Unknown" Reality, Seth invites us to join in and discover the unknown reality for ourselves through a series of exercises geared to illuminate the inner structures upon which our exterior ones depend. Volume One provides the general background and information upon which the exercises and methods in Volume Two are based. From a reader:  "The material brought forth by Seth is always amazing and deeply fundamental. This book is another in the series of Seth teachings and has the same, extraordinary level of perception and wisdom as the other Seth books. It should definitely be included in any reading of Seth, and for those who have read previous material, this adds another segment to this fascinating collection of writings."

Dreams, "Evolution", and Value Fulfillment, Volume 1: A Seth Book by Jane Roberts In Volume One, Seth describes a conscious, self-aware universe where possibilities and potentials generate life-forms. This book answers crucial questions about the significance of

Seth's thought system. From a reader: "Having read hundreds of books on the qualities of consciousness, there are NONE superior to Seth's." This re-issued volume features notes by Jane Robert's husband, Robert F. Butts.

Dreams, "Evolution", and Value Fulfillment, Volume 2: A Seth Book by Jane Roberts In Volume Two, Seth continues his explanation of how the physical world is an ongoing self-creation. He explains how the human species keeps within its genetic bank millions of characteristics that might be needed in various contingencies, and how the soul employs both physical handicaps and advantages as springboards for further achievement. He also expands upon his vision of a thoroughly animate universe where virtually every possibility is not only implicit, but constantly encouraged to achieve its highest potential.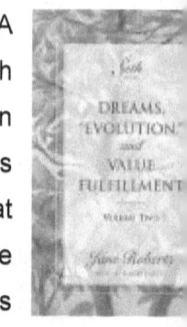

The Magical Approach: Seth Speaks About the Art of Creative Living (A Seth Book) by Jane Roberts Seth invites us to look at the world through another lens — a magical one. Seth reveals the true, magical nature of our deepest levels of being, and explains how we have allowed it to become inhibited by our own beliefs and conventional thinking. The Magical Approach teaches us how to live our lives spontaneously, creatively, and according to our own  natural rhythms. It helps us to discover and tune into our natural, instinctive behavior. By applying the principles in this book, readers will learn to trust their impulses and discover the highest expression of their creativity. "Seth was one of my first metaphysical teachers. He remains a constant source of knowledge and inspiration in my life." -- Marianne Williamson, author of A Return to Love

Chapter 23

OSHO

Many people have an erroneous idea about spirituality and economical wealth; many think that both cannot go hand-in-hand, that the very wealthy cannot reach any level of enlightenment. Nothing can be further from the truth.

To say the least Osho was a very unconventional teacher of spiritual subject. Osho said that he was "the rich man's guru",[54] and that material poverty was not a spiritual value.[55] He was photographed wearing sumptuous clothing and hand-made watches.[51] He drove a different Rolls-Royce each day – his followers reportedly wanted to buy him 365 of them, one for each day of the year.[56] Publicity shots of the Rolls-Royces (more than 90 in the end) appeared in the press.[23]

If you ever wonder why this type of none-religious spiritual teachings has not reached you before, you can blame it in great part to the governments and powerful religions of the world. Osho was persecuted by many governments throughout the world for his teachings.

Osho's Ashram in Pune has become the **Osho International Meditation Resort**,[48] a popular tourist destination[49] that attracts some 200,000 visitors from all over the world each year.[43][50] It is one of the largest spiritual growth centers in the world today.

Today, Osho's books are more popular than ever before, with translations published in 55 different languages.[40][38] After initial rejection, Osho's teachings have now become a part of mainstream culture in India[41] and Nepal. Osho is one of only two authors whose entire works have been placed in the Library of India's National Parliament in New Delhi (the other is Mahatma Gandhi).[42][41] Excerpts and quotes from Osho's works appear regularly in the *Times of India* and many other Indian newspapers. Prominent admirers include the Indian Prime Minister, Dr. Manmohan Singh,[43] the noted Indian novelist and journalist Khushwant Singh[43] and the Indian film star and ex-Minister of State for External Affairs Vinod Khanna.[44] In the West, figures such as the American poet and Rumi translator Coleman Barks,[45] the American novelist Tom Robbins[46] and the German philosopher, author and TV host Peter Sloterdijk[47] have championed Osho.

For further reference visit http://en.wikipedia.org/wiki/Osho

Chapter 24

Rosicrucian Order, AMORC

For thousands of years many knowledge has been the sole province of mystical brotherhoods including Egyptian Priests and Pharaohs, Melchizedek Priests, Arabian Schools, Rabbis, Cabbalists, Indian Yogis, Rosicrucian's, Freemason's, Jewish alchemists and even the catholic church. I chose primarily to write about the Rosicrucian's because their information is readily available to day to those who want it.

The Rosicrucian Order, AMORC, is internationally known as the Ancient Mystical Order Rosae Crucis. We are a nonsectarian body

---

[76] The Invisible college of the Rosicrucians, Theophilus Schweighardt *Speculum sophicum rhodo-stauroticum*, 1618 www.alchemywebsite.com

of men and women devoted to the investigation, study and practical application of natural and spiritual laws. Our purpose is to further the evolution of humanity through the development of the full potential of each individual. Our goal is to enable everyone to live in harmony with creative, cosmic forces for the attainment of health, happiness, and peace.

To assist in this attainment, the Rosicrucian Order offers the world's foremost system of instruction and guidance for exploring the inner self and discovering the universal laws that govern all human endeavor. It is based on the collective ancient wisdom and current knowledge of many of the world's most respected philosophers, artists and scientists.

Our teachings include specific knowledge of metaphysics, mysticism, psychology, parapsychology and science not taught by conventional educational systems or traditional religions. This profound wisdom, carefully preserved by mystery schools for centuries, is transmitted today through the Rosicrucian Order to every sincere person with an open mind and a positive motive.

The Rosicrucian's do not propose a belief system, nor a dogmatic decree, but a personal, practical approach to living that each student must learn and master through their own experiences. Our teachings do not attempt to dictate what you should think -- we want you to think for yourself. What we provide are simply the tools to enable you to accomplish this.

The Rosicrucian Order consists of thousands of men and women in over 100 countries throughout the world. To reach such a diverse membership, AMORC is divided, by language, into jurisdictions called Grand Lodges.

If you would like to receive a Free copy of our introductory booklet "Mastery of Life", please refer to the list above for your language and geographical area and contact the address listed.

Rosicrucian Order, AMORC www.amorc.org FAX 408-947-3677 1342 Naglee Avenue San Jose, CA 95191, USA Phone 408-947-3600

Chapter 25

Eckankar

Eckankar is ancient wisdom for today. Its teachings, which resurfaced in 1965, emphasize the value of personal experiences as the most natural way back to God. Whatever your religious background, they show how to look and listen within yourself—to expand your consciousness and enjoy spiritual freedom. See, perhaps for the first time—how to lead a happy, balanced, and productive life. And put daily concerns into loving perspective.

Eckankar teaches simple spiritual exercises to experience the Light and Sound of God. These exercises also help us Soul Travel, to move into greater states of consciousness. A spiritual exercise can be as simple as relaxing and singing the word HU, an ancient name for God. As we practice these spiritual exercises, we learn to recognize the presence of the Holy Spirit in our lives. We learn that each of us is Soul, a spark of God sent to this world to gain spiritual experience. And as we unfold spiritually, we learn to express the love of God through service to others.

www.eckankar.org

Chapter 26

FALUN DAFA[77]

Falun Dafa is a practice that has brought better health and inner peace to millions around the world. It is a cultivation practice: "cultivation" refers to the improvement of one's heart and mind through the careful study of universal principles based on truthfulness, benevolence, and forbearance; "practice" means doing exercises and meditation to energize the body.

Learning Falun Dafa is easy. The practice is simple, powerful, and absolutely free. The main principles of Falun Dafa are explained in their entirety in the book Zhuan Falun, and in the beginner's text, Falun Gong, both written by Falun Dafa's founder, Mr. Li Hongzhi. Also essential to the practice are the five gentle exercises, including a seated meditation, which you can learn quickly and easily at any of the thousands of practice locations around the world.

Falun Gong (also called Falun Dafa) is an ancient form of qigong, the practice of refining the body and mind through special exercises

---

[77] Dafa (dah-fah)—"The Great Way," or "The Great Law"; short for the name Falun Dafa, "The Great (Cultivation) Way of the Law Wheel."

and meditation. Like tai chi, qigong is a vital part of many people's lives in Asia; almost every Chinese park is brimming by the break of dawn with people practicing these arts.

In just eight years since its public introduction, Falun Dafa has grown to become the most popular form of qigong ever in Chinese history. The major reason for this is that Falun Dafa distinguishes itself from other qigong practices by emphasizing not only physical cultivation, but also cultivation of one's moral character in daily life according to higher principles taught by Mr. Li Hongzhi, Falun Dafa's founder.

Falun Dafa's effectiveness in improving health and its profound principles have quickly made the practice immensely popular throughout the entire world. Since being introduced to the general public in 1992 by Mr. Li, Falun Dafa has attracted tens of millions of people in over 40 countries. Most major cities and universities in the United States, Canada, Australia, and Europe have English-speaking Falun Dafa practice groups.

The people who practice Falun Dafa come from every imaginable walk of life, as Falun Dafa transcends cultural, social, economic, and national boundaries. The practice has spread largely by word of mouth, as those who learn it usually find the benefits simply too good to keep to themselves.

1. The Books and the Exercises

The practice of Falun Dafa is simple, yet profound and effective. It consists primarily of two components: self-improvement through studying Mr. Li's teachings, and performing Falun Dafa's five gentle exercises. The exercises, which include a meditation, are easy to learn, enjoyable, and at the same time both relaxing and energizing. Many students of Falun Dafa enjoy doing them together as a group outdoors. The teachings are articulated in two books, Falun Gong (Law Wheel Qigong) and Zhuan Falun (Turning the Law Wheel), which are available in over a dozen languages, including English.

2. The Principles of the Practice

The benefits of practicing Falun Dafa are numerous and varied, ranging from improved health and newfound energy to mental clarity, stress relief, and peace of mind. Yet Falun Dafa is different from most other qigong practices in that it goes beyond the pursuit of health and fitness to the goal of wisdom and enlightenment. At the heart of the practice are the supreme principles of the universe: Truthfulness, Benevolence, and Forbearance. Through a combination of studying the books and performing the exercises, practitioners strive to become better people by embodying these principles in everything they do.

3. Is This for You?

Millions of people all over the world have chosen to make the practice of Falun Dafa a part of their daily lives. Simply put, they find it a worthy and enjoyable investment of their time towards health, happiness, and meaningful living. All that's required is an open mind and a willing heart. Everyone is welcome, as Falun Dafa is apolitical, informal, and completely free of charge, obligation, and membership. All books are available free at: www.falundafa.org/eng/books.htm We invite you to give this wonderful practice a try and discover it for yourself. To learn about ways to begin, go to: www.falundafa.org/eng/start.htm If you have further questions about the practice in general, go to:

www.falundafa.org/eng/faq.htm to view a discussion of frequently asked questions.

Falun Dafa can be divided in two. One the exercises, which I highly recommend. Two the philosophy.

1 Falun Gong (fah-lun gong)—"Law Wheel Qigong." The names Falun Gong and Falun Dafa are both used to refer to this practice.

1 Falun (fah-lun)—"Law Wheel"   1 gong (gong)—"cultivation energy."

Chapter 27

Feng Shui

Feng shui (say "fung shway"), often called the art of placement, could just as accurately be called "the art of flow." This ancient Chinese practice, literally translated as "wind" and "water," aims to maximize the beneficial movement of chi-the universal life force present in all things-through an environment.

Just as fresh air and clean water nourish our bodies, so does fresh, clean chi nourish our homes and our lives. When the flow of chi through our space is blocked, weak, or misdirected, our relationships, cash flow, creativity, health, and career can suffer. Chi wants to meander gracefully through a space, like a gentle breeze or a winding stream. When it flows too strongly, it becomes like a hurricane or flood. We are likely to feel tossed about by winds of change, unstable, prone to crises, struggling to "keep our heads above water." Where chi is blocked it becomes stale and stagnant, like a pond choked with algae and fallen leaves. We may feel tired, run down, depressed, unable to focus, hampered in our efforts to move forward in our lives.

In a corporate environment, poor feng shui can result in miscommunication between managers and employees, conflicts among team members, and lack of support for key initiatives. Individuals may be overlooked for promotions or deserved raises, suffer damage to their reputation in the company, or even lose their job. The company may have difficulty attracting or keeping key customers.

In a retail store, feng shui problems can block the flow of customers into and through the store, contribute to theft and staffing problems, and have a negative effect on the amount and size of sales.

Feng shui provides tools and guidelines for analyzing and correcting the flow of energy into and through our space. It uses the arrangement of rooms and the placement of furniture to create a smooth pathway for chi through a home, office, or retail location. Blockages and other forms of negative chi are removed or counteracted in order to welcome in opportunities and encourage progress. Colors and shapes associated with the five elements- wood, fire, earth, metal, and water-are used to create movement, balance, or protection, depending on the needs of the client. Imagery and objects such as paintings, photographs, statuary and other accessories are chosen and placed to enhance and reinforce the client's intention.

Feng Shui reminds us that everything is connected, and that our physical surroundings have a significant impact on our mind, body, and spirit. It teaches us to be mindful caretakers of our environments, so that we may be mindful caretakers of our lives.

Feng shui is an ancient practice that originated in China several thousand years ago. The basic "form school" principles are still in use today. For example, the ideal location according to traditional feng shui has an "armchair" configuration: a hill or mountain behind the home on the northern side to provide protection from cold winter winds, with lower hills along either side, the house facing south to catch the sun, and a lake or stream in front to provide water for crops and livestock. This type of landscape configuration is still considered auspicious today. In an urban environment, a larger building to the rear provides a similar kind of protection. Streets and highways act like rivers to provide pathways for chi.

Consider also the effects of your local climate. In central China, for example, feng shui dictated that the kitchen should be located on the southern side of the house. This was because the prevailing winds came from the north, and might extinguish the cooking fire if the kitchen were on that side of the house. Today, some feng shui practitioners have learned this rule that kitchen should be in the south, and will follow it regardless of local conditions. If you live in the southwestern United States, however, where the climate is very hot and dry, your kitchen might be better located on the shadier north side of the home.

Another traditional approach to feng shui is the "eight directions" method. The eight directions are the four cardinal compass points-east, west, north, south-and the points in between-NE, NW, SE, SW. Based on your gender and year of birth, four of these directions will be auspicious for you, and four will be inauspicious and thought to bring illness or bad luck. According to this method of feng shui, the front door of your home should face one of your lucky directions. You should sleep in an auspicious sector of the house, and face one of your lucky directions while you work, and so on. This approach to feng shui is very popular in Europe and is becoming more widely known in the U.S. You are likely to encounter books and magazines that follow this method.

If you are shopping for a new home or apartment, it's worth finding out what your lucky directions are (and those of other family members) and factoring that into your decision. However, just because the front door of a house faces your luckiest direction doesn't mean it's the best choice for you, as it is no guarantee that the house has good feng shui in other aspects. There could be all kinds of feng shui problems on the property that far outweigh the benefits of a "lucky" front door.

If you know your lucky directions, there's no reason not to consider them in your own home, so long as you look at all the factors involved when making decisions about to use and arrange your space. For example, moving your bed so you sleep in a lucky direction won't do you much good if you are now sleeping under an overhead beam or directly in line with the bedroom door, both of which are considered poor feng shui. Feng shui will work best for you if you use it as a basis for making informed decisions, rather than rigidly following guidelines out of context or ignoring the broader implications of your changes.

And just in case you aren't confused enough already, there is also the "compass school" approach to feng shui. This is a complex practice that calculates a detailed "star" chart for the home, based on the year of construction and the precise compass direction the building faces. You can think of this approach as being like having an astrology reading for your home: in addition to the basic chart, there are influences that change every day, month, and year. Some homes will have poor star combinations that will bring bad luck and misfortune to their occupants unless those influences are corrected through specific feng shui "cures," such as placing metal or water in certain areas of the house. Other homes might have a good star chart, only to come under unlucky influences during a particular month or year.

The compass method of feng shui requires that you know the year your house was built, as well as whether and when any significant renovations involving the roof, foundation, or major additions have been made. You also must be able to get an accurate (within a couple of degrees) compass reading on the "facing direction" of your home.

Another complication is that the facing direction is not necessarily the same as the front door, depending on the layout and position of your home. It is sometimes difficult or impossible to get an accurate compass reading, especially in an urban environment. A car parked at the curb in front of your house, a cast iron fence around the front garden of a townhouse, or buried utility lines under your front yard may be enough to throw off your compass reading. When I lived in an apartment in New York City, I took quite a few compass readings over a period of several months; the readings were so varied and inconsistent that I was never able to do an accurate compass analysis of that apartment.

In summary, all of the traditional methods of feng shui offer valuable principles and guidelines-which you may or may not be able to follow or apply to your specific home.

Fortunately, there is another approach, introduced in the United States by Master Lin Yun. Called "Black Sect" or "Black Tibetan Buddhist" feng shui. This and other similar approaches focus on creating a healthy flow of chi through a space. This contemporary Western style of feng shui addresses the need for a method that can be used where compass-oriented rules of placement are difficult or impossible to follow. It can also be used in combination with the other methods to provide a deeper understanding of the energetic qualities and influences of your space.

In this contemporary approach to feng shui, the association of specific areas of the home with specific aspects of your life is based on position relative to the front door-the "mouth of chi." Furniture is arranged to create a safe and comfortable environment, and colors, artwork, and other imagery are chosen to reinforce desired changes. One of the most appealing aspects of this style of feng shui is the emphasis it places on the power of your intention to influence the energy of your home. This makes the practice of feng shui much more personal and unique to each individual, and creates the opportunity to use feng shui as a tool for increased self-awareness and personal growth. "Fast Feng Shui" is my approach to teaching the principles of contemporary western feng shui in a way that is easy to learn and apply. And the best part of this type of feng shui is that anyone can use it for increased prosperity, success and happiness-starting right now, without special equipment or years of training. [78]

---

[78] www.fastfengshui.com

Chapter 28

Psychics, Channelers, Parapsychologists

Even though there are a few real psychics in the world, the changes of you finding one are slim. I for one have only meet one in my life, and a second one that possibly is for real. For the most part rule number one is that a psychic provides it's services for free, will always be a very humble person, who keeps calm regardless of what you say to them, a true psychic never advertises his/her services, because they have way to many people already waiting for there service inline. For example there is one near where I live, for starter this guy lives in a remote and very hard place to find, no street signs, no sign on the door, etc. he dresses quite simple and just like anyone else, his office is quite simply, his service is free, though almost everyone gives him momentary gifts. After years of hearing about him I finally got a friend to arrange a visit, since he is quite difficult to visit, since he has a huge line of people standing outside each day to visit him, in fact he only attends to a portion of the people who wish to see him. Him method is quite simply and to the point, he does not ask a single question, he simply holds your hand and start saying everything that has ever been wrong or is wrong with your health, to my surprise he held my hand for quite a while, probably 5 minutes or so, and simply said you are in perfect health no more no less. Now I was not felling in perfect health, but that was all he had to say for me. Then he went on holding my friends hand, he started by saying that he had had some serious throat infection, that he had gastritis, that his 10 vertebrate from the top had a small injury and that it hurt from time to time, and that he had a brain malfunction that he would have his spirit partner stop by and have it fix, that after it was fix he should stop taking the medication, and proceeded to write a prescription for several herbs. We were both astonished, starting with the throat problem, indeed it had been a severe cough that lasted only a few weeks and we both have forgotten about it, the gastritis was a problem he had and he had not even mentioned it to me, same as the back problem, even though I know him for years and have spent quite a bit of time with him, he had never complaint of either problem. I did know about the brain malfunction, but since he is a top government official, very few people know about this other than his very close family and myself. We were both quite in shock to here this fellow know all this by just holding his hand. A few months had passed and I became very ill, with a severe case of hepatitis, but ALL lab test and eco-sonograms came back negative, doctors had not idea whatsoever what was wrong with me, so I though on giving him a visit, when I got to his office the lights were a bit dim, so I can say he did not see my very yellow skin, again he held my hand for a long time and said you are in perfect health, so I explain to him how ill I though I was, to what he replied, o, no big deal, you will be over all that in a few days, and so I was.

My point to you are a few, one the changes of you finding a real psychic are slim, there are very few and very hard to find, often people travel very far to have an appointment with one. Two if you do find one, it will be free, it will be courteous and you will have NO doubts whatsoever about his or hers abilities, true psychics can spell it out very quickly.

Edgar Cayce (1877-1945)
The Sleeping Prophet

Cayce was born on a farm near Hopkinsville, Kentucky on March 18, 1877. At an early age he gave evidence of his budding talent: he was able to master his school lessons by sleeping on his books. At the age of twenty-one he developed a gradual throat paralysis which threatened the loss of his voice. When doctors were unable to find a cause for his condition, Cayce entered the same hypnotic sleep that had enabled him to learn his school lessons years before. In that state, he was able to recommend a cure which successfully repaired his throat muscles and restored his voice. It was soon discovered that he could do the same for others.

For most of his adult life, Edgar Cayce was able to provide intuitive insights into nearly any question imaginable. When individuals came to him with a question, he would place himself into a sleep-induced sleep state. While in that state he could respond to virtually any question asked. His responses have come to be called "readings". Today his psychic readings constitute one of the largest and most impressive records of intuitive information to emanate from a single individual.

For many years the information dealt mainly with medical problems. Eventually the scope of his readings expanded to include such topics as meditation, dreams, reincarnation, and prophecy. The transcripts have provided the basis for over 300 popular books about Cayce's work.

Mr. Cayce's theories on the end times of this planet are very enlightening and show a global major change in 1998. He prophesized the Sphinx had been built in 10,500 BC and that survivors of Atlantis had concealed beneath it a "Hall of Records" containing all the wisdom of their lost civilization and the true history of the human race. Cayce prophesied that this Hall of Records would be rediscovered and opened between 1996 and 1998. He connected the opening to the second coming of Christ.

Edgar Cayce gave over 14,000 readings between the years 1901 and 1945, covering more than 10,000 topics. Among the topics he channeled was prehistorical civilizations, specifically, Atlantis and its influence on other cultures existing at the time.

He ending every reading by saying, "We are through".

The sleeping prophet, as Cayce has been nicknamed, predicted the beginning and end of both the First and Second World Wars, and the lifting of the Depression in 1933. In the 1920s, he first warned of coming racial strife in the United States, and in 1939 he predicted the deaths of two presidents in office; "Ye are to have turmoils -- ye are to have strife between capital and labor. Ye are to have a division in thy own land, before ye have the second of the Presidents that next will not live through his office... a mob rule!" President Franklin D. Roosevelt died in office in April 1945. In November 1963, President John F. Kennedy was assassinated in Dallas, Texas, when racial tensions in the United States were at their height. "Unless there is more give and take, "Cayce said, "consideration for those who produce, with better division of the excess profits from labor, there must be greater turmoil in the land."

In October 1935, Cayce spoke of the coming holocaust in Europe. The Austrians and Germans, he said, and later the Japanese, would take sides. "Thus an unseen force, gradually growing, must result in an almost direct opposition to the Nazi, or Aryan theme. This will gradually produce a growth of animosities. And unless there is interference by what many call supernatural forces and influences -- which are active in the affairs of nations and peoples -- the whole world as it were... will be set on fire by militaristic groups and people who are for power expansion."

Two of Cayce's major predictions concerned the futures of China and the Soviet Union, the world's great Communist giants. In 1944, he prophesied that China would one day be "the cradle of Christianity as applied in the lives of men." Through Russia, he said "comes the hope of the world. Not in respect to what is sometimes termed Communism or Bolshevism -- no! But freedom -- freedom! That each man will live for his fellow man. The principle has been born there. It will take years for it to be crystallized; yet out of Russia comes again the hope of the world." Russia, he said, would be guided by friendship with the United States. Its attempt to rule "not only the economic, but the mental and spiritual life" of its people was doomed to failure.

Cayce also predicted the possibility of a third world war. He spoke of strifes arising "near the Davis Straits," and "in Libya, and in Egypt, in Ankara, and in Syria; through the straits around those areas above Australia, in the Indian Ocean and the Persian Gulf." When asked in June 1943 whether it would be feasible to work towards an international currency or a stabilization of international exchange levels when the war had ended, Cayce replied that it would be a long, long time before this would happen. Indeed, he said, "there may be another war over just such conditions."

Cayce believed in reincarnation. Each person, in his view, existed in a self-conscious form before birth and would exist again after death. As well as his health readings, Cayce gave many hundreds of so-called "life" readings, during which he would describe his subject's past lives. A number of those readings referred to past incarnations in the legendary lost land of Atlantis. In all, Cayce referred to Atlantis no fewer than seven hundred times in his readings over a span of twenty years.

He maintained that Atlantis had a civilization which was technologically superior to our own, and that its last surviving islands had disappeared in the area of the Caribbean some ten thousand years ago. His most specifically timed forecast was that Atlantis would rise again in 1968 or 1969. Needless to say, Cayce was wrong on that count. [Note: However, it was in that timeframe that the "Bimini Road" was located in the Atlantic Ocean. Whether this is a "road" or "natural, geologic erosion" is being hotly debated.]

Cayce said the size of Atlantis was equal to "that of Europe, including Asia in Europe." He saw visions of a continent which had gone through three major periods of division; the first two about 15,600 BCE, when the mainland was divided into islands. The three main islands Cayce named Poseida, Og and Aryan. He said the Atlanteans had constructed giant laser-like crystals for power plants, and that these had been responsible for the second destruction of the land. Cayce blamed the final destruction on the disintegration of the Atlantean culture through greed and lust. But before the legendary land disappeared under the waves, Cayce believed there was an exodus of many Atlanteans through Egypt and further. Cayce attributed history's Great Flood in part to the sinking of the last huge remnants of Atlantis.

Other predictions were about dramatic changes in the Earth's surface in the period of 1958 to 1998. The cause of these he put down to a tilting in the Earth's rotational axis which he said would begin in 1936.

The first sign of this change in the Earth's core would be the "breaking up of some conditions" in the South Pacific and "sinking or rising" in the Mediterranean or Etna area. Cayce forecast that, by the end of the century, New York, Los Angeles and San Francisco would be destroyed. He said that "the greater portion of Japan must go into the sea" at this time, and that northern Europe would be "changed as in the twinkling of an eye." In 1941, Cayce predicted that lands would appear in the Atlantic and the Pacific in the coming years, and that "the coastline now of many a land will be the bed of the ocean. Even many of the battlefields of (1941) will be ocean, will be the sea, the bays, the lands over which the new order will carry on their trade as with one another."

"Watch New York, Connecticut and the like. Many portions of the east coast will be disturbed, as well as many portions of the west coast, as well as the central portion of the United States. Los Angeles, San Francisco, most of all these will be among those that will be destroyed before New York, or New York City itself, will in the main disappear. This will be another generation though, here; while the southern portions of Carolina, Georgia, these will disappear. This will be much sooner. The waters of the Great Lakes will empty into the Gulf of Mexico."

Cayce prophesied that the Earth's axis would be shifted by the year 2001, bringing on reversals in climate, "so that where there has been a frigid or semi-tropical climate, there will be a more tropical one, and moss and fern will grow." By this time, he indicated, a new cycle would begin.

Edgar Cayce's last reading on 17 September 1944, was for himself. He was now receiving thousands of requests for assistance. His own readings had repeatedly warned him that he should not try to undertake more than two sessions a day. But many of the letters he received were from mothers worried about their sons on the battlefields, and Cayce felt he could not refuse them his aid. His last reading told him that the time had come for him to stop working and rest. On New Year's Day, 1945, he announced that he would be buried on the fifth of January. He was right.

Ten years earlier, Cayce had written a brief account of his work. In it, he said, "The life of a person endowed with such powers is not easy. For more than forty years now I have been giving readings to those who came seeking help. Thirty-five years ago the jeers, scorn and laughter were even louder than today. I have faced the laughter of ignorant crowds, the withering scorn of tabloid headlines, and the cold smirk of self-satisfied intellectuals. But I have also known the wordless happiness of little children who have been helped, the gratitude of fathers and mothers and friends... I believe that the attitude of the scientific world is gradually changing towards these subjects." [79]

---

[79] www.crystalinks.com/edgar_cayce.html

Chapter 29

Dowsing[80], Pendulums, Ouija board[81], Tarot cards[82], Divination, Scrying, Palmistry Chirimancy[83]

There are many tools that work as intermediaries between our 3rd density reality and the 4th density to gather information; they are often referred to as Divination Tools. They are not a requirement to get information from the 4th density, but they are most definitely a

---

[80] www.crystalinks.com/dowsing.html   www.dowsers.com

[81] www.crystalinks.com/ouija.html

[82] www.realmagick.com/articles/00/1600.html

[83] www.crystalinks.com/palmistry.html

means of accessing the 4th density. Any beginner and serious practitioner should take the study and use of them seriously.

A set of Tarot cards is a tool used by Witches and Magicians to interface with the Akashic Hall of Records[84]. You too with some practice can make use of them.

The sword symbolizes mental power by single-pointed thought and focus.

The wand points at the will power, determination and energy necessary to create something new.

The cup tells that he has a passionate desire to perform his magick, and that he feels love and humility towards the laws of nature.

The disk reveals that he is skilled in his magick, and that the combination of concentrated thought, desire, willpower and skill will lead to successful magick.

The I Ching is an ancient Chinese oracle that provides an Oriental philosophical perspective to give insight on situations and problems. "I" means change. "Ching" means book. Therefore I Ching means 'The Book Of Changes'. The I Ching is both a book and a method of divination that represents one of the first efforts of humans to grasp their relationship to nature and society. The I Ching is a book of wisdom that illustrates correct and balanced action in a multitude of

---

[84] See Chapter 12

situations. It is a chart of changes. The basis of the I Ching philosophy is that nothing is static and that our task is to adjust to the ebbs and flows of change. The I Ching has evolved over the centuries and is a mix of Taoist and Confucian philosophy. It is possibly the oldest book in existence. Its origins date back about 5000 years to the time of the ruler Fu Hsi. Fu Hsi was said to have found the eight trigrams that form the sixty-four hexagrams on the shell of a tortoise. Fu Hsi is credited as being the first person to give some order to what was, at that time, an uncivilized culture. Were not written until much later.[85]

Ouija boards are a form of channeling. Like all other forms of channeling - until you understand how to freely communicate with spirit - you must develop some basic skills. The Ouija Board has been around since the time of the Roman Emperor Valens in the fourth century. It is also thought to have been used by the Greeks since before the time of Christ. It is a form of divination. The modern Ouija Board began as a combination of two tools used for scrying. The first was a wheel made up of the letters of the alphabet. The second was a glass, usually a wine glass which is inverted and placed in the middle. The letters are usually written on small pieces of paper which are placed in a circle around the table. It was in 1891 that a patent was granted to Elijah J Bond on the first modern Ouija Board. The following year the rights were purchased by William Fuld. In 1966 the Parker Brothers purchased the rights to the Ouija Board and shifted its manufacturing facilities to Salem,

---

[85] www.crystalinks.com/ching.html

Massachusetts. The Ouija Board ended up outselling the game of Monopoly in its first full year at Salem. Over two million copies of the Ouija Board were shipped. The layout of the Ouija Board seems to vary from country to country and production companies - as other developed an looked to improve their boards to brining clear - more detailed - messages. The original and best layout appears to be to place the Yes at the top of the circle and the No at the bottom. On the basic board - the letters are placed in a circle starting with the letter A next to the word yes and continuing around until the final letter Z ends up on the other side of the word yes. The nine numbers from one to nine should be placed at the bottom next to the no. Many people feel that Ouija Boards are dangerous to use. It depends on who uses them and the entities they attract. Dysfunctional people will attract dysfunctional entities and should never use a ouija board or channel in any way.[86]

There are many tools to guide the user to the other realms of reality. Ultimately in the long run the real truth is that you do not need any tool at all. The fact is that they are just tools to guide your subconscious into communicating for you and with you. Your ultimate goal should always be to find the answer within you, without the use of any outside tools. But if you feel the need, please by all means use them. It is a matter of personal choice. If it works for you, use them.

---

[86] www.crystalinks.com/ouija.html

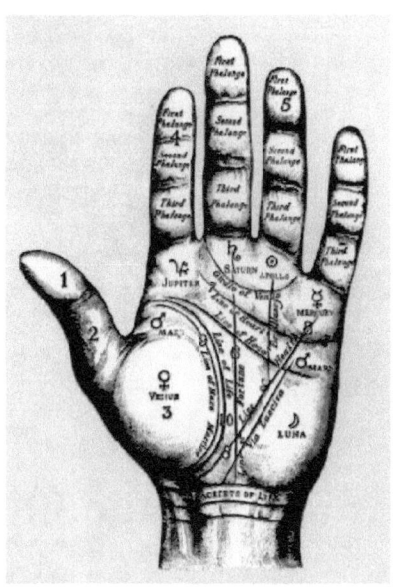

Palmistry is the study of the lines and signs of the hands. Your palm print is the blueprint of your life. It tells everything about you - past, present, future - health - and more. Everything on your palm means something even the nails and color tones of the skin. Once a line is on your hand it does not go away. Lines add on through your lifetime due to the electromagnetic changes sent by your brain. New lines general develop on the dominant hand - the one you write with. The other hand is your destiny, not your past life. Once a line is formed it never disappears. Some people have many deep lines - while others people have the primary lines plus a few branches that extend from them.

Chapter 30

Numerology, Sacred Geometry

Numerology and sacred geometry are two advanced tools worth mentioning, but that I recommend you leave for last, except of course if these subject are of your maximum joy.

Numerology is created from the Latin word 'numerus', which means 'number', and the Greek word 'logos', which means 'word', 'thought', 'expression'. Therefore, the numerology can be defined as 'the science of numbers'. Since ancient times people have used created a mystical relationship between numbers and the character or action of physical objects and living things. Currently numerology is used to predict the future and better understand human behavior patterns.[87]

The term "sacred geometry[88]" is used by archaeologists, anthropologists, and geometricians to encompass the religious, philosophical, and spiritual beliefs that have sprung up around geometry in various cultures during the course of human history. It is a catch-all term covering Pythagorean geometry and neo-Platonic geometry, as well as the perceived relationships between organic curves and logarithmic curves. It is found in the architecture of the universe, in the human body, in a flower, in DNA, in art and it can be used in advanced consciousness creating meditation techniques. The universe is created by a thought consciousness which manifests in physical reality through a geometric blueprint that we call Sacred Geometry which repeats in cycles giving the illusion of linear time.

One of the most amazing things that happens with the use of some drugs like ketamine is seeing all sorts of geometric figures up close. One can spend hours enjoying seeing these figures up close.

Sacred geometry is the study of geometric forms and their metaphorical relationships to human evolution as well as a study in fluid evolutionary transitions of mind, emotions, spirit, and

---

[87] www.crystalinks.com/numerology.html

[88] www.crystalinks.com/sacred_geometry.html

consciousness reflected in the succeeding transition from one sacred geometric form (consciousness state) into another.[89]

Why is Sacred Geometry so important? There are many reasons, but basically, Sacred Geometry is valuable to us because it is a meditation for the logical side of our brain. Most of our meditative experiences are centered in the right hemisphere of our brain – the intuitive, emotional, feeling side of us. When we meditate, it usually 'feels' good. We can sometimes see visions or images in our meditations, hear calming sounds or insightful voices. All of these sensations are located in the right side of our brain; our emotional / intuitive side.

Sacred Geometry speaks of a beauty forgotten to most of us, but ready to be awakened once again. A beauty that is not only known intuitively, but a beauty that is also known logically, and therefore holistically. Shapes and forms remind us of our place in this universe and how we can perceive, move, and create in harmony with the world around us. These forms create the very fabric of our universe.[90]

---

[89] www.floweroflife.org/spiral02.htm

[90] www.floweroflife.org/art-sgbeginners.htm

Chapter 31

Biorhythims

As long as 3000 years ago, the scientists of ancient Greece were recording the regular rhythms of basic bodily functions such as respiration, kidney activity, pulse rate and, of course, the female menstrual cycle. Most of us barely give them a thought; yet these rhythmic cycles affect even the tiniest cells of our organism from the day we are born to the day we die.

Hippocrates, the celebrated Greek physician, noticed that good and bad days fluctuated cyclically in both sick and healthy people. It was only relatively recently, however, that the theory of three internal cycles with a definite effect on behavior patterns gained credibility in our society, and its practical use was appreciated by many people in all walks of life.

In modern times we think of the 'fathers of biorhythm theory as Dr. Wilhem Fliess and Hermanna Swoboda.

A German physician in Berlin, Wilhem Fliess, provided the first tentative explanation for this phenomenon, on the basis of physiological and emotional cycles.

Later an Austrian physician, Prof. Alfred Telcher, further developed the theory identifying a third component, the intellectual cycle.

Hermanna Swoboda was a professor of psychology at the University of Vienna. Dr. Wilhelm Fliess was a nose and throat specialist in Berlin. Like so many important scientific discoveries, both Fliess and Swoboda were working along very similar lines with almost no knowledge of each other's work. It is quite extraordinary that these two scientists, despite doing independent research, came to virtually identical conclusions.

Both Swoboda and Fliess found psychology intriguing and due to books and information beginning to surface at the time, took an interest in human cycles. Swoboda published this paper at the University of Vienna in 1900 - "Life is subject to consistent changes. This understanding does not refer to changes in our destiny or to changes that take place in the course of life. Even if someone lived a life entirely free of outside forces, of anything that could alter his mental and physical state, still his life would not be identical from day to day. The best of physical health does not prevent us from feeling ill sometimes, or less happy than usual."

Analyzing dreams, ideas and creative impulses of his patients, Swoboda noticed very regular patterns or rhythms. Some artists might be familiar with these dry spells and then frenzies of creations with predictable variations. He also observed that new mothers began to show anxiety about their infants whenever a critical day occurred or was about to occur.

Swoboda's discovery of these two basic biorhythms led him to write a succession of distinguished and widely-popular books explaining and developing the ideas of human cycles. First of these books, published in 1904, is titled "The Periods of Human Life" (in their psychological and biological significance). His second book titled "Studies on the Basis of Psychology" further elaborated his work on creativity and the recurrence of dreams. In 1909 he published an instruction booklet which included a slide rule to calculate critical days called "The Critical Days of Man."

Swoboda's best book, and one of his last, was a volume of almost 600 pages titled "The Year of Seven." Much of that work was devoted to proving biorhythm theory by giving a mathematical analysis of how the timing of births tends to be rhythmic and predictable from generation to generation within the same family.

Wilhelm Fliess on the other hand did not get nearly as much gratification from his discovery as Swoboda. He did introduce Sigmund Freud, a friend of his, to Biorhythms around the turn of the century. Freud, well known as the father of modern psychology, was very interested in human behavior and was fascinated by Fliess's work. During the course of five years they wrote over a hundred letters to each other discussing their respective discoveries and research.

Both Fliess and Freud were interested in human bisexuality. Fliess begun to prove cellular bisexuality through his research of Biorhythms realizing that both men and women had an emotional cycle that was the same. He stated that Women are more influenced by the emotional cycle and men are more affected by the physical cycle.

He concluded, due to cellular bisexuality both males and females have both rhythms (saying that men have a pseudo menstrual cycle, if you will). In 1909, Fliess published a book entitled "The Course of

Life," which spurred other doctor, Hans Schlieper, to write a book on Biorhythms called The Year in Space. [91]

---

[91] www.crystalinks.com/biorhythms.html

Chapter 32

Magick, Wish craft, Pagan, Wicca, Voodoo, Shamanism

I bundled Magic, Wish craft, Paganism, Wicca[92] Voodoo, Shamanism among other practices together due to their similarities; neither is considered a religion on its own, due to the fact that they have a very open minded definition of content and standards vs. other religions with strict standards of belief, behavior and acceptability. These practices include acceptance for such a broad array of gods, beliefs, behavior, rituals[93], celebrations, etc. that do not fit under the rigid standards of a religion and often are mix with religious believes. Such is the case of Santeria, a Pagan/Wish craft practice very common in Cuba, brought by the Africans slaves to Cuba. Santeria is very mixed with the Catholic Christianity, in fact they found lots of commonality and decided to use (under the pressure of the Catholic church to convert to Christianity or die) the same god names used by the Catholics for their gods.

---

[92] Wicca is the revitalization of the Old Religion, which pre-dates Christianity by at least 10 thousand years, if not more. Its name, Wicca, means "Wise One", and was derived from the Anglo-Saxon word 'Wicce', which means 'to bend'.

[93] Ritual.- A ritual is a tool of communication with the forces and/or beings of other densities/dimensions.

In many traditional religions people are considered bad from the start, inherently flawed and expected to fail. Because of these negative traits and the acknowledgment of them, folks rally together, form a worship group and placate their God who has made them aware of their flaws and loves them anyway. If they work hard at apologizing for their mistakes, flaws and inherent sinfulness, they may have a shot at redemption and attain a favorable afterlife.

Principles of Wiccan Belief

In the spring Witchmeet held April 1974 in Minneapolis, Minnesota, The Council of American Witches adopted this statement entitled "The Principles of Wiccan Belief."

The statement was created in hopes to bring awareness to the general public as well as to the Wiccan community, and though it was intended for Wiccans in the US, holds true for many Wiccans around the world.

Not all Wiccans have adopted this document, for the few statements included here can not fully encompass ones religion, views and beliefs. These principle statements are more like guidelines than religious "law" and should be understood as such. [94]

---

[94] www.realmagick.com

The Council of American Witches finds it necessary to define modern Witchcraft in terms of the American experience and needs. We are not bound by traditions from other times and other cultures, and owe no alliance to any person or power greater than the Divinity manifest through our own being.

As American Witches, we welcome and respect all life-affirming teachings and traditions, and seek to learn from all our learning's within our Council.

It is in this spirit of welcome and cooperation that we adopt these few principles of Wiccan belief. In seeking to be inclusive, we do not wish to open ourselves to destruction of our group by those on self-serving power trips, or to philosophies and practices contradictory to these principles. In seeking to exclude those whose ways are contradictory to ours, we do not want to deny participation with us to any who are sincerely interested in our knowledge and beliefs, regardless of race, color, sex, age, national or cultural origins, or sexual preference.

We therefore ask only that those who seek to identify with us accept these basic principles:

We practice rites to attune ourselves with the natural rhythm of life forces marked by the phases of the Moon and the seasonal quarters and cross quarters.

We recognize that our intelligence gives us a unique responsibility toward our environment. We seek to live in harmony with Nature, in ecological balance offering fulfillment to life and consciousness within an evolutionary concept.

We acknowledge a depth of power far greater than is apparent to the average person. Because it is far greater than ordinary, it is sometimes called "supernatural," but we see it as lying within that which is naturally potential to all.

We conceive of the Creative Power in the Universe as manifesting through polarity - as masculine and feminine - and that this same creative Power lives in all people, and functions through the interaction of the masculine and feminine. We value neither above the other, knowing each to be supportive of each other. We value sexuality as pleasure, as the symbol and embodiment of Life, and as one of the sources of energies used in magickal practices and religious worship.

We recognize both outer worlds and inner, or psychological worlds - sometimes known as the Spiritual World, the Collective Unconscious, the Inner Planes, etc. - and we see in the interaction of these two dimensions the basis for paranormal phenomena and magickal exercises. We neglect neither dimension for the other, seeing both as necessary for our fulfillment.

We do not recognize any authoritarian hierarchy, but do honor those who teach, respect those who share their greater knowledge and wisdom, and acknowledge those who have courageously given themselves into leadership.

We see religion, magick, and wisdom - in - living as being united in the way one views the world and lives within it - a world view and philosophy of life, which we identify as Witchcraft or the Wiccan Way.

Calling oneself "Witch" does not make a Witch - but neither does heredity itself, or the collecting of titles, degrees, and initiations. A Witch seeks to control the forces within him/herself that make life possible in order to live wisely and well, without harm to others, and in harmony with Nature.

We acknowledge that it is the affirmation and fulfillment of life, in continuation of evolution and development of consciousness, that gives meaning to the Universe we know, and to our personal role within it.

Our only animosity toward Christianity, or toward any other religion or philosophy - of -life, is to the extent that its institutions have claimed to be "the one true right and only way" and have sought to deny freedom to others and to suppress other ways of religious practices and beliefs.

As American Witches, we are not threatened by debates on the history of the Craft, the origins of various terms, the legitimacy of various aspects of different traditions. We are concerned with our present, and our future.

We do not accept the concept of "absolute evil," nor do we worship any entity known as "Satan" or "the Devil" as defined by Christian Tradition. We do not seek power through the suffering of others, nor do we accept the concept that personal benefits can only be derived by denial to another.

We work within Nature for that which is contributory to our health and well - being.

The Ten Native American Commandments

Treat the Earth and all that dwell thereon with respect.

Remain close to the Great Spirit.

Show great respect for your fellow beings.

Work together for the benefit of all Mankind.

Give assistance and kindness wherever needed.

Do what you know to be right.

Look after the well-being of mind and body.

Dedicate a share of your efforts to the greater good.

Be truthful and honest at all times.

Take full responsibility for your actions.

www.ChildrenOfRa.org

Finding a group

If you are looking for a group then going out and meeting people and talking, asking questions and showing your intent of finding a group are the most important steps.

If you stay at home and never mingle with other people then don't expect anything to happen. This is not a 'spoonfed' path to walk, there is a lot of serious work involved and when you do find a group, the work doesn't stop.

Joining a group means giving up a lot of free time, substituting social time for Coven time and spending a lot of time studying and experiencing... So which ever path you follow, and which ever type of group you are seeking - make an effort and be patient.

Chapter 33

Hypnosis

by M. A. Robotham

The word "Hypnosis" is derived form the Greek word "hypnos" meaning sleep, Although hypnosis is not sleep in fact quite the opposite. Hypnosis is a way of accessing the subconscious mind in a controlled and conscious way. There are many ways to use hypnosis and many benefits to be gained from it, form healing to past life regression and achieving out of body experiences. I took a course in hypnotherapy a few years ago so I know quite a bit about the subject.

Hypnosis when utilized brings about a state of mind commonly known as trance, This word sound awful really and hypnosis had been given a bad name because of the way it has been portrayed in films, where people in so called "Trance" have been shown walking around like zombies.

The state of hypnosis is nothing like this at all its actually quite a pleasant experience and varies in depth from a light state of daydreaming to a deep state of somnambulism where the body becomes fully asleep and the mind is fully active.

All of us are in a trance state two or three times a day for example, when driving a car you mind is so focused on the road it produces a trance state, you can drive along and when you get to your destination you seem to have no conscious recollection of the route you took. When this happens our subconscious mind takes over and goes into autopilot and driving becomes automatic. The most common type of trance state is when we watch TV or a Movie we get so absorbed in the story and for a short time become apart of the movie and we loose sense of time and unaware of our surroundings. We cry sometimes if the film is a sad one, become emotional this is because we are in a trance and the subconscious is active which is the right side of the brain which Deals with emotions. Even reading a book can do the same.

The subconscious mind has a lot do with the right side of the brain, its interesting to notice as well that left handed people tend to be more artistic and imaginative, Where as right handed people tend to be more practical. This is because the right side of the brain is connected to the left side of the body and the left side of the brain the right side of the body. The subconscious side is where all the psychic stuff takes place.[95]

---

[95] www.crystalinks.com/hypnotherapy.html

Chapter 34

Ghost, Paranormal

Ghost and the paranormal are simply explained by the fact that there are some people more sensitive than others and can see or sense the 4th density at times with more ease. That there are places on earth where the 3rd density merges with the 4th and opens a window to sense the 4th density better. Some of these places have been created by past activities.

If you are having experiences if this sort and wish to learn more about them in detail, I recommend that you do, but that at the same time you focus on your continued education on the general subjects suggested in this book; they will also help you clarify the science behind the so called paranormal.

Chapter 35

Aliens, UFO's

Do Aliens and UFO's exist? You bet they do. I have met a few and seen quite a few.

In general most UFO can be explained by conventional science and by the understanding of the new science of plasma. Plasma has the peculiar feature that it can be controlled by the mind, especially by the mind of a young person (near the age of puberty) nearby. So you get a combination of two things happening, one the plasma and two the intelligent movement, which comes from a person nearby, these two combined lead to the thought of it being some foreign alien intelligence doing the movement, when in fact it is being moved by one of the observers. Of course this does not explain the seeing of an aircraft such as a flying saucer. Another very common error is people not realizing they had just had an out-of-body experience, and out-of-body experience can be as real as we commonly perceive our waking reality. Many people have had such experiences and believe they had an actual 3rd density experience. Now that leaves us with the less but still quite common actual experiences with real live beings from other densities.

My experiences of UFOs all fall under the category of plasma balls, I have seen from a dozen at a time, that exhibit the common characteristics of intelligence to a huge one that I confused with the sun at 9 PM. I have also seen light fall to the ground and one time I saw a huge lighted tube that went all the way from the ground to the skies. My experiences with live alien beings have all been while traveling in the 4th and other densities.

When analyzing these phenomenon, do not discard them at plain sight, there may be a lot more than meets the eye. I for one know of alien intervention into several peoples personal affairs that are beyond any shadow of a doubt after plenty of investigation with a very analytical and scientific eye. For example I have personally investigated a friend who claims to have had surgery from a alien visitation, to my surprise I found a 2 cm extremely thing scar on the back of his neck, the scar did not have any skin sutures, but I could feel the muscle sutures; he has the type of skin that scars quite easily, in fact he has plenty of scars to prove so, but this scar completely disappeared in a few weeks. Another case I followed quite close was of a lady who I have known for over fifteen years who claims to have been used to carry fetuses on an ongoing basis. She fits all the profiles of an actual carrier; to my surprise she seems quite comfortable with what happens to her.

Crabwood Farm House, nr Winchester, Hampshire August 15

Chapter 36

Crop-circles

How, then, does the debunking media explain that this also has happened literally all over the planet? India alone recently announced the appearance and cataloging of some 10,000 crop formations since the 1970's, and circles have appeared in almost every major country on the globe, whether in rice paddies, grain crops, mud, dry lake beds or even ice.

The astounding complexity of the most recent batch of formations from summer 1997, 98 and 99 defies even the most hardened scientific minds from explaining them away. The old-fashioned explanations of "localized plasma vortices" or "an army of hedgehogs running round and round" simply do not hold weight. In most true crop circles, the stems are usually bent at the growth nodes, not broken, and they exhibit measurable radiation and signs of being heated. This has led most serious crop circle researchers to conclude that they were formed by some sort of microwave radiation that cooked the joints. This cooking turns the water in the crop into steam, which causes the growth nodes to become pliable and bend. (Hessemann, 1996 and others.)

Indeed, seeds and plant fragments are often found that look as though they have been burned in a microwave oven. But how could you possibly use heat on something like dry grass and expect it not to torch up on you? Interestingly enough, large amounts of nearby underground water have been known to spontaneously disappear after a circle is formed. This fact has been confirmed through the use of infrared photography by the crop circle researchers. It certainly appears that the water was being drawn out of the land to keep the fragile crops from burning. No known microwave technology exists that could be beamed and executed with such precision, forming beautiful patterns, while simultaneously drawing upon underground water as a coolant (CCC website.)[96]

---

[96] www.cropcircleconnector.com

Chapter 37

Proofs for Atheist of the existence of soul – the higher language of symbols

Often an atheist will asks for proof of existence of the soul; there are many such proofs available for those who seek them, such as having an out-of-body experience, meeting a reliable true psychic or drugs such as DMT will make you a believer in just a few minutes, but below is one method that I found quite fascinating and interesting when I first noticed it. All you need to do is to notice where your thoughts come from.

While Reading Seth[97]'s book "Seth Speaks[98]" I came across an interesting tidbit. Seth explains that our true native language is one of symbols and not words. That our soul uses symbols, and that it translates them to the words in the language that we use. This explains why one is able to communicate in astral with other beings that not necessarily speak our own language(s) or for that matter do not even have a body that is similar to ours, for example a tree has a soul, and often trees are able to communicate with a complex symbolic vocabulary that we can relate to. In other cases there are

---

[97] Seth was a spirit that channels via Jane Roberts the medium

[98] Seth Speaks – The Eternal Validity of the Soul 1972 ISBN 0-13-807222-1

species such as the Grays who have a limited symbolic language, which for example does not include feelings, therefore making communication with them much more difficult. This also applies to persons of our own species who have not made an effort to improve their vocabulary.

I have noticed that I use a symbolic language behind all my spoken words, including all those I use internally in my minds chattering process. Note: this happens so fast, that it is very difficult to notice, but occasionally with the less used and more complex thought, you may notice a delay while it is being translated from symbols to words, especially if you speak more than one language and you seek to find the words or phrases for your thoughts.

Symbols are the main method used in telepathy and not just plain simple spoken words. Even if you start with words, the words get translated into symbols for the actual transmission. You can think of telepathy as something similar to voice digital transmission through a wire, radio transmitter or fiber-optic cable, the voice is translated from audio into a digital stream of ones and zeros, which actually is a voltage being turned on and off, and travels at a rate many times faster than speech itself. In fact hours of voice communications can be transmitted in fractions of a second with modern fiber-optic technology. Just think about it; less than a hundred years ago if you would have said that all a person has ever spoken could be transmitted in less than a second from one side of the world to other side, they would have laughed at you, but now it is a well known scientific fact that audio and video can be transmitted much faster than it is created.

Spoken language is the process of training our internal soul translator. This is why you may notice in some children an unexplainable quick speed in learning complex terminology, it is because the concept was already known to their soul, and all they needed was to learn the translated word(s) into the language being used. It also explains why it is so difficult for others to learn certain concepts, it is not just the simply spoken word, but the concept behind it that it is not known by their soul, therefore it takes a lot more time for some peoples' souls to learn.

It also explains why Seth complained on several occasions that Jane Roberts was a poor medium for his more complex advanced knowledge he wanted to transmit, in fact he was once asked by Robert Butts Jane's husband why he did not transmit an ancient manuscript through Jane, to which he answered, that it would take Jane at least 5 years studying more vocabulary for her to be able to write the manuscript. In other words, Mediums translate the symbols into spoken words with their own vocabulary, and not the language of the spirit being channeled. This is why Seth often had to s p e l l out some words, because Jane was not familiar with that word and could not translate the symbol into a spoken word.

Bashar[99] has had the opposite problem; (since our human race has it's own uniqueness,) there have been words and phrases from us to Bashar that he (it) was unable to understand for a long time; since the Medium also acts as translator from the heard spoken words into symbols for the spirit worlds, in this case from the person asking the question – to the Medium – to Bashar in the spirit world.

---

[99] A spirit channeled

Since we are such a confused race, we have some very contradicting words and phrases, such as "Yea But." These words and phrases usually come from the more confused people that do not use the language property.

This also explains why one often has a complex thought and has a difficulty finding the words to express it; this happens quite often to the more intelligent souls of children, they even become quite frustrated at not being able to express their thought verbally in a quick efficient way, many times spoken just the looks and facial expression of a child says lots more than their spoken words.

The underling thoughts are there all the time in our subconscious soul, but one has to search for the words to translate them from the symbology used by the soul in order for someone else to understand them, regardless if it's being spoken, written or expressed via body language.

This is why some alien species have opted for telepathic communication and not spoken. In many cases it is not that they cannot speak, but that they find spoken words to be a very inefficient method of communication.

If we truly want to have more contact with advanced aliens, we need to learn how to communicate with the symbolic language better vs. just spoken words. Furthermore the language of symbols is much more compact and efficient method of communicating; it is a language that all species use and it is the language of our souls.

Chapter 38

Tips and tools for improving your life and health

I will give you below some more advice (tools) given by many masters such as Bashar, Seth, Sathia Sai Baba and others on how to live a better life and to evolve (advance) much quicker in addition to some ways to deal with your health.

A lot has been written about health, in fact perhaps a bit too much, but the one thing that only a few ever address is the fact of the mental state and the spiritual aspect as key roles to good health. Not that one should ignore all other great tools provided by modern science. What I am saying is that doctors and patients make a horrendous mistake by ignoring the other two components for health and speedy recovery. TRUE health is like a 3 legged stool, there is no such thing as a one or two legged stool, it must have a minimum of three, same goes with health, one is a medical professional as we know them, especially major kinds of accident, two what you eat and third but not least what you think, yes the spiritual aspect is the most important of them all. In time if you continue to study and practice you will come to understand/believe what will seem completely absurd this moment when I tell you that what you think is ALL that really matters when it comes to health, nothing is more important, absolutely nothing. If you follow this guide book enough you will learn that you can even cure yourself from a broken bone without the help of any doctor whatsoever, I know it is possible since I have done it, this is known to some as miracle, (since science has not labeled it yet) but I can assure that it is NO miracle, the power is ALL within you at this time, it has always been and it will always be. The problem is that you have no clue that you have such powers, and even as your learn that you do, it may (most likely it will) take you a long time to master them. At the same time I was able to cure in a most miraculous way a broken bone on my leg, I failed at curing myself of a common cold. Though this miracle did happen, I still got a long way to go to get to full control of all my body's functions. This is where the other leg comes in handy: the professional medical practitioner and the not so professional alternative medical health practitioners, some that are starting to get recognition such as chiropractors, reiki masters, acupuncturist and many others. Below I will give you pointers to alternative ways of curing yourself from just about any disease that are not very commonly heard of, even in the alternative health circles.

Always keep in mind that there are three (3) components to good health:

Spiritual – Mental – Physical

To have a healthy life you must attend to all of them. You need to make changes in all three aspects of your lifestyle and beliefe system, not just diet and an increase in exercise.

Do a little bit each day of what you really want to do, in other words what your true calling is; after some time you will notice that this is all that you do. It is simple, do what gives you most joy each day, soon you will find that all your activities become what you really like to do, in other words your true calling. Each and every one of us has something different and special, there are not two people alike, we all have a special skill that we came with. If only we allow this very special skill to flourish, we can easily find true happiness, health and wealth.

Do not get mad when something goes wrong, see it as an opportunity for something even better; as an opportunity to learn something new. Take it to the other extreme, give thanks for this new challenge to improve yourself. Keep in mind that ALL happens for our best. Suppose that you have worked very hard towards getting an x job, you prepared for it, you got your recommendation letters, you researched the company well, you know you got the knowledge and education to do it and you desperately want it and even more so, you desperately need it! And you know there are going to be others at the interview, that this job will be filled this day no matter what, but you know you got the best chance of getting it (Sounds familiar) now here is beliefe system one: You put your alarm early, you even meditate and recite all that is possible that you will be asked in the interview, you dress your best, you take all your notes and documentation, you even arrive early at the train station, just to find out that your watch was running low on batteries and that is was not the correct time and you see your train leaving. Now under believe systems one, you start cussing, you get very angry, your blood pressure goes way high, you can almost cry, you kick the floor, you just want to die, tied with all these emotions you run out of the station while you pull your tie off, open your shirt to air and just go home and have a completely miserable day, as you go home you ask yourself what have I done to deserve this??? Again and again. Here is beliefe system two, one that you have heard me say it many times in the story that all happens for the best. The big difference between me and most who have heard me say this story is that I DO believe it AND DO live by it. Back to beliefe system two, you say to yourself "a no big deal, it surely happened for a good reason, my higher self would have warned me, since I do pay attention to what it has to say (more on this below) " and you would have peacefully and calmly decided to take a nice walk home and enjoy the beautiful day vs. take the bus back, as you are leaving the station you feel the hand of someone tap you and as you turn around it is a fellow you once worked with years ago, and he says WOW what a surprise running into you, you are just the person I was thinking of for this job I have, please tell me that you are available; and it all clicks, you say to yourself WOW my higher self is really taking care of me and knows best, as you reach for your well put together documentation and handle it over to him, he takes a quick look at it and says, boy aren't you really dressed for a job interview, what you say we take the next train and go meet the client right now. Later on you find out that this job was many times better. This is how reprogramming of our core belief system works.

I share this with you, because I do believe it. It has taken me close to twenty years to understand this, more so to put it in practice. You and I probably had a conversation at some point about the word "faith" and my lack of understanding it, now I understand the context that religious people use it, and I also understand that they learn this in previous lives, not this one. This is why they used it and not me. For me it has been much harder, since I needed a more technical explanation on how it works; now I have it, now I start using it. There is not necessarily anyone out their looking out for us, though there can be, but our higher-self does this for us if we asked it and allow it to. Here is a personal example of how this works:

Recently the water pump for the house broke once more, needless to tell you this did NOT bother me in the least bit, since I have completely changed my belief systems so this thing automatically do not bother me at all. They simply cannot irritate me, make me mad, angry, depressed, nothing, cause I have a new belief system that I started putting in place the day I was told the story that all happens for the best. So I know the minute that the pump broke that it was for something good... So (as you well know my good technical skills) I completely evaluated what I needed and I headed to the hardware store to get it, (since I have been training myself to ask my higher-self to guide me) I reached over and got one part in my hands, as all the sudden I heard load in very clear "GET TWO" it was so clear that I answer back with my mind and said "NO" I only need one, and I bought it left, and did not think about it any more, until the next day when I started to install the new pump, well you guessed it, yes I needed two of the same part. This is how the miracle (not so miraculous once you understand how it works/ happens; this is how trusting your higher-self (faith) works. It works and it works ALL the time IF you asked it and allow it to. I failed with the part I needed for the pump on part two, which was listen; here is where free will comes in place, even though I had been asking my higher-self to communicate with me, I even argue with it and did not take heed on what it had just told me. It is really quite amazing how clear the communication can be if one allows it, note how clear it was, that I automatically argue with it, like if it had been someone next to me, some natural it all was that I did not take note of what had happen until the next day. Once you start talking to your higher-self, understanding that it exist, that you are not alone ever, and you start trusting it, you realize that then it is time to start rewriting (reprogramming) your belief system with a newer and much more rewarding and efficient one. This is why and how I no longer fear, cause I trust now that my higher-self knows what to do and when. Start by a simple meditation where you say to yourself, please talk to me, AND most important STOP all thoughts and

LISSEN... you may be surprised that it will talk to you loud and clear.

Eating tips

Replace all oils for only olive and/or coconut oil, books have been written on this subject, but you can save a lot of reading, simply by doing it! No if or buts, stop using all oils but olive oil and/or coconut oil.

Awareness of the importance of organic food that does NOT contain herbicides and pesticides. Needless to say one good source of organic food is from your local health food store, but this should not be your only source of healthy food. You should grow some with your own hands, even if it a very small amount.

Deep breathing

No matter what marvels technology may bring us, going back to nature is part of the true key to health and to feeling truly alive. Medical science may make seemingly amazing advances, but the best medicine will always be nature's own healing power. If you live away from nature, then find a way to get back to it, if it is not a permanent move, then make it a very often one. All it takes is the will and beliefe that you can do it. The how will come by itself in a magical way.

There is magic in all we do, most people simply do NOT know this. If you change your daily life from worrying about yourself, your problems and your health to DOING something about other peoples problems, a magical thing will happen after a short while: Your health WILL improve. This is one of the greatest secret mysteries of magic. Notice I did not say worry about other peoples problems/lives; I am specifically saying DO something to help someone else; this may be a child, an elder, your city or town, the environment, whatever you feel a calling to do. For example you may choose to donate some of your time to one of the thousand of foundations throughout the worlds that are working in an array of issues that need solving.

Dr. Andrew Weil has a wonderful book titled "Spontaneous Healing" that relates many experiences of people who managed to cure themselves from seemly impossible deadly diseases. In short Dr. Weil's message is: "If you have the will, you will find the cure, do NOT take NO for an answer."

- Do NOT read negative information about your disease.
- Do not associate yourself with others that are sick and do NOT have a desire to cure themselves.
- Do not talk to others about your sickness. If you do, tell them how much better you are getting, that you expect to be rid of it in a short time. There is magic in this.
- Look at your disease as a temporary problem. It is a problem of your body, NOT you.
- Do NOT watch the local news every day. Reduce your TV and newspaper news to a maximum of one hour per week. If something big happens that may be of interest to you, you will find out in time.
- Start living like a billionaire. That is right, a billionaire can only use one pillow at a time, buy the best one, you probably can afford it; same goes for many other things in your life, such as your bed, food you eat, books you read, etc.

If you have email, I highly recommend getting a few inspirational newsletters and your daily horoscope. Agora, Inc. is a great source of free and paid newsletters.

To start receiving your own copy of the HSI e-Alert, visit: http://www.hsiealert.com/freecopy.html Or forward this e-mail to a friend so they can sign-up to receive their own copy of the HSI e-Alert.

The science of being well is a must read FREE book found at: www.scienceofbeingwell.net

One of my favorite authors is Dr. Deepak Chopra. He has written many books on many medical and business subjects. The reason I mention him several times in this book, is because Dr. Chopra is also a traditional medical doctor with a traditional education. Dr. Chopra has had the vision of knowing how to combine both sciences, the traditional and the spiritual. Among his many books I highly recommend the following:

"Ageless Body, Timeless Mind," "The Quantum Alternative to Growing Old," and "The way of the Wizard." These books are guaranteed to improve your health in more than one way.

Classical music is often ignored by many people, since they have note developed a liking for it. If you are one of them, I highly recommend that you start listening to some. Classical music from the main famous authors has a healing property not known by most. Music has a vibration to it that is understood by the bodies' cells. One of the biggest discoveries being made in medical science is that specific sound affects the body's healing properties. Be in the lookout for these technologies. They do work. Here is a brief experience that I had:

In the early nineties I made friends with a fellow that seemed to me at first as a professional scam artist, he had this portable small piece of equipment that he wanted to reverse engineer. He told me that the inventor had died and had left him the only prototype and that the schematics had been lost, that it was a small scaled down model from a much larger and older machine, of which he showed me a picture, but I could not make out from the picture what it was. At first I ignored him, but he was quite persistent, and I had no choice that to listen to him since he shared a house with a good friend of mine that at the time I was visiting often. He was extremely possessive of this machine and would not let me take it to my lab, in fact I needed to take it to another friends lab and he refused to let me take it and I was not willing to take my lab and my friends lab to his home, so we were at a standstill. But I did take a look inside and it became obvious that it was some sort of a simply ultrasonic equipment, no more no less, except for the fact that it had some knobs to set a modulation to the ultrasonic and this was labeled clearly in the human audio frequencies. He kept on telling me of all the miraculous healing properties that it had, that it cured cancer, and all sorts of health problems, including joint pains. At the time I had a mild pain that had lasted over ten years on my lower back from a motorcycle accident, the type of pain you know you are going to live a lifetime with, never went away, I just mentally blocked, but I knew quite well it was there. So one day I say o what the hell, lets try this dumb thing, so I turned it on and placed the pad on my back, since I had no instructions of how it was supposed to work if it in fact did, I tried all the setting and ever combination I could dial up. To my surprise after about 5-10 minutes the pain started to go away and it has been gone till to date. As life has its turns, by the time I started to take this guy seriously, I became very busy in my work and one day I got the news that he had died from a massive unexpected heart attack. So I tried to get a hold of this equipment from his family, but all knew it had some value, even though they had no idea what to do with it, and I was not able to convince them to give it to me.

On another occasion while doing some consulting work, I met briefly an engineer that worked as a missile guidance radar designer for Scientific Atlanta, the last person on earth you would think was involved in weird science as I refer to it in those days. He mentioned that he was getting information from the Akashic Records on a audio device to trigger healing of any disease, he strongly believed that in the future all disease were going to be cured with this simple technology. Needless to say the subject was way too bizarre for my taste in conversation at the time, therefore I ignored it.

Aromatherapy

Historically aromatherapy has been used for thousands of years for healing and spiritual rituals. Aromatherapy and its various uses was a sacred practice in most traditional cultures including the Persian, Hebrew, Mayan, Greek, Egyptian and Chinese.

Today, aromatherapy is a very active movement in Europe, especially in France where it is now a recognized medicine reimbursed by medical insurance.

Plants from all over the world contain useful essential oils. These highly volatile oily substances to which the plant owes its perfume and flavor, are present between the cells and act as plant hormones, regulators, and catalysts. They may be considered as representing the vital elements or life force within the plant.

Extraction methods are of utmost importance with purity being imperative in order to obtain good therapeutic results.

Breathing in these essentials oils is what gets the required results.

Aromatherapy requires an extremely high quality of essential oils. Synthetic substances cannot replace the real product. There are hundreds of chemical components in essential oils. Most of them are in minute quantities, and yet it is the precise combinations and ratios of elements which render each oil powerful.

Because of that, solvents or preservatives are not used in the preparation of first-quality essential oils. A steam-distillation method of extraction is used instead. This process consists of sending steam throughout the plants, which evaporates oils.

The steam is then condensed and the oils separate from the water. This method yields high quality oil. The best oils come from wild organic plants.

The amount of oils found in each plant varies greatly and this is reflected in the price. [100]

---

[100] www.crystalinks.com

Ayurveda (which is pronounced Aa-yer-vay-da) means "knowledge of life". It is a holistic system of healing from ancient India; thought to be the oldest healing system on our planet, as old as 5000 years. Ayurveda is the knowledge of all aspects of life - mental, physical, emotional, and spiritual. It gives us the formulas for living long lives filled with joy. [101]

Ayurveda stresses the concept of balance in healing. One can learn to heal themselves or remain healthy by staying in balance.

Ayurveda said to be a world medicine, is the most holistic or comprehensive medical system available.

Five thousand years ago in the Himalayas, one of the greatest sages of India, Srila Vyasadeva wrote down the Vedas for the first time, this included a limb of which is called Ayurveda: "The science of Life" (Ayur means life and Veda means science). The Vedas came from an oral tradition that reached back into antiquity. Srila Vyasadev entrusted the original copies of the texts with his most erudite and enlightened disciples, who, along with other great sages, inaugurated a very long sacrificial ceremony for hundreds of years for the purification and blessings of the entire world. Remember people lived for one to two thousand years back then. During that time, they studied and discussed these ancient texts with their own disciples, who wrote commentaries, and expanded

---

[101] www.ayurvedaplus.com

and developed these original and eternal truths without ever altering them.

Ayurveda is a science that teaches how to live in a true and natural balance. This is not limited to the proper functioning of our mind, body and soul but extends further in establishing a natural and balanced relationship with the nature as a whole.

This includes a balanced relationship between us and all the creatures, our family members, our friends, our colleagues at the place of work and also the work, the climate and the society we live in, our ideas and customs, and finally with truth and God.

Ayurveda teaches how to maintain this balance. As long as we can maintain this balance we are healthy and when there is imbalance there is disease, unhappiness and misery.

Ayurveda is considered by many scholars to be the oldest healing science. It is a Sanskrit word which means "The Science of Life." Ayurvedic knowledge originated in India more than 5,000 years ago and is often called the "Mother of All Healing". It stems from the ancient Vedic culture and was taught for many thousands of years in an oral tradition from accomplished masters to their disciples. Some of this knowledge was set to print a few thousand years ago, but much of it is inaccessible.

The principles of many, if not all, natural healing systems now familiar in the West, such as Homeopathy and Polarity Therapy, have their roots in Ayurveda.

Ayurveda places great emphasis on prevention and encourages maintaining health by paying close attention to balance in one's life through right thinking, diet, lifestyle and herbs. Knowledge of Ayurveda enables one to understand how to create balance of body, mind and consciousness according to one's own individual constitution and how to make lifestyle changes to bring about and maintain this balance.

Just as everyone has an individual face or thumb print, according to Ayurveda, each person has a particular pattern of energy--an individual combination of physical, mental and emotional characteristics--which is his or her constitution. This constitution is determined at conception by a number of factors and is the same throughout one's life.

Many factors, both internal and external, act upon us to disturb this balance and are reflected as a change in one's constitution from the balanced state. Examples of some of these emotional and physical stresses are: one's emotional state, diet and food choices, seasons and weather, physical trauma, work and family relationships.

Once these factors that can cause imbalance are understood, one can take appropriate actions to nullify or minimize their effects or eliminate the causes, and re-establish one's original constitution.

Balance is the natural order; imbalance is disorder. Health is order; disease is disorder. Within the body there is a constant interaction between order and disorder. Once one understands the nature and structure of disorder, one can re-establish order.

Ayurveda identifies three basic types of energy or functional principles that are present in everybody and everything.

There are no single words in English to describe these principles, so we use the original Sanskrit words Vata, Pitta and Kapha. Energy is required to create movement so that fluids and nutrients get to the cells, enabling the body to function.

Energy is also required to metabolize the nutrients in the cells, and is called for to lubricate and maintain cellular structure.

Vata is the energy of movement, Pitta the energy of digestion or metabolism and Kapha the energy of lubrication and structure.

All people have vata, pitta and kapha, but one is usually primary, one secondary and the third least prominent.

The cause of disease in Ayurveda is viewed as the lack of proper cellular function because of an excess or deficiency of vata, pitta or kapha and/or the presence of toxins. In Ayurveda, body, mind and consciousness work together in maintaining balance. They are simply viewed as different facets of one's being.

To learn how to balance the body, mind and consciousness then requires an understanding how vata, pitta and kapha work together.

According to Ayurvedic philosophy the entire cosmos is an interplay of the energies of the five great elements--Space, Air, Fire, Water and Earth. Vata, pitta and kapha are combinations and permutations of these five elements that manifest as patterns present in all creation. [102]

The Zapper. [103] The first inexpensive, effective electro medicine to destroy parasites (worms, bacteria, viruses, fungi, etc.) throughout the body. All parasites and diseased tissues are positively charged. The zapper introduces negative ions through the skin and into the body's living tissue, killing the parasites by reversing their polarity and also helping to heal the diseased tissue. Healthy tissue is negatively charged.

Hypnotherapy. Hypnotherapy is the use of hypnosis in a therapeutic context. Hypnotherapy goes past the conscious mind and taps into the emotional body - the inner child - the place in which we store issues that we have to deal with, but are not ready. To heal physically, one must heal the emotional aspect of the issue first or it will resurface in another way. Please remember that not everyone is a candidate for hypnotherapy. There is usually a goal for each patient such as overcoming the fear of something. In some cases the therapy is successful. Post hypnotic suggestions given create a desire to satisfy the suggested behavior. The person feels like doing what the hypnotist suggests, provided that what is suggested does not generate conflict with their belief systems.

---

[102] www.crystalinks.com/ayurveda.html

[103] www.worldwithoutparasites.org

When doing hypnosis it is necessary to use the brain's natural ability to produce a deeply relaxed state. Hypnosis occurs primarily in the alpha and theta states, but can occur during any of the brain wave patterns.

> Beta - the fastest of the brain waves. It is the waking state
>
> Alpha - the restful state with a sense of relaxation. Hypnosis induces this state.
>
> Theta - this is a deep state of relaxation. Deep hypnosis occurs at this state.
>
> Delta - this is the sleeping state. It is a deeper state of mental relaxation than meditation in which the person is aware of their surroundings.

Hypnotherapy can be used to explore past/parallel lives, during which time blockages created in other lifetimes can be viewed and released. As a certified hypnotherapist I have used this technique to help patients release phobias and blockages on all levels - physical - mental - and emotional.

Desired changes may include:

- Weight Management
- Treating Anxiety and Panic Disorders
- Overcoming Phobic Disorders
- Stop Smoking
- Improvement of Self-Esteem
- Pain Management after diagnosis from a physician Improved Concentration

- Reliving something from the patient's past that blocks them from moving on [104]

---

[104] www.crystalinks.com/hypnotherapy.html

This material has created such a stir that the United States Government has entered into the affair, due to so-called national security interests, and the "US Patent and Trademark Office" recently denied approval for various patents pending concerning the manufacture of ORMUS. The reason for this is astounding when viewed from a scientific standpoint. ORMUS, it appears, is a superconductor that operates (unlike other superconductors) at room temperature. ORMUS has the potential to completely revolutionize the energy industries and may prove to be the actual warp-drive (Star Gate) factor featured in so many episodes of Star Trek and Star Wars movies and other science fiction stories. *The Myth, Magic & Murder of ORMUS, By Elder H. Alfred Goolsbee*

Chapter 39

ORMUS/ORMES/m-state[105]

THERE IS NO MEDICAL ADVICE HERE!

The information you will find here is for information and research purposes only. Self-help requires intelligence, common sense, and the ability to take responsibility for your own actions. By reading this chapter you agree to hold yourself FULLY responsible FOR yourself.

I will start this chapter from a quote by Barry Carter, "I predict that the study of the ORMUS elements will change what we know in every scientific field including meteorology, astrophysics, quantum physics, chemistry, medicine, psychology, parapsychology, geology and all aspects of technology. If only 10% of what we have

---

[105] **ORMUS** is an *exotic* form of elemental matter. It is believed that the various unusual properties of ORMUS make it difficult to detect using standard analysis methods. Some of these ORMUS (or m-state) elements have superconductive properties and are capable of "tunneling". (Such as seeping through the bottom of glass containers.) The (so far) known various ORMUS elements are: cobalt, nickel, copper, ruthenium, rhodium, palladium, silver, osmium, iridium, platinum, gold and mercury. Many of these elements can be very biologically toxic in their various standard forms but have proven to have a wide array of uses and benefits in their m-state forms, according to the overwhelming majority of reports. www.ormusvortex.info

observed about ORMUS proves out, ORMUS will be the greatest scientific discovery in human history."

And a quote from David Hudson in this specific regard, he stated: "I'm not a doctor, so I can't practice medicine. Anything that is administered to someone for the purpose of curing a disease is medicine ... My purpose in this was not to cure diseases and illness, but I did want to know: Does it work? ... I can tell you, it's been used on Lou Gehrig's disease; it's been used on MS; it's been used on MD; it's been used on arthritis ... I can tell you that at 2 mg. a day it totally has gotten rid of Karposi Sarcomas (KS) on AIDS patients (there's 32,000mg. in an ounce, 2mg. is nothing). And it gets rid of KS. I can tell you that for people who have taken it at 2mg. injections, within 2 hours their white blood cell count goes from 2,500 to 6,500. I can tell you that Stage-4 cancer patients have taken it orally, and after 45 days have no cancer any place in their body."

And yet one more quote from www.ormusvortex.info What is ORMUS good for? This is no small question! ORMUS has many useful properties. It has applications in science, energy, transport, agriculture, health, healing, anti-aging and spirituality, just for starters. Many open minded people are beginning to investigate the many possibilities in these exciting areas of research. There are many different personal reports of a wide variety of health benefits, as well as many reports of psychic or spiritual enhancements. There is much evidence that plants grown in soil amended with forms of ORMUS have reduced disease, accelerated maturation and greatly increased production. Applications in science will be very exciting considering the superconductive properties of certain ORMUS elements. It is believed that fields such as communication, computing, transportation will be revolutionized and that green, renewable energy production could be vital in solving many serious ecological issues. Spiritual and/or psychic benefits could also possibly have a dramatic positive impact on humankind in general if benefits such as increased empathy and sensitivity could be realized! These are only some of the possibilities of these materials.

The texts of the Old Kingdom gave the Philosophers' Stone many names. It was called the golden tear from the eye of Horus, that which issues from the mouth of the Creator (the Christian Word), and the spittle or the semen of the Father in Heaven. With the rise of the Heliopolian Amun, it later became the hidden Light: the unknowable name of the God whose title was Amun and whose symbol was the ram. The modern name is ORMUS,[106] ORME and White-Gold, it has also been known as an elixir,[107] Manna, Shewbread, the snot, monoatomic elements, AuM, the polymers, m-state, shemana, microclusters, superdeformed high-spin elements, exotic atoms, Semen of the Gods, Schefa Food, Shem-an-na,

---

[106] ORMUS.- Orbitally Rearranged Mono-atomic Elements. ORMEs are virtually undetectable by conventional means because they lack a d-orbital electron. However, they do show a distinguishing infrared doublet located between 1400 and 1600 cm-1.

[107] Elixir.- The Elixir of the alchemists is essentially a liquid version of the Philosopher's Stone and has the same ability to perfect any substance. When applied to the human body, the Elixir cures diseases and restores youth.

Bread of the Presence of God, MFKZT, Elixer of Life, the lapis, the Sophic Hydrolith of the Wise, Erinaes Philothes Philolithes, What then is it?", dew, occult gold, hrysopoeia, aurum potable, water of gold, WhiteGold, The Philosophers' Stone[108] and many more name are all part of alchemy[109] an ancient chemistry science now being studied. This and various other names have been used by Alchemists and by high priests of ancient civilizations for that which

---

[108] The Philosophers' Stone.- Was sought as a wonderful medicine that had the power to repair the human body and thereby increase life almost indefinitely. The Bible itself declared the Melchizedek the King of Salem, who first possessed the Philosophers' Stone, would live forever... The Philosopher's Stone was an alchemical "medicine" sought by alchemists in order to bring about a permanent transmutation of base metals into gold. The Philosopher's Stone had several names, including the "materia prima" and the "magnum opus" . Many "recipes" for the Philosopher's Stone were concocted throughout the centuries, usually either containing a silver or gold alloy which could be changed again into the pure metal, making alchemists believe that the metal had been transformed, or a "white or yellow metallic alloy superficially resembling silver or gold". Only a small quantity of the Philosopher's Stone was said to be required in order to transform large quantities of base metals into gold.

[109] Alchemy.- The word is derived from the Arabian phrase "al-kimia," which refers to the preparation of the Stone or Elixir by the Egyptians. The Arabic root "kimia" comes from the Coptic "khem" that alluded to the fertile black soil of the Nile delta. Esoterically and hieroglyphically, the word refers to the dark mystery of the primordial or First Matter (the Khem), the One Thing through which all creation manifests. Alchemy, then, is the Great Work of nature that perfects this chaotic matter, whether it be expressed as the metals, the cosmos, or the substance of our souls.

feeds the Light Body. NOTE: There is still more to it than what is describe above; Alchemist describe other formulas that go together with the above mentioned new discoveries; hint: oil of wine, do your homework...

Dr. Immanuel Velikovsky in his book "Worlds in Collision," where he explains what happen last time Planet X passed near earth. This by the way is predicted by many will happen again between 2009-2015, says the following: The tail of a comet is composed of carbon and hydrogen gases, and these elements were in suspension in the earth's atmosphere after the comet departed. The Hindu Vedas, the Egyptian papyri, and the Hebrew legends say that the wind smelled sweet, and eventually the carbohydrates combining in the air precipitated. mankind fed on morning dew, say the Icelandic traditions, and the Vedas tell of the honey-lash falling - as the Greeks say ambrosia all fell - from the clouds. Where the honey-frost fell on the waters, it turned them milky and sweet. Ovid, the Vedas, and the Egyptians say the rivers flowed with milk and honey. The precipitate also fell among the Israelites, they called it Manna.

More than a decade ago, David Hudson, a farmer in Phoenix Arizona, stumbled upon the fabulous Philosophers' Stone while trying to mine and refine gold on his farm. He realized with some excitement that he had discovered a repeatable formula. Even better, his formula could be scaled-up from a laboratory to a chemical plant. This was something that had eluded alchemists for at least three thousand years. Hudson's discovery is now a controversial subject at the forefront of pharmaceutical and industrial technologies based on high spin state mono-atomic or single atom elements of iridium, rhodium and gold. He has developed high spin mono-atomic states for many of the transition elements including gold. David Hudson believes that White-gold is unique among the monatomic elements because it is able to correct DNA deficiencies by a denaturing process. He hypothesizes that eating larger doses of monatomic elements may decelerate the aging process and perhaps even reverse it. White-gold would relax the damaged DNA and allow it to correct and recombine.

In March of 1988, David Hudson filed U.S. and worldwide patents on eleven orbitally rearranged monatomic elements, ORMES, which he discovered in a form not previously recognized. This is a totally new form of matter, the confirmation of which will be presented by Mr. Hudson with scientific references and data compiled by some of the most acclaimed research laboratories in the world.

David Hudson is a fourth generation Arizona farmer who became interested in extracting gold and silver from the tailings of old mining sites near his 675 acre farm. When he began the recovery process he soon discovered that gold and silver were being lost because of the buildup of a powdery substance referred to as "ghost gold" by many miners and metallurgists. Hudson's curiosity led him to work with spectroscopist's at Cornell University and other labs to discover the elemental ingredients of this powder. Initial findings of the sample yielded iron, silica, and aluminum. Further extraction of these elements left 98% of the powder intact. The surprise was that this 98% consisted of nothing which could be identified through normal spectroscopic analysis.

Hudson knew that this "nothing" could be seen, felt, tasted and weighed. It had to be SOMETHING and he was determined to find out what IT was. In the course of his research he found a paper from the Soviet Academy of Sciences stating that proper spectroscopic analysis requires a 300 second burn instead of the 15 second burn used in the United States. Utilizing the Soviet technique of fractional vaporization, Hudson discovered that his sample contained the elements palladium, platinum, ruthenium, rhodium, iridium and osmium.

Even more astounding was his discovery that each of the nonmetallic elemental forms was a superconductor, a substance which allows an electric current to flow without resistance even in the absence of a continually applied potential. Hudson continued his research and found four papers by the U.S.

Naval Research Facility showing that cells of living tissues communicate with each other by a process identical to superconductivity, but the nature of the superconducting substance was unknown. On a hunch, Hudson analyzed the brain tissue of pigs and cattle and found the brain dry matter weight was 5% rhodium and irridium!

As a result of Hudson's research, he knew that the electrons flowing through a superconductor pair off and are converted to a light frequency in the process. He theorized that this might be the same process occuring in human cells. Hudson discovered papers published by Bristol-Myers-Squibb Laboratories and others which indicated intense experimentation was being done utilizing precious elements in the treatment of cancer. These elements were shown to interact with the cell by a vibrational frequency or by light transfer to correct the mutant DNA. When Hudson applied his proprietary method of analysis to Essiac Tea (an alternative treatment for cancer), he discovered high levels of rhodium and irridium. He also found that Acemannan, a derivative of the aloe Vera plant currently being tested on AIDS patients, is 90% rhodium!

David Hudson's life took an abrupt turn in 1990 when his uncle brought him a Time-Life book, "Secrets of the Alchemists." The goal of the alchemists was to make a white powder of gold that would serve as the container of the "light of life". This search for the white powders has been termed the search for the philosopher's stone. Encyclopedia Britannica says: "The stone, also referred to as the 'tincture' or 'powder'... was allied to an elixir of life... Inasmuch as alchemy was concerned not only with the search for a method of upgrading less valuable metals, but also of perfecting the human soul, the philosopher's stone was thought to cure illness, prolong life, and bring about spiritual revitalization."

A new line of thought consumed David Hudson. He read over 500 books on alchemy and its history. He reread the Bible, finding many references to the white powder. He talked to Rabbis well versed in the ancient secrets of Judaism, who told him of white powders available only to the priests of Solomon's Temple. This is referred to as "mana", food of the gods. Hudson's research has led him to believe that ingesting the manna enabled the priests to approach the Ark of the Covenant without being killed.

In his lecture, Hudson will give fascinating details about the Ark and a scientific explanation behind manna's protection. He also will discuss where the priests obtained their formula for making the white powders and how this formula was lost after the Temple was destroyed. He will explain his theories about the Essenes and why he thinks Mary was given the white powders of gold in preparation for the conception and birth of Jesus. Nostradamus predicted that by 1999 "occult gold" would be known to science. Other prophecies indicate the discovery of this "occult gold" would be made by a direct descendant of the Davidic blood line. According to the book, "Holy Blood, Holy Grail", the Davidic blood line is continued today in the French de Guise family name. Long after his research into the white powders began, David Hudson discovered that he was a direct descendant of this French family.

Could David Hudson be the one chosen to fulfill these ancient prophecies? [110] Perhaps he has already done so. David Hudson retired from the ORMES/m-state business years ago, but his legend is still told as the modern founder.

So what can ORMUS/ORMES/m-state do for you? Here is a short list: perfect telepathy, the ability to know good and evil when it's present, and to project thoughts into another person's mind. There is also the ability to levitate, or to walk on water. By excluding all external magnetic fields (including the Earth's gravity), the white powder of gold takes one beyond the four dimensional space time continuum, and the individual becomes a fifth dimensional being. They can literally think where they would like to be, and go there. They can heal by the laying on of hands, and can cleanse and resurrect the dead within two or three days after they died. They have so much energy that they can literally embrace people and bring light and energy back into them. But there is a catch to the above statements. ORMUS is only part of the equation to be able to do all these things and gain all these benefits. You will also have to advance/ascend quite bit as an individual spiritual being that you

---

[110] A special thanks to Dan Haley, Jerry Decker Cheyenne Turner for background information used in this chapter.

are. You will also have to research several other secrets well guarded by the alchemist throughout history and till to date. Here goes the saying "The master will appear when the student is ready." I can say that this has been my case many times. When I thought I was running out of information, by pure magic someone came into my life and handled me a bunch more books.

In Revelations, it says, "Blessed be the man who shall overcome, for he shall be given the hidden manna, the white stone of the purest kind upon which will be written a new name." He will not be the same person. [Obviously!]

Before obtaining the privilege White-gold may bring, it is well to remember the Rabbis' warning that the powder can be used for good or evil and it is incumbent upon all to learn to control our own dark side before partaking:[111] Here is a key. Perhaps you will use it to open a new door. Beware! Once through the door you will find the pursuit of Wisdom demands either your fulltime attention or none at all. If you become a philosopher, your friends may think you have become a little mad. Indeed, what would be made of you? Glassyeyed, preoccupied, strange friends, muttering about ancient

---

[111] 27 Schwaller De Lubicz, p197

history, the Good and the Righteous, and chemistry. Things most people simply don't think about. THE ALCHEMY KEY[112]

ORMES is obtained from the Precious Metals (Rhodium (Rh), Silver (Ag), Iridium (Ir), and Gold (Au). The other four Precious Metals (Ruthenium, Palladium, Osmium, and Platinum.) Superdeformation of Nuclei[113] of these precious elements, results in a monoatomic, superconducting, high spin, low energy state, wherein -- in accordance with ORME Physics[114] and ORME Biology[115] -- the extraordinary characteristics of the white powder of gold can be manifested.

I also want you to note that this substance ALSO has MANY industrial process applications, such as levitation of objects and the production of very low cost energy also known as free energy. Keep an eye open in the years to come for these rediscovered technologies. All this is part of new modern science know as "quantum physics" which will eventually be accepted as part of our

---

[112] THE ALCHEMY KEY Unraveling the Single Tangible Secret in all Mysteries by STUART NETTLETON I S B N: 0 - 6 4 6 - 3 4 0 2 2 – 0 a FREE 559 page book that you can download from http://members.optusnet.com.au/skyecn

[113] www.halexandria.org/dward164.htm

[114] www.halexandria.org/dward471.htm

[115] www.halexandria.org/dward476.htm

modern chemistry methodology. These puzzle pieces are being described using modern observational tools like electron microscopes, analytical chemistry and spectrographic analysis but they are also being described using yogic or psychic vision and ancient historic records.

What we can see of the finished picture at this point--looks like it could connect science and spirit. Some of the pieces of this puzzle come from scientific observation; some come from Judeo-Christian, Hindu or Chinese scriptures. Some come from theoretical quantum physicists and others come from practical alchemists. [116]

"Given the facilities of today's scientific advancement and our knowledge of atoms and nuclei, is it possible (as it was in the distant past) to convert gold [and other precious metals] into a sweet-tasting, ingestible white powder? Is it possible for that powder to outweigh its optimum weight of gold? Is it also possible for that same powder to under-weigh itself and to weigh less than nothing? Under such circumstances, is it possible that the powder can disappear from sight into another dimension of space-time and then be returned to its original state? The answer to each of these questions is YES -- for this is the post-Star Fire mystery of the phoenix, and it is the key to the Messianic bloodline enhancement through the fire-stone." Laurence Gardner

---

[116] The Matrix of Consciousness, by Barry Carter

The May 1995 issue of Scientific American discussed the effects of ruthenium (one of the precious metals), by noting that a single ruthenium atom placed at each end of the double-helix DNA increases the conductivity of the strand by a factor of 10,000, causing the DNA to become, in effect, a "superconductor". Based on a synthesis of additional historical, philosophical, mythological, and scientific evidence, David Hudson has determined that the ORME is truly the "Tree of Life". Hudson has noted in the _Scientific Literature_ (http://www.halexandria.org/dward477.htm) (Guidice, et al), the basis for human cells being able to exhibit Superconductivity_ (http://www.halexandria.org/dward156.htm) and the extensive amount of research being conducted on treating cancer and other diseases with precious metals. These precious elements appear to be correcting the DNA, literally "flowing the light of life" within the body.

The Platinum Metals Review includes articles which discuss the treatment of cancers using platinum, iridium and ruthenium. Apparently, the application of a platinum compound to an altered DNA state (as in the case of a cancer) will cause the DNA to relax and become corrected. It is known that both iridium and rhodium have anti-aging properties, that ruthenium and platinum compounds interact with DNA, and that gold and the precious metals can activate the endocrinal glandular system in a way that heightens awareness and aptitude to extraordinary levels.

Here is a short list of websites to get started on the subject of ORMUS:

www.subtleenergies.com/ormus/tw/toc.htm

www.subtleenergies.com/ormus/manual.htm

www.pleiadian.org/products/

www.pleiadian.org/alchemy

http://whitegold.twentythree.us

ORMUS/ORMES discussion forums

The oldest ORMUS forum is called the WhiteGold Forum. The WhiteGold Forum is a moderated email list. This means that the moderator of the list reviews every post you send to the list before it gets sent on to the whole list. WhiteGold List: http://zz.com/WhiteGoldWeb

Since its inception in February of 1996 it has been the policy of the WhiteGold Forum to keep the names and contact information of its subscribers as private as those subscribers wish to be. We determine whether a person wishes to make this kind of information available to the entire list by whether or not they include this kind of information in the body of their post or in their signature lines. If you include only your first name at the bottom of your post that is all that will be included in the "From:" line in the header.

The WhiteGold List is for the sharing of personal experiences with the ORMUS substances. There is some scientific discussion but we discourage religious and political discussion because of the great diversity of people who are interested in ORMUS. The WhiteGold List averages about 25 messages per day. To join the WhiteGold list send a message to WhiteGold-request@zz.com with the subject Subscribe. The WhiteGold list is a very active list. Folks on the list are generally quite willing to answer questions so you may generate some interesting responses by posting your questions to this list.

The largest ORMUS forum list is:

http://groups.yahoo.com/group/ORMUS forum. This forum has over a thousand members and is quite active with over thirty messages per day. This forum is also for primarily for sharing of personal experiences with the ORMUS substances. There is some scientific discussion but here again we discourage religious and political discussion because of the great diversity of people who are interested in ORMUS. Membership on this forum is by request. It is not moderated or anonymous.

The ORMUS http://groups.yahoo.com/group/ORMUSandSpirit forum was created as a place where people can freely discuss religious and spiritual issues. Anyone can join this list and it is not moderated or anonymous. This forum averages a few message per day.

The ORMUS Politics

http://groups.yahoo.com/group/ORMUS_Politics list was created for ORMUS related political discussion. Membership on this forum is by request. It is not moderated or anonymous. This forum averages about one message a month.

The ORMUS Scientific Workgroup

http://groups.yahoo.com/group/ORMUS_SWG email forum was created for scientific discussion of ORMUS related things.

Membership on this forum is by request. It is not moderated or anonymous. This forum averages about 7 messages per day.

http://groups.yahoo.com/group/ORMES This is one of the most recent forums; it was created by a true scientist, one that seeks to use proper scientific definitions methods. There has been an ongoing very long discussion regarding proper scientific definitions, but there has not been an agreement on how to properly define these newly discovered substances; even though they all seem to behave in similar ways, it does not mean they are the same thing. Note that there are many formulas, all leading to a somewhat similar product, but not necessarily the same. Some start with sea water, others with salt, others with rocks from various sources, and many with pure precious metals. Later some have other procedures done to it, like charging, which yet produces another variation that may need is own classification. Overall this is all a newly rediscovered sciences that is in its infancy stage.

In addition to these forums there are dozens of local area ORMUS email lists. These local ORMUS lists were created so that people can meet in person to work together on ORMUS related stuff. I also post information about upcoming ORMUS related meetings and lectures when they are to occur in a local area. For a list of all forums go here:

www.subtleenergies.com/ormus/tw/forums.htm

ORMUS Book list

Robert Cox, Stuart Nettleton and Laurence Gardner. These three gentlemen have written fine books with the ORMUS materials as a main subject. Rob's book The Pillar of Celestial Fire discusses these materials primarily from the Hindu and Egyptian historical perspectives. Stuart's book The Alchemy Key[117] discusses these materials primarily from the Middle Eastern and Masonic historical perspectives. And Laurence Gardner's books Genesis of the Grail Kings and Lost Secrets of the Sacred Ark[118] discuss these materials from the perspective of the Sumerian, Egyptian and Hebrew traditions.

Here are some quotes from Laurence Gardner[119]: "So, given the facilities of today's scientific advancement and our knowledge of atoms and nuclei, is it possible (as it was in the distant past) to convert gold into a sweet-tasting, ingestible white powder? Is it possible for that powder to outweigh its optimum weight of gold? Is it also possible for that same powder to underweight itself and to weigh less than nothing? Under such circumstances, is it possible that the powder can disappear from sight into another dimension of space-time and then be returned to its original state? The answers to each of these questions is 'yes' — for this is the post-Star Fire mystery of the Phoenix, and it is the key to the Messianic bloodline enhancement through the fire-stone. As to why the fire-stone was called 'highward' by the ancient Mesopotamians, we shall now

---

[117] The Alchemy Key can be downloaded for free at:

http://members.optusnet.com.au/skyecn/

[118] Lost Secrets of the Sacred Ark: http://www.Graal.co.uk/lostsecrets.html

[119] Laurence Gardner official website: www.graal.co.uk

discover as we enter the realm of highspin metallurgy. (Then he goes on to discuss David Hudson)"

The 17th-century philosopher, Eirenaeus Philalethes (revered by Isaac Newton, Robert Boyle, Elias Ashmole and other Royal Society colleagues of his era), produced a work in 1667 entitled 'Secrets Revealed'. In this treatise he discussed the nature of the Philosophers' Stone, which was commonly thought to transmute base metal into gold.

Setting the record straight, Philalethes made the point that the Stone was itself made from gold, and that the philosopher's art was in perfecting this process. He stated: "Our Stone is nothing but gold digested to the highest degree of purity and subtle fixation. It is called a stone by virtue of its fixed nature; it resists the action of fire as successfully as any stone. In species it is gold, more pure than the purest; it is fixed and incombustible like a stone, but its appearance is that of a very fine powder".

Some time earlier, in 1416, the noted French chemist Nicolas Flamel wrote that when the noble metal was perfectly prepared, it made a fine 'powder of gold', which is the Philosophers' Stone.

Barry Carter's books titled "The Matrix of Consciousness" and the "The Matrix of Reality" neither of these books is available yet.

ORMUS Vendors

Today, there are a number of companies manufacturing products said to contain ORMUS/ORMES//M-state substances. Some are working from a pure gold base, while others are using platinum group trace elements from sea sediments and volcanic or meteoric earth sources, others use new energy devices that are yet to be classified by proper science methodology. The extent to which these products might individually approach the fully charged superconductive state, however, is unknown at this time since the enigmatic powders do not react to conventional analysis as do the metallic elements from which they derive. In other words, NO one is providing clear definition on what these new products really are. Note that ORMES is a well defined substance that to the best of my knowledge no one is selling at this time.

In respect of these products, I am not making specific recommendations as such, nor am I suggesting any particular product for any specific purpose - but I cite below some of the 30+ companies selling ORMUS/m-state products. Please note that since at the time of writing this book there are NO proper scientific definitions, the names ORMUS, ORMES, M-state are used by vendors without a clear definition of what they mean by them. Almost all reports have been positive from all these vendors. I myself have consumed several of them and only have good things to say, but this by no means says that the vendors have any clear scientific definitions, nor are really sure of what is it that they are selling. Many hold their formula secret, therefore no one really knows what is it...

Ambrosia Technology for highly perfected m-state products from deep sea water and selected organic sources www.liquid-chi.com This Company uses a structured course level approach for its product range.

Ascension Alchemy formulates ORMUS powder and sublingual products from pure gold www.asc-alchemy.com Also m-state products from the Great Salt Lake, the Dead Sea and plants. I highly recommend this company for those seeking spiritual advancement.

White Powder Gold made from 24k gold, and held in a liquid suspension for precisely measured dosage. This site incorporates numerous links and helpful background information. www.whitepowdergold.com

Priestess Alchemy for superior Quintessential Elixirs, formulated to bring ancient science into the new millennium. Uniquely devised skin care and cosmetic products also available. I highly recommend their skin care products. www.priestessalchemy.com

Pureganic Mineral Company for frequency charged PureGold suspension and regenerative Liquid Manna. Also m-state mineral powder for plant growth and soil enhancement. www.Pureganic.com

Harmonic Innerprizes energy medicines. Naturally occurring monatomic minerals from volcanic seabed Including Etherium Gold, Chamae Rose and others. www.harmonicinnerprizes.com

Energetic Nutrition are suppliers of Etherium Gold and energy field formulations. Some useful information regarding biofeedback and EEG reports. www.energeticnutrition.com/hi/gold.html

ZeroPoint Technologies for optimized super health and energy products from gold, silver and platinum groups http://zptech.net/ High energy range also features the revolutionary mineral, indium.

Monét Cosmetics synergistic anti-aging cream. A unique formulation of natural ingredients for all skin types. With m-state elements and electrically charged water soluble minerals. www.monetcosmetics.co.uk

Resonance Health are UK supplies of Etherium Gold and other energy field formulations. Range includes Star Stuff with bee pollen and m-state elements. www.resonance-health.biz

Life Enthusiast Co-op for Tamahi Minerals with magma water, m-state and nano elements. Also featured is Golden Life-Force Ambrosia. www.life-enthusiast.com

Nu Tech Energies has been highly praised in the forums, yet same as the rest their definition is not based on standard scientific methodology, therefore no one really knows what it is or what it should be scientifically called. www.nutechenergies.com

For an updated list of vendors go to:

www.subtleenergies.com/ormus/tw/sources.htm

Chapter 40

ORGONE

Orgone energy was originally observed by Wilhelm Reich, MD, a psychoanalyst in the late 1920s, as a bio-electrical charge whose flow within the body could be visibly seen as waves passing through his clinical patients as they were experiencing intense emotional breakthroughs. (1) Later, in the 1930s, to confirm his visual observations, Reich was able to objectively measure the movements of this energy by using a very sensitive millivolt meter with sensors attached to the body to record subtle bio-electric charge. He found the energy flowed from the inside body core to the outside surface (towards the world) when a person felt pleasure or expansion; and conversely, it flowed from the surface to the interior (away from the world) during states of anxiety, fear, and contraction. (2)

Reich also noted that the conditions of expansion and contraction affected a person, not only emotionally, but down to the autonomic nervous system, to the cellular, and even chemical levels. (3) States of expansion produce parasympathetic conditions associated with dilation of the blood vessels and increased circulation, pain relief, better digestion and peristalsis, lower blood pressure; and the stimulation of potassium and lecithin production; along with creating a sense of well-being, and sexual excitement. States of contraction, however, produce sympathetic effects: constricted blood vessels, less blood flow, and often pain. In addition, the contracted condition increases blood pressure and heart beat rate, adrenaline flow and cholesterol; it inhibits digestion and blood supply to the genitals and is associated with the emotions of anxiety and "stress".

The ability of the body to expand and contract and not become "stuck" in one mode, created what Reich called the pulsation of life which distinguished the living from the non-living. This pulsation of expansion and contraction also followed a specific four-beat rhythm: Tension - Charge - Discharge – Relaxation Reich observed this energy pattern within the organs of the body: from the beat of the heart, to peristaltic movements of the intestine, the bladder, and especially obvious in the sexual function of orgastic discharge. He called this pulsating pattern the function of the orgasm or the Life Formula. www.orgonics.com

Dr. Wilhelm Reich who lived in Austria, Germany, Denmark, Sweden, Norway, New York, and finally Rangeley, Maine from 1944-1957 until his death. Orgonomy covers many topics but begins with the theories of neurosis in humans as they are related to the natural flow of life energy being blocked in the body by traumatic experiences in life. Many also caused sexual impotency. Dr. Reich worked closely with Sigmund Freud during this work and the results are written in his books "The Function of the Orgasm - 1927" and "Character Analysis - 1933". Vegetative-therapy (Reichian therapy) was developed and created by Dr. Reich in the 1920's to 1930's and it is used in part by many of the current therapies practiced today such as gestalt therapy, bioenergetics, rolfing therapy, and primal scream therapy to name a few. His study of neurosis was applied to the masses in his work "The Mass Psychology of Fascism - 1933", "People in Trouble - 1936" and also in his books titled "The Invasion of Compulsory Sex-Morality - 1931", "The Sexual Revolution- 1935", "The Murder of Christ - 1951" and "Listen Little Man -1948". His work continued in the area of "The Bion Experiments" -- creation of life from inorganic matter. "His work continued with further studies into orgone energy (also known as chi, prana, and other eastern names). Wilhelm Reich performed several scientific experiments that objectified the presence of orgone energy - "The Cancer Biopathy - 1948". Many of his articles were written in journals including "Annals of the Orgone Institute", "International Journal of Sex-Economy and Orgone Research", "Orgone Energy Bulletin", and "Core" (Cosmic Orgone Engineering).......... as well as the book "Ether God and Devil / Cosmic Superimposition - 1951". He created instruments to accumulate orgone energy (orgone accumulators which speeded up natural healing of the body). He experimented with the reaction of orgone energy with nuclear radiation "The Oranur Experiment - 1951" which demonstrated the significant health dangers of low level radiation. He also created instruments that could return self-regulation to weather (the cloud buster) "Contact With Space - 1957". He did research on the source of ufo's energy, and discovered a motor force from orgone energy. He should be remembered most for his work for children. Through the entire period from the 1920's through the 1950s , he advocated for natural child-birth, natural parenting, self-regulation and for the sexual rights of youth and adults. www.orgone.org

www.orgonelab.org Dr. James DeMeo's research web site, and home page for the Orgone Biophysical Research Laboratory. DeMeo has been investigating the work of the late Dr. Wilhelm Reich since 1970, and founded OBRL in 1978. With cooperative assistance from a network of professionals and institutes supportive of Wilhelm Reich's original discoveries, OBRL has grown to become one of the world's primary centers for genuine and uncompromised research and educational programs focused upon Orgonomy, the science of orgone (life) energy functions in nature, as developed by Reich in the first half of the 20th Century.

Starting in 1977, as part of his graduate research at the University of Kansas, DeMeo undertook replication studies of Reich's biophysical research -- specifically, a systematic evaluation of the Reich cloudbuster which yielded positive results. The acceptance of DeMeo's work by the KU faculty constituted the first time any aspect of Reich's controversial biophysical research had been validated by peer-review within a mainstream academic institution. Through the organizational structure of OBRL, and with the cooperative assistance and support of many other individuals and groups dedicated to Reich's works, DeMeo has since directed field applications of the cloudbuster apparatus, successfully ending droughts across the USA and overseas as well, with applications towards reducing the energetic stagnation characteristic of wetter regions suffering from chronic air pollution and forest-death. A number of Desert Greening expeditions have also been organized and directed by DeMeo within the arid zones of the Southwestern USA, and into the dry regions of Namibia and Israel, producing a dramatic verification of Reich's earlier findings on the ability of the cloudbuster to bring rains under even extremely dry conditions. With the support of local governments, a five-year desert-greening experiment was also undertaken in the 1990s, in the East African Sahel region adjacent to the hyperarid Sahara Desert. All of these projects have produced significantly positive results with sometimes-dramatic increases in rainfall, ending dry episodes of sometimes decades duration, filling reservoirs and greening parched landscapes.

Chapter 41

New Energy Truth and Lies of Omission

Dr. Brian O'Leary, Ph.D. April 26, 2007, www.brianoleary.com and www.brian-oleary.com

George Orwell has said that the biggest lies are lies of omission. The manifold manipulations of the Bush administration and its media mouthpieces bring this deception to a fine art. They skillfully manage our perceptions by selecting themselves as the sole "newsmakers" on important issues while avoiding any deeper context or greater truth.

Hidden from view are both drastic corruption and exciting possibilities that lie outside any serious consideration by the collective mainstream. But the consensus perception is just now coming to grips about the *problems*, which will inevitably lead to understanding their deeper roots. This is a process of "truth and reconciliation" which is only beginning to reach the awareness of some people and select politicians.

We can begin to sense the principle that "if the people lead, the leaders will follow". Sooner or later, the truth will come out. But the process of truth-telling appears to be much too slow for us to be able to plan our futures in a timely and rational way.

For example, I'm struck by the collective's lie-by-omission about radical innovation in clean energy and other sustainable solutions. Sadly, the lie is shared even by the most progressive scientists, politicians, journalists and environmentalists. To them, there can be no clean energy breakthroughs, period. Only when pressed, these mainstream scientists and pundits claim advanced energy technologies are not even worth researching because "we all know you can't break the laws of thermodynamics." They are wrong.

This is a lie because those laws are broken many, many times under nonequilibrium conditions, for example, by quantum experiments and by research on various devices that show anomalous energy coming from electromagnetic, plasma, solid state, and electrochemical devices. These experiments are systematically debunked by some of the most vocal and powerful physicists who really don't know what they're talking about. But these high priests of a decadent materialistic physics provide a convenient and effective censorship on bold new breakthroughs as the oil barons laugh all the way to the bank and the planet descends into ecological, political and economic tyranny.

The schools of Richard Heinberg *(The Party's Over)*, George Monbiot *(Heat)*, Michael Ruppert *(Crossing the Rubicon)*, James Lovelock *(The Revenge of Gaia)*, Tim Flannery *(The Weather Makers)*, Ross Gelbspan *(The Boiling Point)*, Michael Klare *(Blood and Oil)*, and countless academic scientists excel at stating the problems of global climate change and dwindling supplies of oil. Their despondency about the lack of viable solutions beyond sacrifice and imminent global collapse show on virtually every page of their writings.

But many of these authors can only scoff at considering even the remotest chance we could violate any of the sacrosanct "laws" of physics, that we must evermore live with existing technologies to obtain our energy. Needless to say, their prognosis is truly grim— as it should be, under the limiting assumptions they themselves have placed on their analyses.

The sad result is an unwitting alliance between the powers-that-be and those partial truth-tellers who are articulate about the crisis itself but are woefully ignorant about the full range of solutions. Layers of truth unfurl at a frustratingly slow pace.

We all lose from this creep of perceived credibility. Greater truths seem to be embraced only in fleeting moments of tiny bite-sized increments, but drown in the cacophony of hubris and kitsch. We are led to believe that our awareness can only take on so much at a time. We are also led to believe that any true energy breakthrough could only occur in the distant future, at best.

As we move through each unfurling layer of illusion-to-truth and its propagation out through the collective consciousness, the Earth clock ticks ever onward towards exhaustion. Our growing biocide and genocide moves much faster than we can respond. This censorship of underlying truth, especially by those who should know, is but another deception, a lie of omission, which pre-empts rational discussion of the wide variety of choices we really do have.

What we see happening now is that the wave of consensus awareness sweeps through the culture first towards those "solutions" which are really nonsolutions in the long run. Clean coal. Nuclear. Natural gas. Biofuels. Hydrogen fuel cells. Electric cars. Solar. Wind. Waves. Tides. Ocean thermal gradients.

Macroengineering boondoggles such as carbon dioxide emissions sequestration caves, the injection of sun-screening toxic particles into the atmosphere, gigantic Tokomak nuclear reactors that don't work, HAARP, etc. etc..

Upon intelligent examination, none of these alternatives by themselves or even in combination could adequately replace hydrocarbons to meet current demands without serious economic and ecological consequences. Yet they're the only ones allowed to be discussed in the public domain because they represent only what we now know and have a vested interest in.

History teaches us the same dynamics of the denial of new possibilities again and again. Many wise people such as Thomas Jefferson, Abraham Lincoln, Mark Twain, Aldous Huxley, Martin Luther King, Albert Einstein, Franklin D. Roosevelt, John F. Kennedy, Bertrand Russell, Albert Schweitzer, Buckminster Fuller, George Bernard Shaw, Arthur C. Clarke, Margaret Mead, and the whole genre of science fiction point out time after time that new ideas are often not considered seriously until it's too late to implement them wisely or peacefully. Out of fear and ignorance, we give our power away to those who are defending an old paradigm which could kill us all. We shut off our imaginations, our vision. We all collaborate in committing lies of omission.

I know about the resistance to discussing real change only too well. Even though my scientific credentials and long research career are impeccable, my presentations on new energy possibilities are most often ignored or debunked by my former academic colleagues, the media and a bewildered general public.

For example, I was recently invited by a BBC producer to talk about new energy on a special on future energy alternatives, but then uninvited when an executive producer decreed that they would cover only nuclear "hot" fusion Tokomak reactors as the one "credible" new energy option. This research, long supported by the scientific establishment, has so far turned up nothing, yet has so far cost governments tens of billions of dollars. Some of these same scientists have fraudulently debunked, defunded and derailed early experiments by some electrochemists suggesting that clean and cheap energy could come from low temperature catalytic nuclear reactions in water and heavy water solutions ("cold fusion").

The frauds, the lies and the cover-ups can only get worse as the truth marches on, polarizing the culture ever more. We are on a collision course towards an unprecedented revolution in which either the people awaken to deeper truths to be acted upon, or we all perish and bring down nature with us. My new energy colleagues and I keep getting muzzled and debunked because the corporate cartel running the world want more and more control over our energy policy. Meanwhile, I feel that the closer I get to the truth, the further I feel pushed away from the culture.

Once again, censorship has almost totally cut off my access to the media, which I used to enjoy as a mainstream scientist for decades. This is a grievous lie of omission. Hundreds of publishers have also turned me down in spite of a productive and profitable background of authorship. They too lie by omission. So how is the collective mind to ever learn about these possibilities with all these media blackouts?

To the censors, I've become a heretic who has abandoned his comfortable positions at prestigious universities to tilt at windmills in exile, one who uses bad science to bolster some extraordinary claims. Worse, I am one of those conspiracy theorists not worth listening to, for surely the existing world-views must prevail for us to mold our future. It's all a Catch-22, a mix-mash of fuzzy thinking, obfuscation, denial, careerism, and self-protection. "Better the devil we know than the devil we don't know, so leave me alone and let me do my work" is the usual refrain.

Progressives, mainstream scientists, environmentalists and Al Gore alike have stopped far too short of telling us how to meet the mandates of the climate crisis and the depletion of fossil fuels. My attempts to engage most of these spokespeople about new energy remain unanswered, in spite of broaching the discussions only as a hypothetical possibility, as a what-if. Admirable as their critiques of current energy policy might be, they speak to only part of the truth and so cover up the real solutions.

In the big picture, these people lie by omission almost as much as the oligarchs, and by default, the rest of us. New energy truth will emerge in time, but we do not have the luxury of time to keep the charade of believing "new energy cannot exist" going indefinitely. Our leading scientists and communicators are going to have to stop riding the slow wave of unfolding layers of partial truth in such politically correct ways—or step aside and let others take over. We need to make it safe to accelerate the process of unraveling truth. We need to be willing to suspend disbelief.

If we want to uncover deeper truths we must develop a new perspective, we must reframe the issues, we must be willing to be perceived as being wrong, in short, as being heretics. For years I had a bumper sticker that read, "The truth will set you free but first it will piss you off." That's fine. But then we will need to muster the courage to face the truth with action. We can begin to do that by creating a greater context from which to ask our questions.

The necessary re-framing begins with leaving our prior beliefs at the door (even if only for a moment). We must be willing to have discussions we've never had before. It begins with a simple neutral statement like: "Say we spend a small amount of our collective resources on exploring *the possibility* of having clean, cheap, decentralized energy for all humankind. Is this worth the effort? If so, how can we implement this research, development and deployment?

There are at least two important reasons why we need to have this discussion.

First, we can begin to address the full range of possibilities for a clean energy future and a sustainable Earth. How can we make informed decisions based on incomplete information? Is there not *any* acknowledgement of energy innovation? Why is this topic so taboo, especially in the face of such a planetary crisis?

The second reason is just as important: Who will benefit by going to this or that energy choice? A new energy future must be able to benefit all of humankind, all of nature. Therefore, we cannot, *must not,* give this one away to the oligarchy who have benefited so much from controlling nonrenewable resources and destroying our environment.

Those who run the world know this best. They have structured things to suppress real solutions. They optimize fear while they optimize profits, wanting to squeeze out every last drop of oil, natural gas, uranium, water, wood, topsoil, crops, coal or anything else we all need until these resources are utterly exhausted. History tells us that if we wait too long, a time might come when they take their last profit and they run for the hills moments before being lynched by a just-awakened mob, or they'll blow us all up in a World War III. And the rest of us, in our silence, are complicit with this madness. In such a case, we lose our freedoms, our environment, our health, our peace.

To summarize the statement of the problem of our unabated thirst for hydrocarbons under the ground, two communities are forming a consensus about two pressing issues that mandate a drastic reduction in our consumption of oil, gas and coal. One community is made up of competent climate scientists who warn us that we must drastically cut back carbon dioxide emissions very soon if we are ever to reverse drastic climate change. The second community, made up of oil geologists and economists, warn us that the decreasing supply of available oil and other resources in the face of increasing demands (the "peak oil" movement) will create such international havoc that wars, poverty and economic collapse are inevitable—unless we quickly switch to viable energy alternatives.

The irony here is that, those same experts who justifiably warn us of the grim consequences of our actions also deny the full range of possible solutions such as new energy. Meanwhile, some progressives working within the system are slow to respond to the problem and have not the foggiest idea about how to really solve it. Others surely do know but lie-by-omission to stay in the good graces with their powerful corporate sponsors.

Politics is about the art of what's possible, not the science of what's real. In the U.S. and other western capitalist "democracies" we are sacrificing the truth on the altar of economic expediency. The accumulation of money and power for the privileged few is what runs the world. These oligarchs perceive that authentic democracy in energy independence as a threat, because they would lose their power if new clean, cheap energy were to become available. We are talking about supplanting a multi-trillion dollar economy that underlies their immense power. That's why they are lying by omission, that's why so many inventors have been threatened and assassinated.

New energy can be introduced for the benefit of humankind by a common revolution by the people themselves. But only through a cultural-political process of truth and reconciliation can we reveal the answers with which we must develop a new consensus.

We are entering an era of truth-telling coming from the people, not from any politician or mainstream media "source": 9/11 truth, Constitutional truth, electoral fraud truth, war pretext truth, depleted uranium truth, UFO truth, consciousness science truth, and many others. If new energy truth is to take its place among this list, we are going to have to organize ourselves as activists to force the body politic to embrace truth, cutting across many issues and forming alliances. Otherwise, we will surely enter a Dark Age of enormous proportions and most all species will die off from human folly.

Just as important as truth-telling is the reconciliation of our past with our future. The ending of apartheid in South Africa and the falling of the Berlin Wall are modern examples of truth and reconciliation. We must not only serve justice upon those who have knowingly lied for their own benefit and to the detriment of humans and nature, we must reconcile ourselves with our past, with one another and with all creation. New energy truth and reconciliation are key elements in these times of great change.

This essay underlies speeches presented in May 2007 at the International Institute of Integral Human Sciences in Montreal, Canada (www.iiihs.org) and on the May PQI Mediterranean cruise Q3 advanced course (www.pqievents.com).

Chapter 42

Alchemy

ALCHEMY REDISCOVERED AND RESTORED By Archibald Cockren www.sacred-texts.com/alc/arr/index.htm

Alchemy Is a Science (from Alchemy by Franz Hartmann)

Alchemy is a Science of Soul that results from an understanding of God, Nature, and Man. A perfect knowledge of any of one them cannot be obtained without the knowledge of the other two, for these three are one and inseparable. Alchemy is not merely an intellectual but a spiritual science, because that which belongs to

---

[120] 17th century engraving of distillation apparatus. www.alchemywebsite.com

the spirit can only be spiritually known. Nevertheless, it is also a science dealing with material things, for spirit and matter are only two opposite manifestations or poles of the eternal One.

Alchemy in its more material aspect teaches how minerals, metals, plants, animals, and men may be generated or made to grow from their "seeds." In other words, how that generation, which is accomplished during long periods of time in the due course of the action of evolution and natural law, may be accomplished in a comparatively short time, if these natural laws are guided and supplied with the proper material by the spiritual knowledge of man. There is no doubt that gold can be made to grow by alchemical means, though it requires an alchemist to make the experiment succeed, and he who is attracted by the material power of gold will not obtain possession of the spiritual power necessary to practice the art.

It is therefore a grave mistake to confuse alchemy with chemistry. Modern chemistry is an artificial science that deals only with the external forms in which the elements of matter are manifesting themselves. It never produces anything truly new to creation; it can only recombine atoms and molecules into different substances. We may mix and compound and decompose chemical bodies an unlimited number of times and cause them to appear in various different forms, but at the end, we will have no augmentation of the underlying substances nor anything more than the recombination of the substances that have been employed at the beginning. Alchemy does not mix or compound anything; it causes that which already pre-exists in a latent state to become active and grow. Alchemy is, therefore, more comparable to biology than to chemistry; and, in fact, the growth of a plant, a tree, or an animal or the evolution of whole species are alchemical processes going on in the laboratory of nature, and performed by the Great Alchemist -- the power of the divine Mind acting in nature.

Alchemy Is an Art

Alchemy is also an art, and as every art requires an artist to exercise it, likewise this divine science and art can be practiced only by those who are in possession of the divine power necessary for that purpose. It is true that the external manipulations required for the production of certain alchemical preparations may, like an ordinary chemical process, be taught to anybody capable of reasoning. However, the results that such a person would accomplish would be without life, for only he in whom the true life has awakened can awaken it from its sleep in matter and cause visible forms to grow from the primordial Chaos of nature.

Alchemy in its highest aspect deals with the spiritual regeneration of man and teaches how a god may be made out of a human being or, to express it more correctly, how to establish the conditions necessary for the development of divine powers in man, so that a human being may became a god by the power of God in the same sense that a seed becomes a plant by the aid of the Four Elements and the action of the invisible Fifth Element (the Quintessence or Life Force).

What Else Did the Alchemists Know?

They were right about lead to gold; what other secrets did the Alchemists have? In 1926, the alchemical initiate Fulcanelli, whose real identity is still unknown, claimed that the secret of alchemy was openly displayed on the walls of the Gothic Cathedrals. Victor Hugo and many others have written of the hermetic symbolism of the cathedrals, however Fulcanelli went a step further and produced a masterpiece, Le Mystere des Cathedrales. This book is a guided tour of the esoteric tradition in the west as displayed on the walls of certain cathedrals and private homes in Gothic style.

What Did Fulcanelli Know?

A couple of years ago, two researcher's went back and took a closer look at the messages revealed by Fulcanelli. They found a prediction regarding the year 2002. Of course this date has come and gone, but the authors have some interesting things to say about that on their web page.[121] The authors were convinced that the catastrophe will be related to the superwaves of Paul LaViolette. Paul has made many predictions that have been fulfilled[122] so perhaps this one will also come to pass. I have my own prediction about weather on Earth. I believe that Dr. Robert Gagosian's theory about the gulf stream stopping[123] is correct and that it will happen before 2012. And I am amazed that our scientists are trying to convince us that our wild weather is due to global warming. Just look at all these dramatic increases in sun related catastrophes.[124]

---

[121] www.vincentbridges.com/RaisingtheDjed.htm

[122] www.etheric.com/LaViolette/Predict.html

[123] www.whoi.edu/institutes/occi/currenttopics/climatechange_wef.html

[124] www.handpen.com/Bio/sun_freaks.html

The sun is freaking out and nobody is talking about it. The changes in the sun are due to the fact that our solar system has traveled into an area of interstellar space that contains more ions of hydrogen, helium, and hydroxyl. This has caused the appearance of new states, and activity regimes, of the sun. But, I digress, for more information about out sun's problems, read Dmitriev,[125] the man has all the info.

The interview was conducted by Mark Stavish[126] a long-time student of esotericism

Stavish: What are some of the practical benefits of alchemy?

Dubuis: This is a very complicated problem. I think that with alchemy, or if you start with cabbala, or with a good Hermetic initiatic discipline, you can find your inner path within a very short period of time. It is difficult for the mundane world to understand, but if you don't take one of these paths, you will "go back up" in millions or billions of years. What the alchemist, cabbalist, or other hermeticist must try and do is shorten the suffering of humanity. Not through soft-heartedness, to save lives or things like that, in details, but to put humanity back on the path that will allow it to go very rapidly to its own realization. After which, all of the trouble that appears in our material world disappears.

---

[125] www.tmgnow.com/repository/global/planetophysical1.html

[126] www.hermetic.com/stavish/default.htm

Stavish: What is the basic philosophy of alchemy?

Dubuis: It is the Science of Life, of Consciousness. The alchemist knows that there is a very solid link between matter, life, and consciousness. Alchemy is the art of manipulating life and consciousness in matter to help it evolve or to solve problems of inner disharmony.

Matter exists only because it is created by the human seed. The human seed, the original man, created matter in order to involute and evolve. You see, if we go beyond what I said, the absolute being is an auto-created being, and we must become in its image auto-created men. That is from a seed of the origin we are self-created.

Stavish: How do you define God?

Dubuis: I can't define it because I don't think it exists in the personal sense. There is a Universal State of Being that is completely impersonal. The answer to this question comes for some people who make the Experiment of Eternity... They then know that things are as they are, because they can't be otherwise. But no personal god acts on things. The only god in the universe is man.

Chapter 43

Intentional Communities

You might think that communes are something that became extinct back in the sixties and seventies. Actually, many people live communally today, in intentional communities[127], Eco-villages[128], group marriages[129], co-ops[130], ashrams[131], co-housing[132] groups, even in survivalist and radical religious colonies.

Communal living is an excellent choice for people who enjoy deep, intimate companionship with more than one person. It is often very difficult to form and maintain a healthy, mutually satisfying and beneficial relationship with the random assortment of personalities that comprise a typical family. An intentional community can be looked at as a "chosen family," in the respect that it is made up of people who came together intentionally based on "commonalties"

---

[127] www.ic.org

[128] www.gaia.org

[129] www.polyamory.org

[130] www.cooperative.org

[131] www.alignment.org

[132] www.cohousing.org

other than biological (or adoptive) accident. An intentional community differs from a family in the important respect that no one in an intentional community will ever legitimately feel "stuck" with it. Thus, communal living can supply people whose conventional family relationships are dysfunctional or nonexistent with the best a family has to offer, a circle of connected, loving co-experiences with whom to share life.

There can be practical advantages to communal living. Often, a member of an expense-sharing group can live more cheaply than a single person can. People who live in group housing are freer to travel, as there are always going to be others about to water plants, take in the mail, pay the bills, keep company to those who stay behind, and so on. Most important, an intentional community is a social network. The chances are good that someone will usually be available to go out for lunch; to share a movie; to look over a final draft; to try the lunch seasoning; to listen to a cool idea; to join in on a magnificent undertaking; to take a walk in the sunset; to practice a sport or hobby; to fall in love with; to learn and to teach something to. Last but not least, maintenance chores are always more pleasant, and less demanding, when shared.

Obviously, communal living can never be as private as a person's own home. However, parameters can be set to maximize the possibility that adequate privacy will be available for those who sometimes require it. People who need a lot of privacy probably do not belong in a communal setting. People who thrive on human interaction probably do.

Communal living is a remarkably viable means for enriching our lives with interpersonal adventure and fun. As a group we have the resources, practical and personal, to actualize the very best of what we can imagine. After all as a group we will know more than individually we could. The sharing and maximizing of resources will improve greatly our quality of life as well as healing our planet.

Instead of owning many of any one product, we will own less, but share a wider range of items. Communal living can be a potent and powerful medium for free, creative, experimental, sustainable, ecological, and fulfilling way of life.

By pooling our money, creativity, skills, assets, ideas and resources; and thereby supplying our basic needs through communal energies, we find there are both an abundance of all things available to us all, and an optimization in the efficiency of their use. For example, sharing the use of automobiles, and making a communal dinner each evening. One car can serve numerous people, thus requiring fewer of them; and not only does everyone get a wholesome, nutritious meal each night, but they also only have to cook and cleanup once a month, or less, for example and then only as part of a team.

I believe that together we will achieve things we never, in our secular lives would have dreamed of, for example: operating large natural shops, bakeries, production of tinctures, teas and organic herbs, writing and performing music, publishing books, creating a seed bank, producing videos, setting up radio stations, promoting Eco-tourism, setting up a health center, and much more; the possibilities are endless. Operating a natural, organic food restaurant where everyone contributed their energy, and equally shared in the returns. While at the same time, contributing a service to the community as a valuable foundation in our lifestyle, coming out of the usury money orientation, which is antithesis of sharing and breeds fear of loss and distrust and moving into a money-less society. We will be changing the program from moment to moment, from one of the secular insecure world of getting-for-self, to a world of "Love, as Service Done". We put our sharing words and actions into the morphogenetic field for playback, and were automatically lifted to the higher consciousness of "all for one and one for all."

The aberrations in our relationships and in our society come from the conditioning each of us has experienced in this and/or other lifetimes, not to mention the brainwashing of upside down society by the media, the corrupt government and the powerful selfish multinationals on their greedy rat race. Positive conditioning by the right environment will create a new breed of peaceful, secure, loving beings. The big error is competition, which makes each the enemy of every other; and the backward, ungodly usury money system, which programs the people to be in a fearful, getting-for-self consciousness. Thus, the unnatural fear of lack and the self-defeating abnormality of judging one another and ourselves, when in truth, we are all subject to the perverse collective consciousness, programmed predominantly in duality and which the status quo communications media perpetuates. This limited consciousness has blocked us from being able to transcend into the knowing of our oneness with the all-knowing, omnipotent, omnipresent Universal Mind, which fills all space in a Universe of symbiotic perfection.

To learn more about Intentional Communities around the world, I recommend you start by reading a few books on the subject, visiting a few and by going to the following website on the Internet.

Utopian EcoVillage Network Federation[133]

Comunidad Los Visionarios[134]

---

[133] www.uevn.org

[134] www.LosVisionarios.org

Chapter 44

Additional Books, Newsgroups, Web Pages

Now a days it is impossible to get all the facts and details without the use of the Internet. If you do not have Internet access, do yourself a favor, get it.

There are many other sources of information to help you expand your point of view of reality. Among them is what is really going on with governments throughout the world, especially the US government. The mass media is part of the government; it should not be your single source of information.

Recommended Web pages

I highly recommend your get an offline explorer to download to your computer and save your favorite web pages, Meta Products makes a very nice one. www.MetaProducts.com

If you are not already familiar with newsgroups such as http://groups.yahoo.com I highly recommend you become familiar with this technology. Newsgroups are perhaps the second best source of information on this 3rd dimensional reality. Second only to web pages and books.

www.rense.com for the TRUE story in the news. ALL of the major media only give entertainment report to amaze the masses, and quite often does not provide the real true story, even though there are plenty of facts. Rense is one of the better places to judge for yourself what is true and what is not.

www.unknowncountry.com

www.educate-yourself.org   Educate-Yourself.org is a free educational forum dedicated to the dissemination of accurate information in the use of natural, non-pharmaceutical medicines and alternative healing therapies in the treatment of disease conditions. Free Energy, Earth Changes, and the growing reality of Big Brother are also explored since survival itself in the very near future may well depend on self acquired skills to face the growing threats of bioterrorism, emerging diseases, and the continuing abridgement of constitutional liberties. It is strongly recommended that visitors to this web site print out hard copies of the information that is of interest. Do not assume that your hard drive, this web site, or even the Internet itself will always be there to serve you.

www.dowsers.com   This is yet one more subject that seems incredible but that has a lot of truth. Dowsing is the art of letting your inner-being guide you to what you are searching for, be it water, gold, or whatever is that you seek.

www.halexandria.org if not the best it is definitely one of the best compilation of information on the internet. It is much more than a book, it is a live document that is continually updated with new up to date relevant information. It has lot of information on spiritual matters, especially information that comes from the scientific community. The Library of Halexandria is a Synthesis of new physics, sacred geometry, ancient and modern history, multiple universes & realities,

consciousness, the Ha Qabala and ORME, extraterrestrials, corporate rule and politics, law, order and entropy, trial by jury, astronomy, monetary policy, scientific anomalies, and a whole host of other subjects ranging from astrology and astrophysics to superstrings and sonoluminesence to biblical and geologic histories to numerology, the Tarot, and creating your own reality. It is an attempt at bridging of the Age of Pisces and the Age of Aquarius.

Halexandria is, in essence, putting all of the pieces together. It is based primarily on fact and documented evidence, with a liberal dose of rational, logical speculation, as well as several diversions into reality-based fictional treatments. In all cases, Halexandria makes the assumption -- an assumption which will be mathematically proven within these pages -- that all aspects of the universe are connected and that there are no limits to what we can possess or what we can become.

This then is the Pharos, the lighthouse to attract the wandering net-surfer, to encourage the browser to view one after the other the scrolls of this modern, compacted, esoteric library, akin in design or aim to that of Egypt's ancient Alexandria, and its famed Library, Mouseion and center of wisdom. From hence, one can choose a variety of options in which to rush in where angels (and used car salesmen) dare not tread. For example.,.

Halexandria is in all respects a journey, The Fool's Journey, which begins from diverse locations, but always leading to a comprehension of the magnificent whole. Depending upon your preferences, you may initiate your journey, your destined path, from any point of the above modified Tree of Life (or Tree of Knowledge of Good and Evil). Your only prerequisite will be the possession of an open mind and a sense of humor -- possibly even a warped sense of humor. Or warped mind. Whichever.

Inasmuch as Halexandria is, above all, about choices, it is not necessary to read the Synthesis (aka the Executive Summary) first, and thereafter select one of the other Nine pathways briefly described above -- or to decipher the Website Road Map (which has the notable advantage that it does not require refolding) -- or to plunge into any of the almost 800 web pages of this website relatively unaware.

www.crystalinks.com   This is yet another must read library of all sorts of information ranging from ancient lost civilizations to extraterrestrials to healing to psychic and spiritual development, etc.

www.mysticweb.org   I mention twice in this book, it is an excellent place to get started on your education. Once more: "follow your highest joy" when the time comes to move on to other sources of information do so, by NO means am I saying be lazy and not finish what you started, if you start a course finish it, but if your heart (highest joy) is not there, only then move on.

www.whatthebleepdoweknow.com   Has many links and information from spiritual scientists. I coin this term "spiritual scientist" because to me, these scientists have already crossed the link of science into the spiritual realm which in true reality is science anyhow. One day we may use one single word to describe both.

Recommended Books

There are so many books, that when one starts searching it is hard to figure out which one to get. You have many older ones that are hard to understand and then you have many new ones that are empty of direct and clear information and then you have the manuals type that do not say they are a manual into one single subject. So below I will list them in the order I see them.

There are a few places in the Internet to download thousands of books at a time from many different subjects, among them there are the following worth mentioning:

www.ascension2000.com   www.divinecosmos.com   THE CONVERGENCE 3 BOOK SERIES: A SCIENTIFIC CASE FOR "ASCENSION" Scientific Proof for Ascension – A Discrete, Heretofore Unrecognized Astrophysical Event in our Near Future with Profound Spiritual Implications. NEW! Posted Dec. 6, 2000, Revised 10/20/02. This is David Wilcock's heavily revised and updated "tour de force" that synthesizes scientific and metaphysical data into a comprehensive thesis. Topics include hyperdimensional physics, the Global Grid, harmonics, Atlantis, the true meaning of crop circle formations, the Mayan Calendar, the Great Pyramid, secret societies, hidden planetary, solar and galactic time cycles, the Hall of Records, the archeo-matrix of Carl Munck, geometric dynamic structures in the Stock Market, 12,000-year old submerged pyramids in Japan, the Martian Monuments, quotes from the Seth Material, Ra Material, Edgar Cayce, Walter Russell and the Wilcock Readings, and more. A staggering amount of rarely seen information is beautifully tied together in 21 chapters to arrive at a provocative conclusion: That Earth is about to undergo a literal dimensional shift. Thousands of Emailers agree that this book is GUARANTEED to satisfy you – and best of all, it's posted FREE.

ABSTRACT OF BOOK TWO: Every system level of our universe, from subatomic to stellar as well as all commonly recognized forms of life, will be revealed as the visible result of a unified "aether" of space-time energy that vibrates multi-dimensionally according to specific, numerically-based harmonic principles of light, sound and geometry. The inherent harmonic organization of this aether forms a series of stresses in space and time that produce dynamic forces such as gravity and electromagnetism, measurable effects in the passage of "linear" time as well as far more subtle effects relating to consciousness. Our Solar System is now completing its passage through a "major" 25,920-year harmonic time cycle of these stresses relative to our positioning in the Galaxy, producing precise, visible changes in the Earth, Sun and elsewhere. The end product of this inevitable movement through the underlying material of space and time will be a complete transformation of our reality on all levels- physical, mental and spiritual. Furthermore, we will show that the knowledge of this harmonic system has been well-known and actively utilized by ancient civilizations, current governments and higher forms of intelligence operating around us today, and that comprehensive efforts have been made to preserve this knowledge on our behalf in many different ways- including mythologies, spiritual traditions, modern "crop circles" and archeological sites on Earth and abroad.

NOTES: FROM BOOK 3: THE ENERGETIC TRANSFORMATION OF OUR ENTIRE SOLAR SYSTEM is now underway, and we are already feeling the effects – which the US Environmental Protection Agency admitted in a front-page New York Times article in 2002, (which Bush later dubbed "an act of the bureaucracy") but is attempting to blame on global warming. This is by far the most facile and under-informed opinion about what is going on, though human pollution is certainly causing considerable damage to the Earth's biosphere.

In this book, we go miles beyond either of our previous two books in the Convergence series... The Shift of the Ages and The Science of Oneness. If you liked these books... just wait. When we wrote these books, we had not yet discovered the entirely new world of Russian physics... and once we found it, ALL the pieces fit together.

We now present a completely Unified model, showing how the same energetic fields are at work on all levels of size, from the quantum to intergalactic. This proves that the Universe is holographic and / or fractal in its very nature. This model has never existed in such a complete form in any of our recent history, at least overtly. Many annoying paradoxes of science have now been resolved into one single, stable multi-dimensional cosmology – which has dazzling implications for our immediate future.

The information contained within this book has waited long enough. It keeps banging on the door, because it wants a hot meal and a warm place to sleep in your mind. Start learning what a part of you already knows -- come and discover The Divine Cosmos.

And so, these books are NOT of fantasy or science fiction. These books could not have been written until now, without the power of the Internet to bring the world's frontier researchers together so that such collaboration could take place. Not simply another piece of the puzzle, it is an assembly of the puzzle: the first of its kind, fusing vast amounts of data together to reconstruct the Universe in a new "hyperdimensional" model that is precisely unified from the quantum all the way up to the universe itself, and written at a level that does not exclude any readers with technical gibberish. And it is also the story of a discrete astrophysical event in our near future that we have labeled as "The Time of Global Shift," since it seems to have direct spiritual implications for humanity – the long-awaited shift from the Age of Pisces into the Age of Aquarius.

www.davidicke.com British author David Icke has written 16 books and traveled to over 40 countries since 1990. His research exposes the Big Brother fascist dictatorship predicted by George Orwell in his book, 1984, and charts the history of the Illuminati with its connections to unseen forces in other dimensions of reality that some call 'extraterrestrials'. Icke refers to this as the 'Reptilian Agenda'. His books reveal how a Hidden Hand is behind world-changing events like the attacks of 9/11 and the manufactured wars in the Middle East, as part of a mass mind manipulation technique he has dubbed problem, reaction, solution. What David Icke wrote about in the 20th century has proved to be so astonishingly accurate in predicting the events of the 21st and continues to be so.

Nowhere else is there such a unique library of information showing how all of these apparently diverse subjects are part of a Global Agenda from the Origination, History, Symbolism and Bloodlines of the Illuminati; Secret Societies; Big Brother Surveillance; the Manipulation of Wars, Politics, Business, Banking, and Media; Microchipping; Problem-Reaction-Solution; the truth about 9/11; the 'War on Terror'; Mind Control; Religion, the Reptilian Agenda and so much more. David Icke also reveals how we live in a virtual-reality dream world, very much like the one portrayed in the Matrix movies.

If you are ready Read on and discover the truth!

www.michaelmandeville.com An excellent set of 7 books that complement the above www.ascension2000.com website and books. These books complement the above books. Michael Mandeville also provides the Earth Changes Bulletin, a timely bulletin with prediction on coming earthquakes and other earth changes. Here is THE ONLY complete anthology of the prophecies of Edgar Cayce about the 20th and 21st Centuries. No work comes close to presenting the real Edgar Cayce, his life, his work, his detailed predictions, and why this psychic is the most important prophet of our times. Unmatched anywhere, here is an extraordinary vision of the future, including the "Great Leveling" of the "classes and masses" which must occur to create true justice and democracy, the advent of spiritual values which will transform the Earth, the catastrophic Earth Changes which will culminate in geological upheavals and a catastrophic shifting of the Earth's Spin Axis, the opening of the "Hall of Records" which will reveal the true origin and history of humanity, the Destiny of America, Russia, Japan, and China, and much much more. Through the 3 books of the Trilogy, Cayce's observations, teachings, and predictions are brought together into a story line of the "World Epic" which defines the looming Change In The Earth which has been and will transform all aspects of the environment and human civilization between 1936 and 2030.

www.archive.org or www.gutenberg.net Project Gutenberg is the premier online free book project on the internet and perhaps the world's largest FREE electronic book library at the time. You will find over 10,000 FREE electronic books on just about every subject and the list continues to grow each day. If you like it and you use it, please send them a small donation.

http://books.mirror.org This index is a guide to available online editions of great books. It has links to many internet sites that have online free books. A must add to your list of online book resources.

www.soilandhealth.org This is a specialist library about holistic agriculture, holistic health and self-sufficient homestead living. Most of the titles in this library are out of print. Many are quite hard to find.

When comprehended as an inter-related whole this library constitutes a self-guided course of study or a self-teaching curriculum that connects agricultural methods to the health of animals and humans, shows how to prevent and heal disease and increase longevity.

This is a free public library. No membership payment is required to get full access to its contents. However, donations are solicited.

The Soil and Health Library has four major sections:

Radical Agriculture. The nutritional qualities of food and consequently the health of the animals and humans eating that food are determined by soil fertility. This section's interest is far wider than organic gardening and farming; other health-determined approaches to food-raising are also included. Go to the Agriculture Library[135]

The Restoration and Maintenance of Health. Nutritional medicine heals disease, builds and maintains health with diet—and sometimes heals with fasting or other forms of dietary restriction. There are many approaches represented in this collection. There is

---

[135] www.soilandhealth.org/01aglibrary/01principles.html

also a collection concerning longevity and nutritional anthropology. Go to the Health Library.[136]

Achieving Personal Sovereignty. Physical, mental, and spiritual health are linked to one's lifestyle. This collection focuses on liberating activities, especially homesteading and the skills it takes to do that—small-scale entrepreneuring, financial independence, frugality, and voluntary simplicity. There is also a collection of social criticism, especially from a back-to-the-land point of view. Go to the Personal Sovereignty Library.[137]

Achieving Spiritual Freedom. There are many seemingly-different self-betterment roads. The books in this collection seek to empower a person to effect their own development in an independent manner. Go to the Spiritual Freedom Library.[138]

www.wie.org What Is Enlightenment magazine is striving to catalyze a new way of thinking, one that integrates our highest spiritual aspirations with the demand to transform the world.

www.sacred-texts.com The Internet Sacred Text Archive CD-ROM includes electronic texts of nearly a thousand of the most important books and articles ever written, including over two hundred

---

[136] www.soilandhealth.org/02/02principles.html

[137] www.soilandhealth.org/03sov/03principles.html

[138] www.soilandhealth.org/03sov/0304spiritpsych/0304principles.html

transcribed specially for sacred-texts. Years of extensive research and scholarship went into this CD-ROM: all the core texts of religion, mythology, folklore and the esoteric are on one disk.

This collection includes the full text of each book, many with footnotes and illustrations. To buy all of these books you would have to spend tens of thousands of dollars, even if you could find them: many are out of print and hard to obtain at any price.

The disk has a massive and comprehensive set of scriptures from Hinduism, Buddhism, Confucianism, Taoism, Sikhism, and other eastern religions. The disk includes English translations of all of the Vedas, together for the first time. Read the beloved Hindu epics, the Mahabharata and Ramayana. Included are many volumes of the renowned Sacred Books of the East series, including the Upanishads, the Bhagavad Gita, Taoist Texts, the Dhammapada, the Lotus Sutra, I Ching and the Confucian Canon. You can also read the historical sources of Wicca, New Age beliefs, and even Atheism. Whatever your religious beliefs, this CD-ROM is a must-have if you want to understand world religions. No other religion CD-ROM is as comprehensive or well-organized.

The CD-ROM includes hundreds of books about oral traditions and folklore that go back to the dawn of humanity. Take a trip to the Kalahari, Siberia, or the Australian outback and hear the oldest stories in the world from tribal elders and shamans. Sail with the ancient Polynesians from New Zealand to Hawaii and Easter Island. Follow the adventures of tricksters, culture heroes and animals from Native America. Journey back to ancient Rome and Greece and feast on rich classical mythology. Enjoy the legends and sagas of the European dark ages, and wonderful Celtic folklore of gods, heroes and fairies. The disk includes all of the primary sources of

Tolkien's Lord of the Rings, including the Kalevala and the Eddas. Open up dusty--and very authentic--books of magic, peer into the future with Nostradamus, get a Tarot reading, visit legendary lost continents and learn occult secrets--if you dare. The CD-ROM includes material not found at the website; bonus sections include the complete plays of Shakespeare and the writings of philosophers through the ages from Plato to Thoreau. All of these and more are included on the CD-ROM.

"Three Magic Words," by U.S. Anderson. This book was also sold by the title "The Key to Power and Personal Peace" and it could easily be sold by twenty different titles, since even though it is a book of only 320 pages it covers exceptionally well many subjects. It is literally a compendium on how to think, live life and prosper. It provides much more details on many of the subjects I provided an introduction to in this book, such as Faith, how to create attraction to the things we want, intuition, our false illusions and much more. This book is a must read, if you do not get it all at first, read every six months or so, until you get it.

Advanced psychology manuals

"Gods in every man" by Jean Shinoda Bolen, M.D. and "Goddesses in every woman" by the same author. These two books give a very nice explanation of all of our basic physiological behaviors, and more important a tool on how to deal with oneself and with others. A way of how to quickly understand and predict other peoples behaviors.

Books that cover many subjects

"The Seven Mysteries of Life" by Guy Morchie gives a broad view of many mysteries of life, good reading to start with and to read to a child.

Spiritual novel
fun to read, teaches a principal in a fun way

"The Celestine Vision" by James Redfield. An excellent novel that touches on much truth. You be the judge on what is (if any) fantasy and what is not. Definitely a FUN book to read. And a best seller too... Now in movie too www.thecelestineprophecymovie.com

www.realityshifters.com/pages/reviews.html Has an excellent book recommendation list that covers spiritual, new age, healing, or consciousness.

Movies

WHAT THE BLEEP DO WE KNOW?! is a new type of film. It is part documentary, part story, and part elaborate and inspiring visual effects and animations. The protagonist, Amanda, played by Marlee Matlin, finds herself in a fantastic Alice in Wonderland experience when her daily, uninspired life literally begins to unravel, revealing the uncertain world of the quantum field hidden behind what we consider to be our normal, waking reality.

She is literally plunged into a swirl of chaotic occurrences, while the characters she encounters on this odyssey reveal the deeper, hidden knowledge she doesn't even realize she has asked for. Like every hero, Amanda is thrown into crisis, questioning the fundamental premises of her life – that the reality she has believed in about how men are, how relationships with others should be, and how her emotions are affecting her work isn't reality at all!

As Amanda learns to relax into the experience, she conquers her fears, gains wisdom, and wins the keys to the great secrets of the ages, all in the most entertaining way. She is then no longer the victim of circumstances, but she is on the way to being the creative force in her life. Her life will never be the same.

The fourteen top scientists and mystics interviewed in documentary style serve as a modern day Greek Chorus. In an artful filmic dance, their ideas are woven together as a tapestry of truth. The thoughts and words of one member of the chorus blend into those of the next, adding further emphasis to the film's underlying concept of the interconnectedness of all things.

The chorus members act as hosts who live outside of the story, and from this Olympian view, comment on the actions of the characters below. They are also there to introduce the Great Questions framed by both science and religion, which divides the film into a series of acts. Through the course of the film, the distinction between science and religion becomes increasingly blurred, since we realize that, in essence, both science and religion describe the same phenomena.

The film employs animation to realize the radical knowledge that modern science has unearthed in recent years. Powerful cinematic sequences explore the inner-workings of the human brain. Quirky animation introduces us to the smallest form of consciousness in the body – the cell. Dazzling visuals reinforce the film's message in an exciting, powerful way. Done with humor, precision, and irreverence, these scenes are only part of what makes this film unique in the history of cinema, and a true box-office winner.

*** www.whatthebleepdoweknow.com ***

Another movie coming soon to look for is from the famous modern author of "The Celestine Prophesies," name the same.

The Secret is released to the world! This ground-breaking feature length movie presentation reveals The Great Secret of the universe. It has been passed throughout the ages, traveling through centuries... to reach you, mankind, and humankind.

This is The Secret to everything - the secret to unlimited joy, health, money, relationships, love, youth: everything you have ever wanted.

In this astonishing program are ALL the resources you will ever need to understand and live The Secret. For the first time in history, the world's leading scientists, authors, and philosophers will reveal The Secret that utterly transformed the lives of every person who ever knew it... Plato, Newton, Carnegie, Beethoven, Shakespeare, Einstein.

Now YOU will know **The Secret.** And it could change your life forever.

*** www.TheSecret.tv ***

*** www.WhatIsTheSecret.tv ***

One of my favorites is the mini-series titled "The Matrix" The Matrix seems like just a sci-fi movie, but it is much more. It goes deep into the subject that nothing is really real.

CONVERGENCE the film. David's scientific work, thoroughly documented for free public consumption on www.divinecosmos.com, is now being realized into a feature Hollywood documentary film, CONVERGENCE. Convergence is timely, salient and of true benefit to humanity.

Our planet is undergoing extreme changes while a great portion of humanity lives in stress and anxiety. At the same time, amazing discoveries are being made that have the potential to transform our lives in a way that is nothing short of remarkable. Unfortunately, the majority of people have not received these findings, and oftentimes when they do, the information is fragmented and difficult to comprehend.

Convergence is a trilogy about the latest findings from experts, accompanied with scientific verification and graphics about the true nature of, and our direct impact upon, the universe. It presents interviews with leading scientists, physicians and researchers in the fields of physics, the mind, astronomy, ancient history and noetics.

The potential for great advances are mitigated by the potential for great disasters. This movie is presented so that we may all move forward into the greatest renaissance in humanity's history: the evolution of consciousness and true peace.

There is still a lot more. Here are a few words that you can enter in your favorite Internet search engine: Blood electrification, places with spiritual energy, retreats, shrines, healing ceremonies, surrendering to your higher self, urine therapy, ozone therapy, structure water, tantric sex, yoga.

Chapter 45

Where to start?

This is very simple, start one issue at the time. Do NOT try to understand it all at once, but do start TODAY with one issue, work on it for a while, until it BECOMES your new belief system. For example, every day when you wake up, ask (also known as prayer) your higher-self to surprise you with a little bit of magic, a wake up call of what is really going on; that is all. Just say to your higher-self (just like if you were talking to someone) "Higher-self of mine, please show me that you do exist, give me a sign of some sort this day, I promise to do my best to notice." That is it, nothing too complicated.

For example I was once asked by this lady in front of a camera that was interviewing me, that if I had a genie right there and then offer to grant me a wish, what would I asked for? I quickly answered WISDOM. It has been many years, and my wish has been coming true, granted it has taken many years, but true wisdom is not something learned in one book nor on a short period of time and it only goes to those who truly seek it.

A few years later a friend and I visited a parapsychologist named Iris Saltzman in Miami, Florida USA who told me that I was going to be granted with the gift of knowing many secrets, it has happened; my request to that genie that day, was in fact a request to my higher-self that was there listening all along all the time, just waiting for me to ask.

Ask your genie to guide you, and then listen to it when it speaks, if it speaks to you by means of guiding you to what gives you the most joy, then listen up and DO what gives you the most joy and STOP once and for ALL doing the things that do NOT give you the most joy, those things are based on FEAR. STOP living in fear and move over to the light of living in joy. This of course takes a quantum leap of faith and trust or you can get there one step at a time. Slowly at first you will start noticing miracles on your every day life, this will give you the will to take a quantum leap jump, and start living the life of miracles.

Bashar explains that we have only two motivators, and that NO one lacks motivation. One is the search for Joy and the other is Fear. That we program our belief systems with these two, and that from our belief systems we make all our decisions automatically. That the key is to reprogram out belief systems, by the means of evaluation what is it that we really belief in. For example, the fear of not having, of getting older and not have a stash of money, therefore when the time comes to make a decision it is easy to make it, since your belief system responds for you. Now if you change your belief system to knowing that you are all inclusive, all loving and all powerful, then you will know that all you will ever need will come to you as and when you need it.

As a Chinese proverb (or is it curse?) says:

"May you live

in

interesting times"

Joel Segurola Gonzalez

x-athiest@LosVisionarios.org

www.LosVisionarios.org

DONATIONS

Unfortunately institutions that seek ecological and social changes are quite often poorly financed. Ours is in this situation. We have many projects including the promotion of this book for which we seek funding. We accept www.paypal.com our account is: donations@condorhuana.org or feel free to email us for details on how to donate and how we will use the funds.

INDEX

1

10th planet

    Planet X · 192

12th Planet · 191

2

2012 · 17, 84, 158, 163, 164, 176, 180, 181, 183, 185, 186, 187, 189, 191, 343

A

abundance · 111, 203, 210, 215, 348

Age of Aquarius · 353, 358

Age of Pisces · 353, 358

Akashic Records · 130, 292

Akasic Records · 130

alchemy · 18, 106, 306, 310, 316, 321, 341, 342, 344, 345

Alchemy · 306, 319, 321, 322, 340, 341, 342, 345

apparitions · 18

Apparitions · 85

Aromatherapy · 292, 293

Astral · 20, 86, 124, 125, 126, 127

astral travel · 18, 56, 74, 124, 129

Astral Travel · 86, 124

astrology · 18, 49, 52, 53, 99, 102, 103, 104, 105, 164, 241, 353

Astrology · 48, 52, 100, 101, 105

astronomy · 353

astrophysics · 303, 353

Atheist · 2, 279

aura · 18

auras · 49, 127

Ayurveda · 294, 295, 296, 297

Ayurvedic · 295, 297

B

Bashar · 84, 218, 219, 220, 281, 283, 370

believe system · 24, 113, 285, 369, 370

Believe System · 108

Bhagavad Gita · 149, 362

C

Carlos Castañeda · 123

Christ · 84, 134, 142, 144, 145, 149, 150, 247, 326

Clairaudience · 85

Clairvoyance · 85

cloudbuster · 327

Conscious creation

conscious creation · 33

Conscious Creation · 29, 108

consciousness · 106, 153, 182, 202, 210, 233, 349, 353, 356, 364

Cosmos · 111, 132, 133, 182, 183, 357

D

DARMA · 156

Déjà Vu · 85

density/dimension · 57, 65, 67, 68, 73, 74, 84, 134, 163, 164, 185, 186, 187, 188

DMT

Spirit Molecule · 122, 279

dowsing · 18

Dowsing · 352

Drugs · 123

E

Earth Changes · 352

Eckankar · 233

Edgar Cayce · 18, 355

Cayce · 18, 163, 166, 246, 247, 251, 359

ego · 24, 156, 198, 211, 212, 213, 214, 215

extraterrestrials · 353

F

faith · 64, 84, 109, 111, 112, 286, 287, 370

Falun Dafa · 234, 235, 236, 237

Father

    father · 133, 212, 305

Feng shui · 238, 239, 240, 241

Free Energy · 352

Fulcanelli · 342, 343

G

ghost · 18, 60, 308

GNOSIS · 211

god

    GOD, God · 24, 43, 66, 70, 210, 265

GOD · 132

God, god · 85

Grays · 280

H

Higher-self · 111, 369

hyperdimensional · 355, 357

hypnosis · 18, 78, 272, 298, 299

Hypnosis · 272

Hypnotherapy · 298, 299

I

Intentional Communities · 346, 350

J

Jane Roberts · 112, 279, 281

K

KARMA · 156

ketamine · 259

Ketamine · 122

Krishna · 144, 149

Kundalini

   kundalini · 134, 212

M

Magic · 20

Manna · 305, 307, 322

Mayan calendar · 163

meditation · 50, 83, 84, 202, 208, 217, 234, 235, 287

Medium · 281

Mother

   mother · 133, 212, 214

multiple universes · 352

N

near death experiences · 18, 124

new physics · 352

numerology · 353

O

OBE · 125

orgone · 326, 327

ORME · 86, 303, 305, 313, 353

ORMUS · 86, 303, 305, 318

Ouija board · 18, 253

P

parapsychologist · 53, 369

parapsychology · 18, 53, 231, 303

past lives · 77, 78, 79

Planet X · 165, 168, 170, 191, 192, 193, 307

pole shift · 165, 192

prayer · 194, 203, 369

Precognition · 85

prophecies · 162, 182

Psychic Dreams · 85

Psychokinesis · 85

Q

Qabala · 353

R

Ramalu · 213

Reincarnation · 76

Remote Visions

    Remote Sensing · 85

Rosicrucian · 47, 230, 231, 232

S

sacred geometry · 352

Sacred geometry · 61

Sai Baba · 134, 143, 144, 149, 216, 217

Samael Aun Weor · 211, 212, 213, 215

Seth · 112, 113, 221, 279, 281, 283, 355

SEX · 368

Sumerian · 170, 191, 192, 319

symbols · 279, 280, 281, 282

T

Tarot · 353

tarot cards · 18

Telekinesis · 85

telepathic · 51

Telepathic Sensing · 85

Telepathy · 85

The Law of Attraction · 111

The Philosophers' Stone · 306

The Time of Global Shift · 357

U

Universal Subconscious Mind · 111, 132, 133

W

Wicca · 18, 195, 265, 362

Wiccan · 266, 267, 268

Wishcraft · 18, 49, 195, 265

Witches · 254, 266, 267, 269

Y

yoga · 18

YOGA · 368

Z

Zodiac · 105